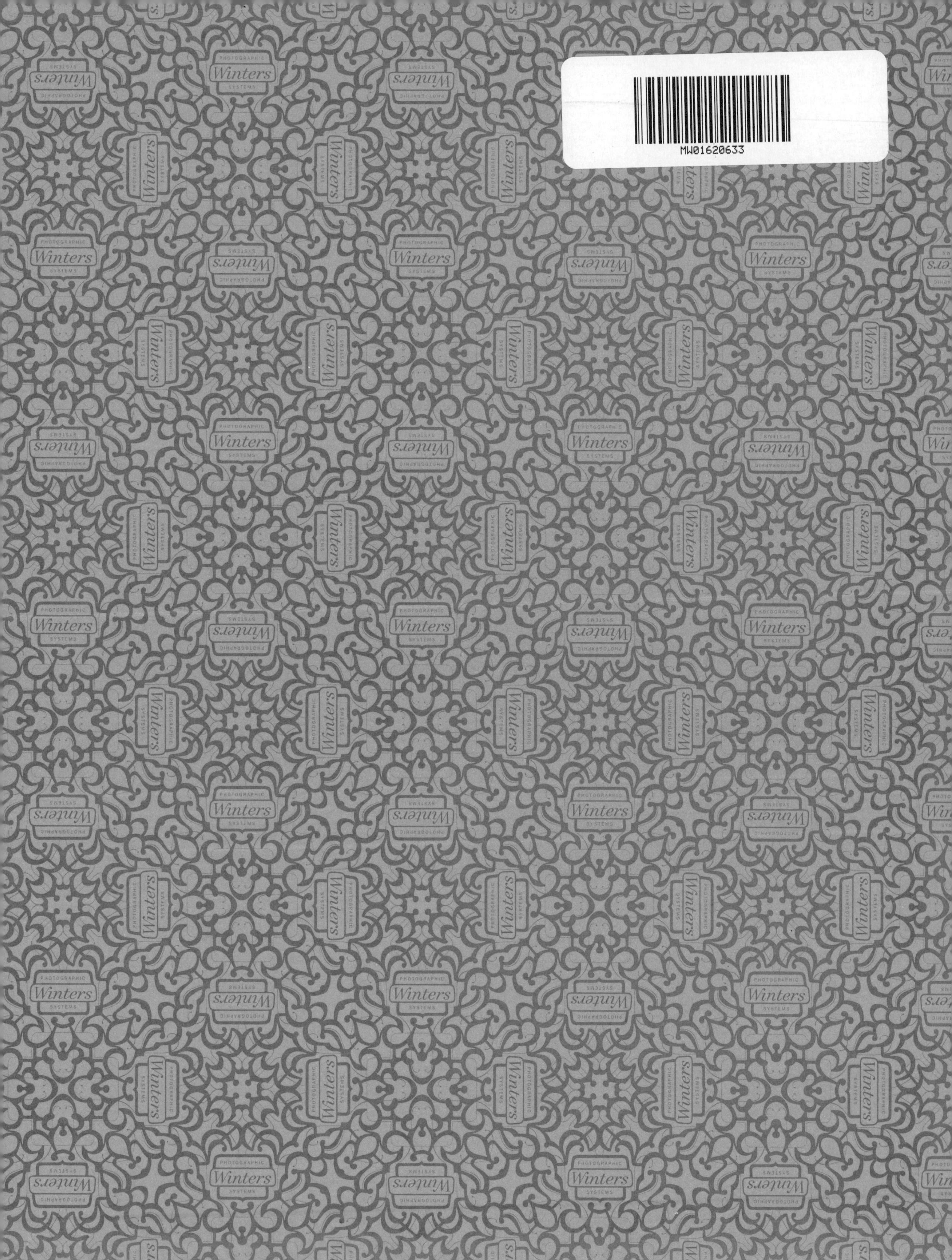

MW01620633

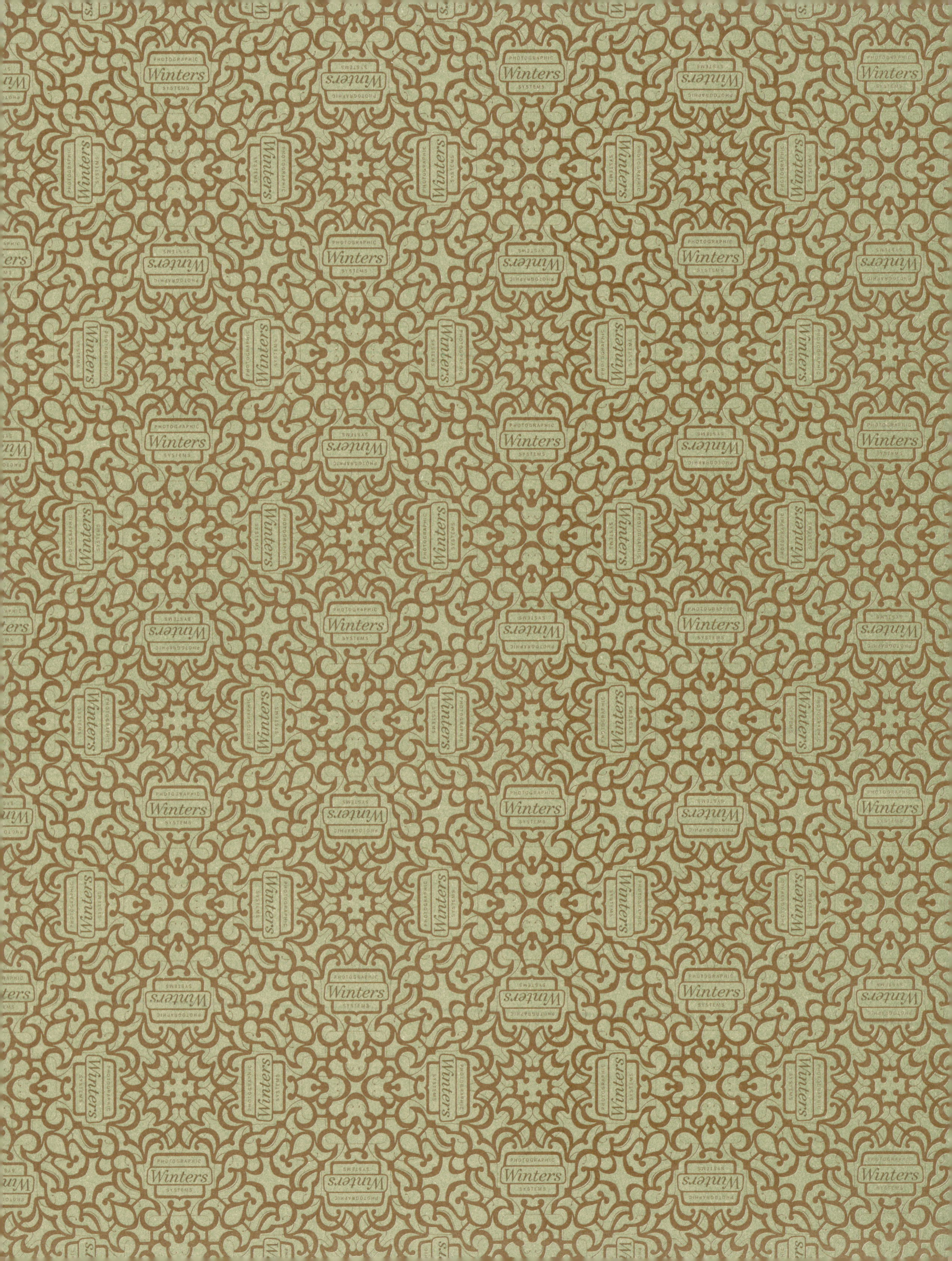
PHOTOGRAPHIC
Winters
SYSTEMS

Perio

Dan Winters

odical

Kodak 160VC 2 4031

Photo

Dan Winters

Foreword by Lynn Hirschberg

aperture

ograph

S

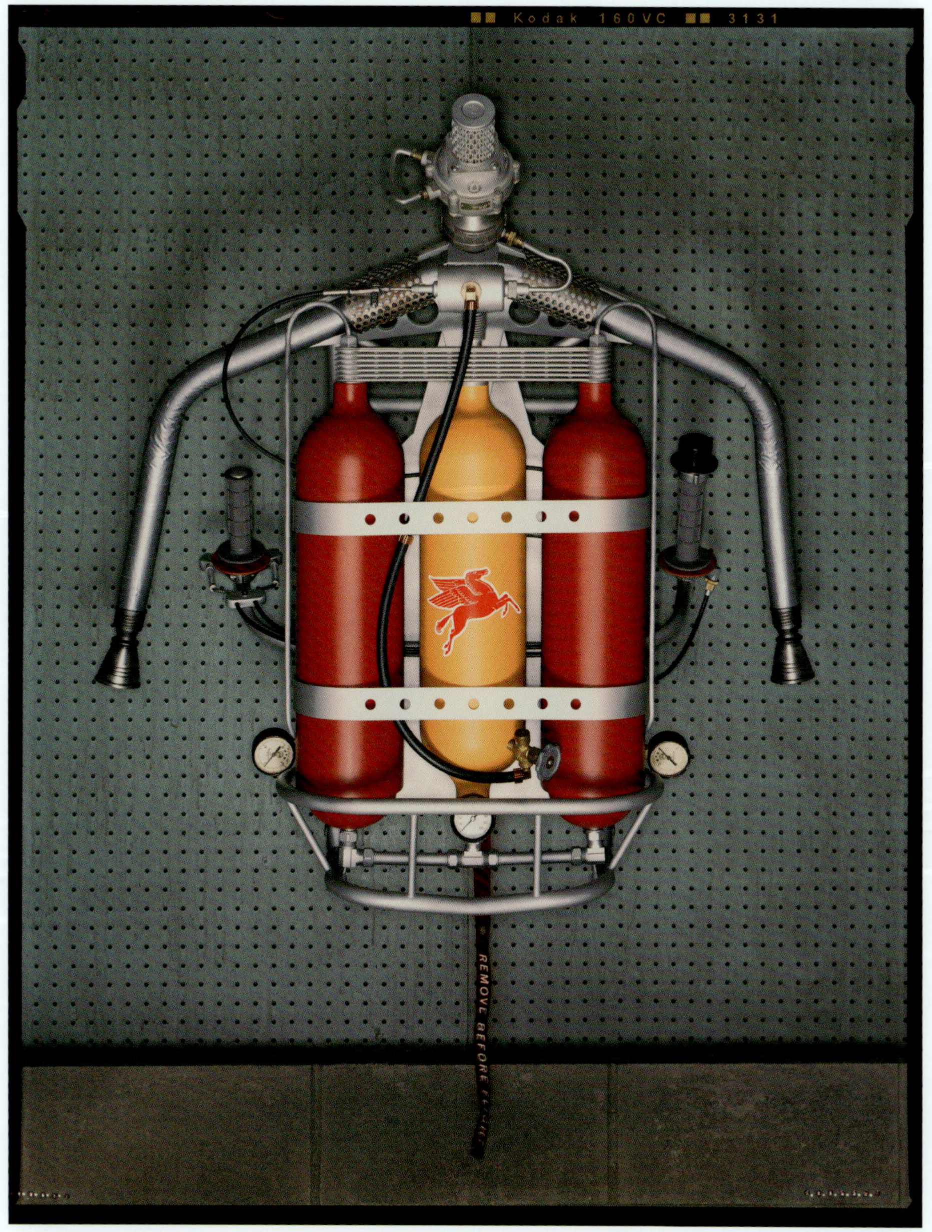

for Kathryn + Dylan

Foreword | *by* Lynn Hirschberg

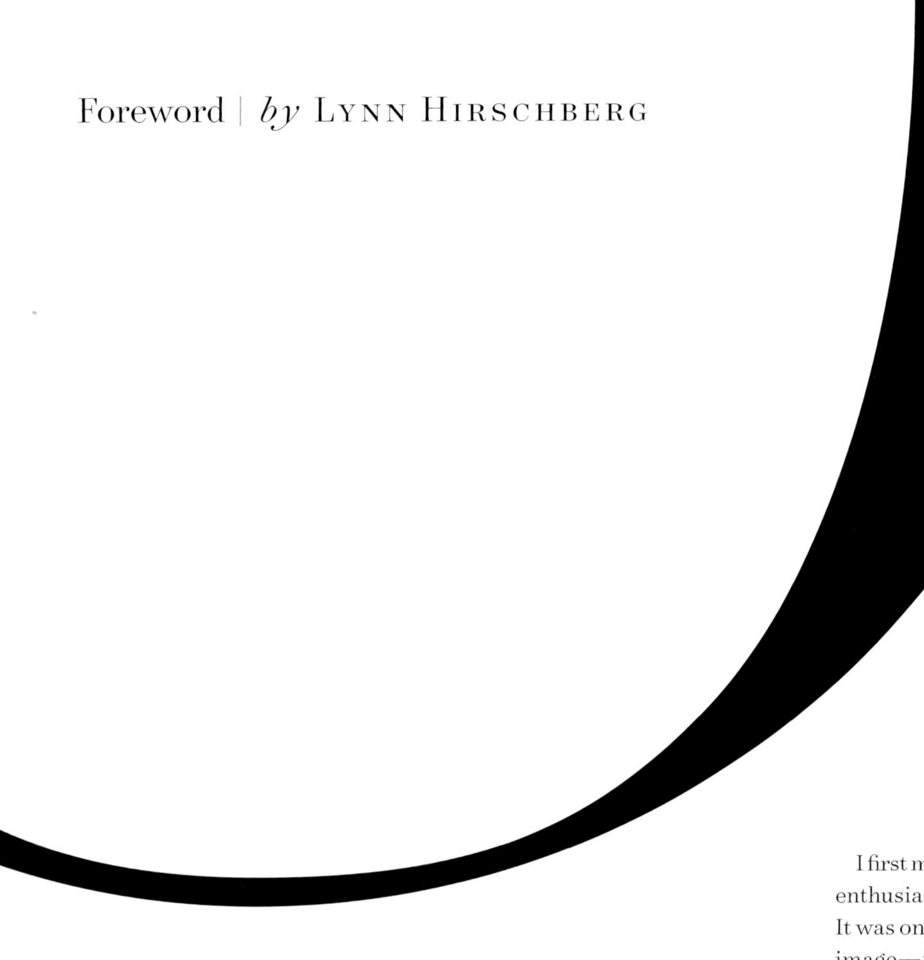

On July 16, 1969, when Dan Winters was seven, his father took a picture of the Apollo 11 launch. He aimed his camera (and his flash) at his television set in Ventura County, California, eager to capture history in a visual moment. Unfortunately, technology blocked his ambition: the resulting photograph is of a cloudy TV, the picture indistinct. But it was an important shot: that photo—how to take it, the subject matter, the sense of timeliness—intrigued Dan Winters and arguably launched his career as one of the most important chroniclers of America in the last two decades. "It was a galvanizing moment," Winters told me at the end of a long shooting day in New York City. "I grew up with the space program, and my father's picture, however flawed, was in the tradition of creating a document, a reminder of that second in time. And that's what I've always tried to do in my career—document my surroundings, whether it is a study of someone's face or the best angle of a bee. I have no grand idea about doing a project, in India, for example—I am fascinated by an American sensibility. That's my passion."

I first met Winters long after I had enthusiastically admired his work. It was one of those things where an image—in my case, I think it was a photograph of the actress Kate Winslet looking down, her expression one of great beauty tinged with a tentativeness that seemed to perfectly illustrate the precarious nature of the movie business—stopped me cold, and I stared at it for many minutes, unable to turn the page. As a magazine writer, I've always been conscious of the power of photography. I long for the picture that accompanies my piece to captivate the reader and enlarge what I have written. Again and again, Winters has taken my rather basic desire much further: his portraits of movie stars, pop icons and inspirational personalities, as well as his "portraits" of subjects like a rusty car stuck in the woods, Mr. Rogers's red zip-up cardigan, or a mid-century photo booth, are closer to paintings than to photography. Winters's sense of composition and lighting has a poignant elegance: even the humblest subjects—a bee, candy bars, a toupee—are imbued through his sensibility, with a stillness and grace. Like great paintings, these photographs are rich in nuance—the wariness in Leonardo DiCaprio's eyes is reminiscent of the men in Dutch Masters' paintings; the sad, knowing expression of Willie Nelson immediately brings to mind a twist on the heroic work of Frederick Remington. And yet, Winters's work is wholly original; he seems to distill the emotional truth of his subjects, whether it be the artist/provocateur Jeff Koons, whom he depicts with two sets of eyes, or Angelina Jolie, her luscious mouth caught somewhere between a smile and a scream, or the recording-industry mogul Rick Rubin, shrouded in a white blanket like an all-knowing guru.

That photo accompanied a story I wrote about Rubin for the *New York Times Magazine*, for which Winters has done some of his most striking work. As often happens, the story wasn't yet completed when Dan took the photo, yet he still managed to enliven all my theories about Rubin. He's uncanny that way. He had for years revealed the essence of the personalities that I was profiling before I finally met him. The meeting was regarding another of my pieces—a cover story in 2006 about an actress named Vera Farmiga that had the working title, "What Ever Happened to Wanting to Be Meryl Streep?" Farmiga, a virtually unknown actress, to me represented the frustrations of all actresses who were attempting to do great and challenging work. Thankfully, Winters (who has his pick of magazine assignments) was compelled by this idea.

Well, Winters was so wonderfully not what I expected when I met him to discuss Farmiga. I thought he'd be small and hipsterish. Instead, he is tall and expansive and handsome in a uniquely American way. He has the glow of the thoroughly engaged. It was immediately apparent why his subjects respond to his gaze; he was both commanding and embracing—and he does his homework. Despite the fact that Farmiga was not famous, he had spent hours studying the contours of her face in order to discover what made her captivating. "Celebrity portraiture strives to create intrigue and allure," he told me later. "I tell the subjects to think of a shoot with me as a portrait session, not a photo shoot. They'll say to me, 'Can you shoot my left profile?' Or, 'This is my best look.' But that's like going to a doctor and telling him what to do. They have to trust me. I can find their best look."

Although strikingly pretty, Farmiga was not particularly photogenic, but like a surgeon, Winters diagnosed the problem. "Every face has its complexities," he explained. "Look at George Clooney—he is the handsomest guy in the room, and you'd think that the pictures are going to take themselves. But, actually, his face is asymmetrical. You have to rotate him slightly to get the best shot. He's still the best-looking guy in the room, but even his face is challenging."

Winters stripped Farmiga down, both literally and figuratively, erasing the language of fashion and creating a portrait that is both sad and hopeful. Her hands are particularly evocative—they underscore her contemplative and confused state of mind, which I reflected in my cover story. While Farmiga's face was probably not known to readers, Winters's image—which reminded me of Edward Hopper's paintings of lone, starry-eyed women—attracted their interest. Just as I had wished, the photo made readers ask, "Who is that girl?"

Throughout his photographic career Winters has managed to deftly fuse journalism with art, without sacrificing either approach. This may have something to do with his multifaceted background. Initially, Dan wanted to be a filmmaker, and at the same time, he was fascinated by entomology, internal combustion engines, and livestock. It was in 4-H Club that he was first introduced to photography (by Clarence Dalyremple, a former Vietnam war photographer). "I had a Steinbeckian upbringing," he recalled. "My family was very conservative and very rural, but I wasn't a hick even when I was a hick. I was a restless kid, and I was always looking for a way to experience life outside of Ventura County. Magazines were a window to the world for me."

By 1977, when he was sixteen, he embarked on a three-year project that studied the protective response of the Eleodes beetle. For two straight years he won first prize in his regional science fair, and went on to win again in the state's science fair, all the while pursuing his interest in motion picture special effects.

Winters attended classes at Moorpark College in Ventura and, perhaps more important, began poring over the work of photography's masters: Irving Penn, Richard Avedon, Diane Arbus, and others. "I was particularly impressed by a small book of photos by Harry Callahan published by El Mochuelo Gallery, Santa Barbara, back in 1964," he said. "I became addicted to still photography," he recalled. "I'm still happiest in the darkroom." By twenty, Winters was certain that he wanted photography to be his life's work. "Pursuing a career in the arts was not part of my parents' vocabulary," he confirmed. "But they still supported me. Although, one year, when I was starting out, I wanted a particular lens for Christmas, and my mother bought me a microwave oven instead. She thought I needed to eat more than I needed that lens."

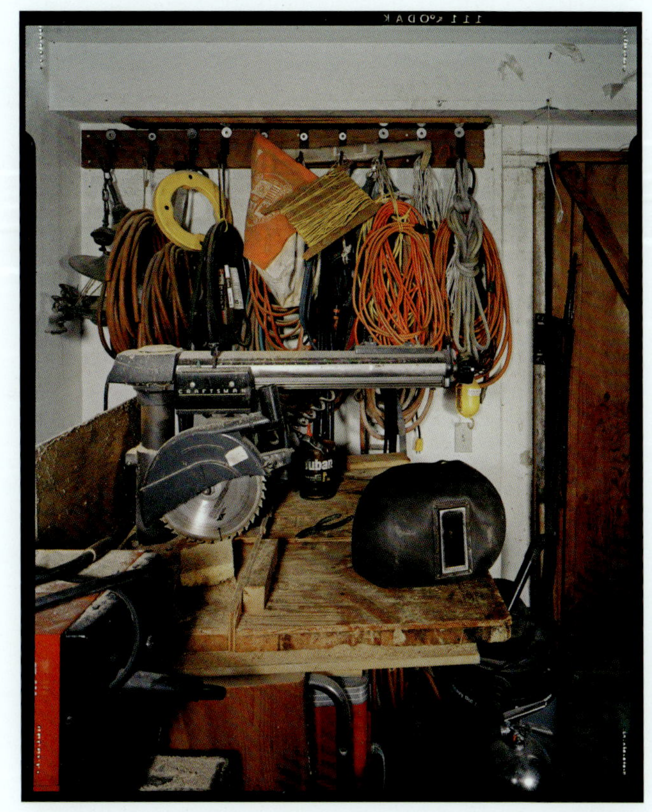

THE WORKBENCH OF LARRY WINTERS, Ventura County, California, 1994

At first, Winters was interested only in working in black and white. In 1986, he went to work for the *Thousand Oaks News Chronicle* as a general assignment photographer. "The front page was color, and I hated it," he recalled. "We all hated it. But I had to make my peace with color. I came to see it as my mission to give color photography the same power as black and white. Now I think about the famous black-and-white photos that Brady took of Abraham Lincoln. They are stunning, but it would be really amazing to see them in color. With color, you feel more connected to the photo."

Winters's sense of color is fascinating: he has learned how to light and direct a shot so that the palette looks both natural and necessary. Look at his Laura Dern photo on the cover of this book: the red of her lipstick intensifies the pop of the picture and contrasts vividly with the white of the pearls around her neck. She looks at once glamorous and terrified. Similarly, in the picture of Natalie Portman, the subtle browns and grays emphasize the sense that she resembles a woodland creature. Winters is able to create the image of a serene, but pearl-gray sky behind Sandra Bullock as she sways in the ocean, or illuminate the dawning day behind Al Gore as he contemplates an uncertain future. If these photos were in black and white, they would not possess the same depth. "I still shoot black and white all the time," he maintained. "But I like the way color becomes a character in the shoot. It requires another layer of thought."

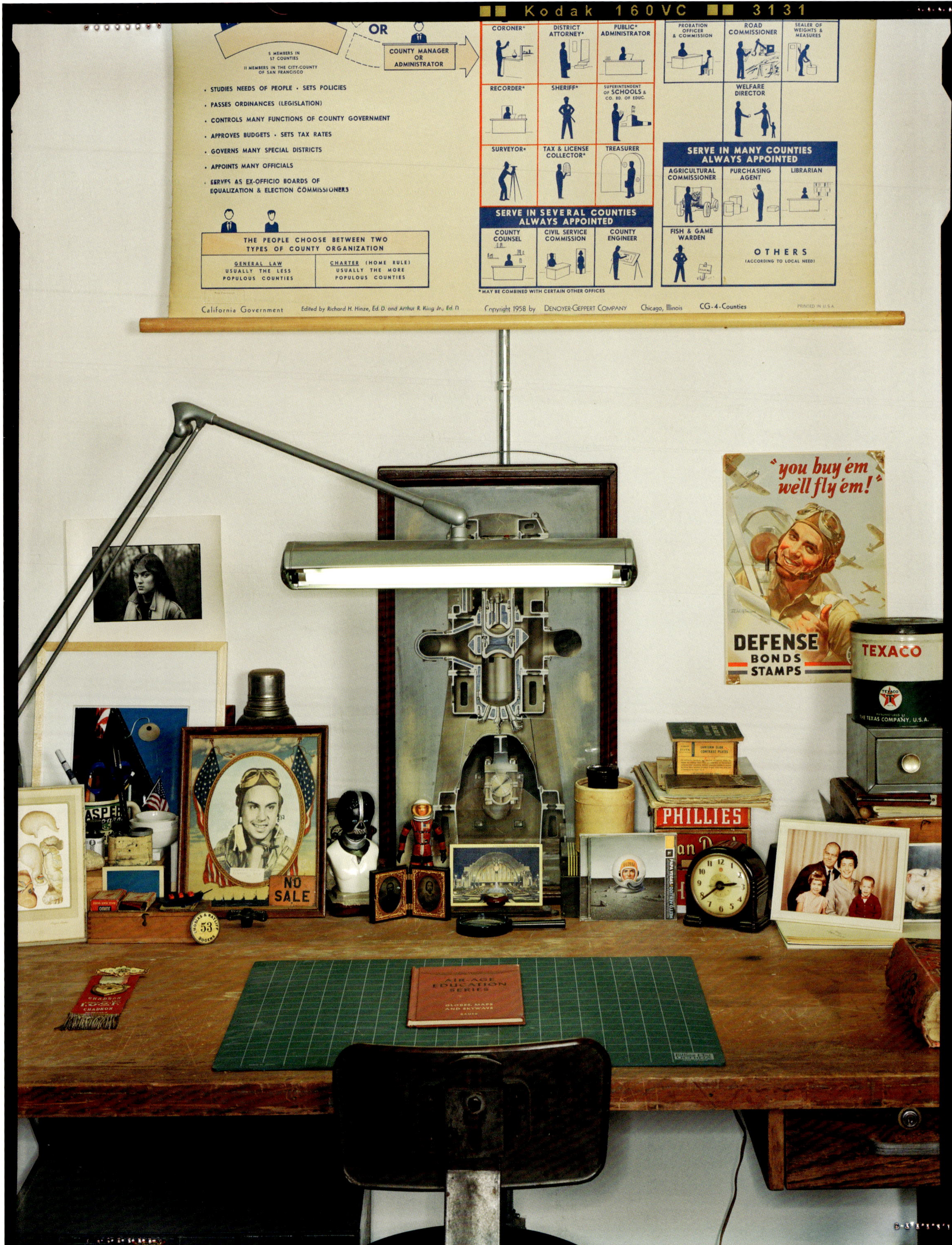
Kodak 160VC 3131
OR
COUNTY MANAGER OR ADMINISTRATOR
5 MEMBERS IN 57 COUNTIES
11 MEMBERS IN THE CITY-COUNTY OF SAN FRANCISCO
• STUDIES NEEDS OF PEOPLE • SETS POLICIES
• PASSES ORDINANCES (LEGISLATION)
• CONTROLS MANY FUNCTIONS OF COUNTY GOVERNMENT
• APPROVES BUDGETS • SETS TAX RATES
• GOVERNS MANY SPECIAL DISTRICTS
• APPOINTS MANY OFFICIALS
• SERVES AS EX-OFFICIO BOARDS OF EQUALIZATION & ELECTION COMMISSIONERS
THE PEOPLE CHOOSE BETWEEN TWO TYPES OF COUNTY ORGANIZATION
GENERAL LAW
USUALLY THE LESS POPULOUS COUNTIES
CHARTER (HOME RULE)
USUALLY THE MORE POPULOUS COUNTIES
CORONER*
DISTRICT ATTORNEY*
PUBLIC* ADMINISTRATOR
RECORDER*
SHERIFF*
SUPERINTENDENT OF SCHOOLS & CO. BD. OF EDUC.
SURVEYOR*
TAX & LICENSE COLLECTOR*
TREASURER
SERVE IN SEVERAL COUNTIES ALWAYS APPOINTED
COUNTY COUNSEL
CIVIL SERVICE COMMISSION
COUNTY ENGINEER
*MAY BE COMBINED WITH CERTAIN OTHER OFFICES
PROBATION OFFICER & COMMISSION
ROAD COMMISSIONER
SEALER OF WEIGHTS & MEASURES
WELFARE DIRECTOR
SERVE IN MANY COUNTIES ALWAYS APPOINTED
AGRICULTURAL COMMISSIONER
PURCHASING AGENT
LIBRARIAN
FISH & GAME WARDEN
OTHERS
(ACCORDING TO LOCAL NEED)
California Government
Edited by Richard H. Hinze, Ed. D. and Arthur R. King Jr., Ed. D.
Copyright 1958 by DENOYER-GEPPERT COMPANY Chicago, Illinois
CG-4-Counties
PRINTED IN U.S.A.
"you buy 'em we'll fly 'em!"
DEFENSE
BONDS
STAMPS
TEXACO
THE TEXAS COMPANY, U.S.A.
PHILLIES
NO SALE
53
AIR AGE EDUCATION SERIES
GLOBES, MAPS AND SKYWAYS

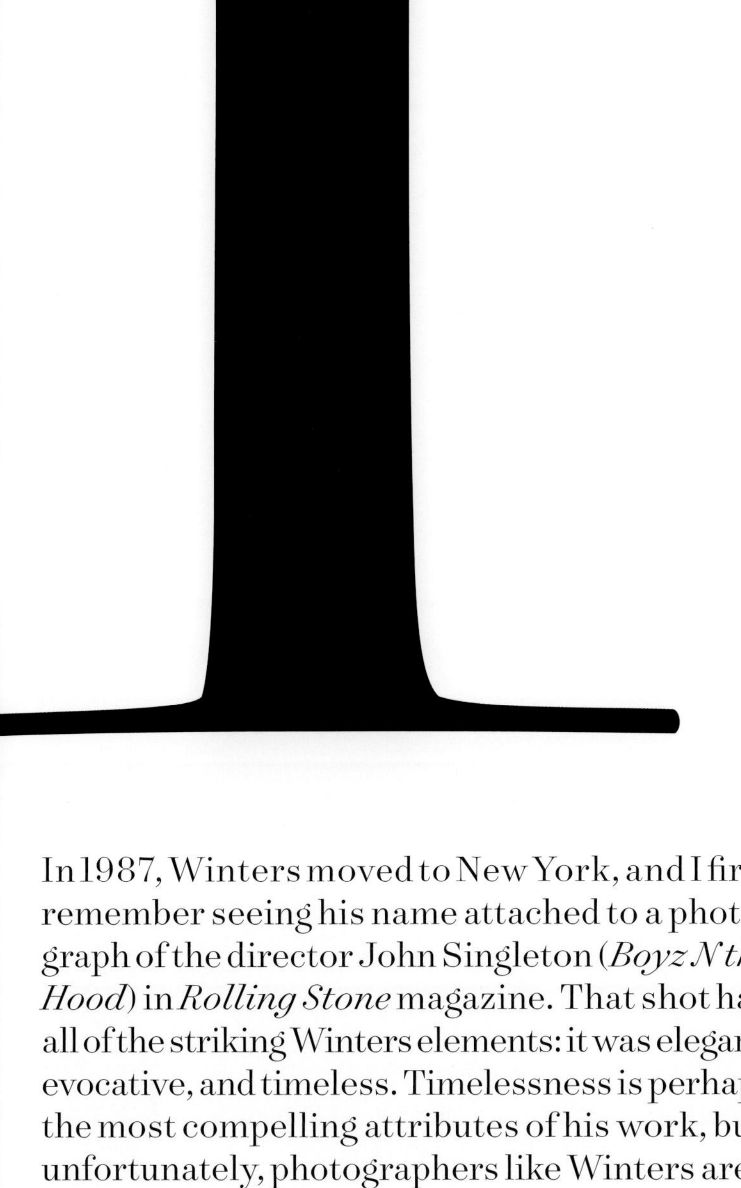

« Dan Winters's Desk, Driftwood, Texas, 2006

In 1987, Winters moved to New York, and I first remember seeing his name attached to a photograph of the director John Singleton (*Boyz N the Hood*) in *Rolling Stone* magazine. That shot had all of the striking Winters elements: it was elegant, evocative, and timeless. Timelessness is perhaps the most compelling attributes of his work, but, unfortunately, photographers like Winters are a dying breed: one of the current problems with celebrity portraiture is a tendency to turn the photograph into a brand-oriented fashion picture. The editor Tina Brown started it at *Vanity Fair* in the '80s, and it rapidly caught on at other magazines, mostly because fashion equals credits, equals advertising revenue. This sort of fashion/celebrity photography may help the bottom line, but it has been largely detrimental for portraiture. ¶ When we negotiated a shoot for the *New York Times Magazine* as recently as four years ago, it was rare for an actor to demand hair and makeup experts to groom them for their pictures, and stylists, who decide on the look of the subject, were not part of a shoot. When you add a stylist to a photo shoot it instantly changes. There are stylists who insist on particular clothes, hair, and makeup to create the mood and look they desire, and that image is then grafted onto the subject. The photographer then shoots that image, rather than an image of his own making. Celebrities are often insecure and have come to rely on what they view as the stylist's expertise. But just as he mastered the complications of color photography, Winters has adapted to the team aspect of today's celebrity journalism. The Helen Mirren portrait for example, was created with a stylist. But Winters controlled the shoot—the portrait is informed by emotion, not fashion.

"When I shoot someone well known, I try to Google their image, and I study paparazzi pictures, which are not retouched, to figure out their face," Winters explained. "That's the only way to find an unaltered image. And I only shoot people I like. If there is a stylist, it's usually someone I know, and there will never be a rack of clothes a mile long. It's important to reveal people without making them uncomfortable. I'll put on Miles Davis or John Coltrane—something that will help the mood. But even so, it's becoming more of a challenge: the control that we strive for is harder to find, and the photography will suffer."

Winters has also resisted the pitfalls of digital photography, which has had a huge impact on the medium. "If I want the sky less blue, I can change it digitally, but I'd rather know how to do it with lighting. Digital tools have made a great contribution to color printing, but they can make people lazy," Winters said. More disturbing is the impact digital retouching has had on portraiture. Features are adjusted; limbs are slimmed and transplanted from one frame to the next; facial expressions are smoothed and altered—all these changes are designed to create a more "ideal" picture. In it, most images of the famous are massaged to the point of robotic dullness, and most are forgettable. "I'm not interested in that sort of digital enhancement," Winters said. "I find it diminishes character, and character is why we are fascinated by these people in the first place. I can change a person's face through lighting or positioning." He uses his portrait of Gwyneth Paltrow as an example. "I'm trying to achieve a definitive likeness," he said. "If you pull her chin up or down, it will completely change her face. I can show what's fantastic about her face without using any digital tricks."

Winters left New York for Los Angeles in 1991, when he married Kathryn Fouts, who eventually became his business partner. When their son, Dylan, was born in 1993, Winters dreamed of moving to somewhere more rural, so that his son could have the same kind of upbringing that he did. In 2000, the family moved to Austin, and Winters, who collects WWII memorabilia and all sorts of artifacts from mid-century America, set up a studio in Driftwood, Texas (population twenty-seven). Although Winters has won more than a hundred national and international awards for his photography, he does not have any of the trappings of the weary been-there-done-that pro. Rather, he seems like a small-town guy with a multitude of interests. If you look at the photo of his desktop, a still life that he curates and changes regularly, you get a sense of his fascination with the last sixty years of America. The photographs in this book have the same historical resonance: they are true evocations of people and things that define their time. The power of these photos is their ability to trigger emotion, identification and, finally, a sort of collective memory.

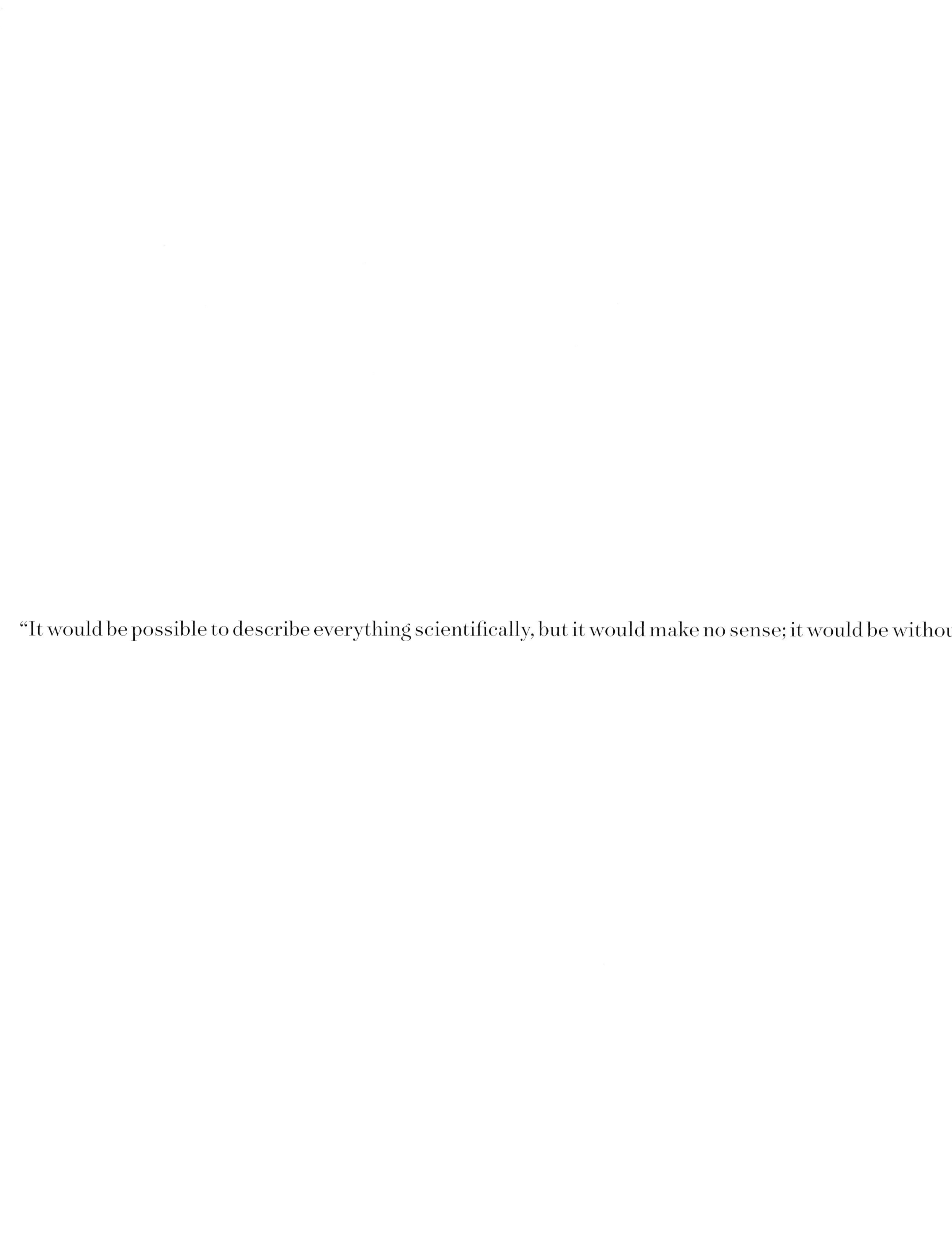

“It would be possible to describe everything scientifically, but it would make no sense; it would be withou

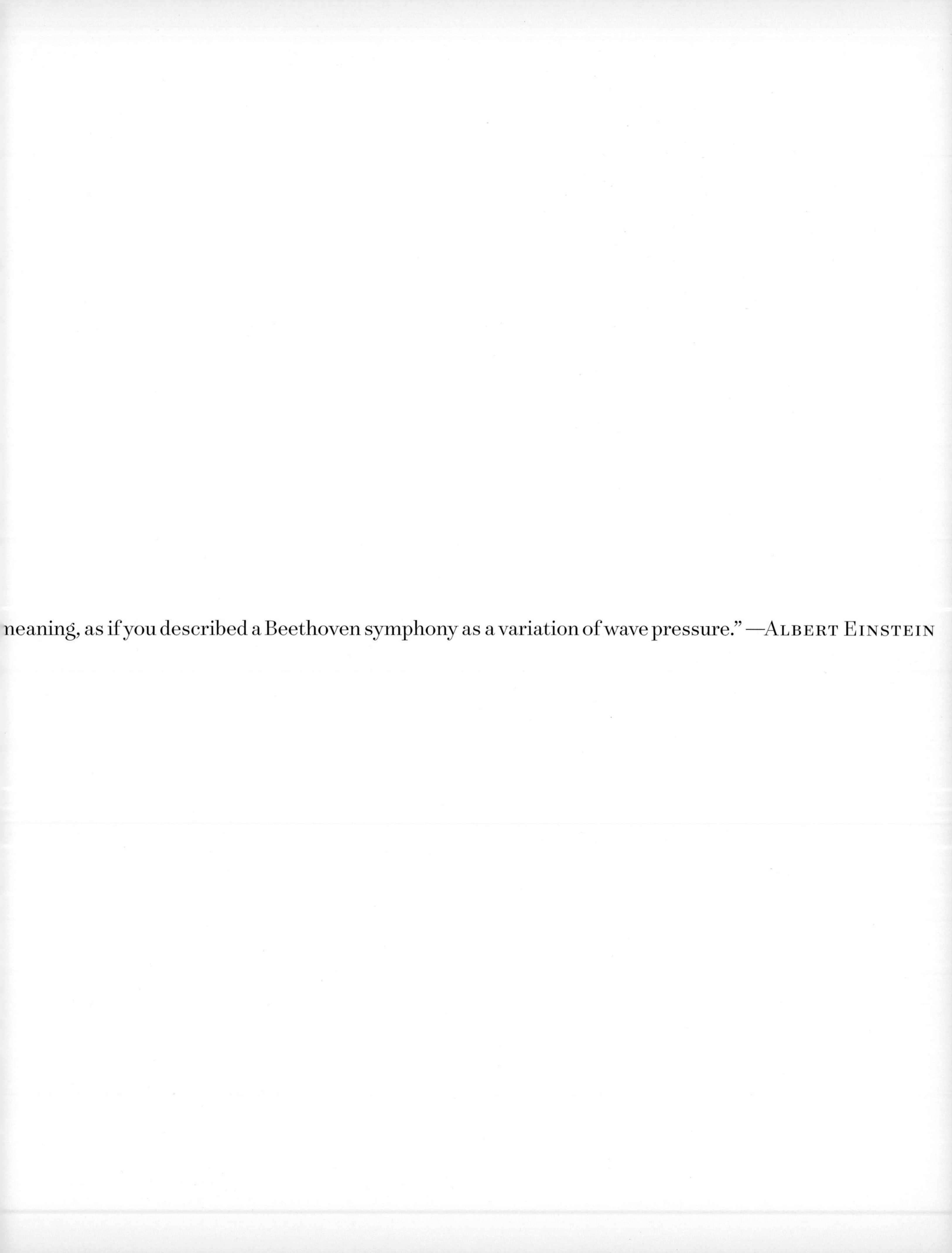

meaning, as if you described a Beethoven symphony as a variation of wave pressure." —Albert Einstein

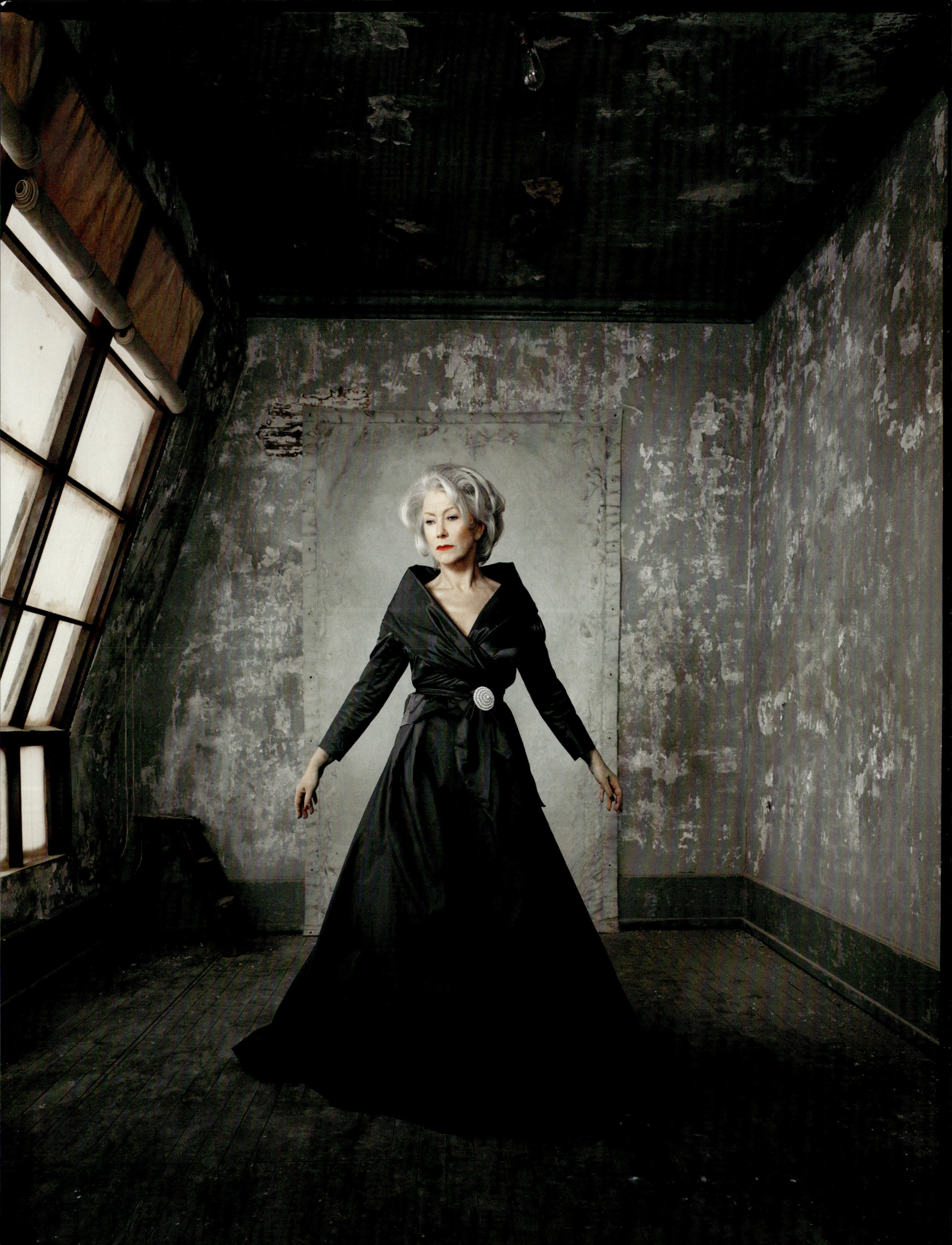

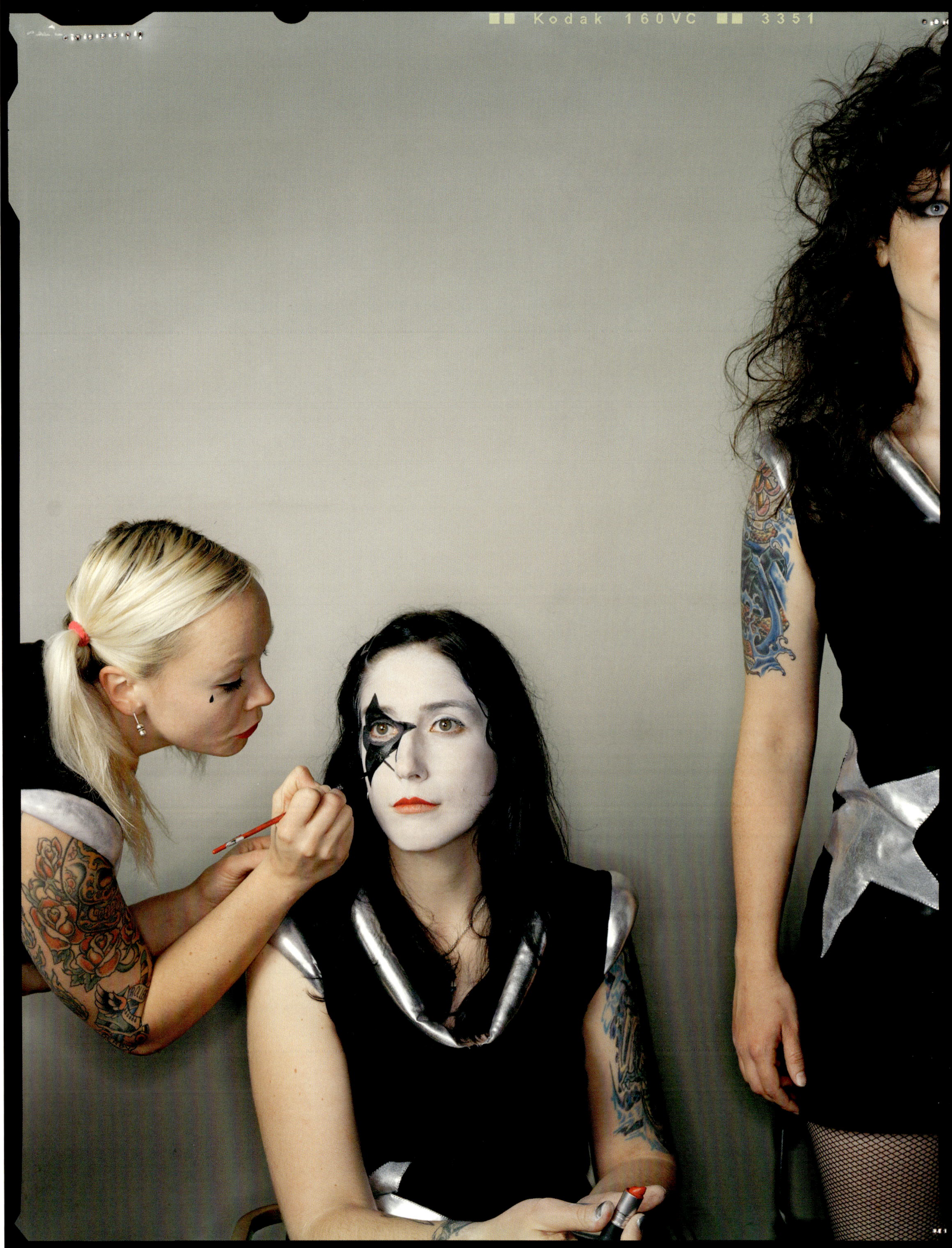
Kodak 160VC 3351

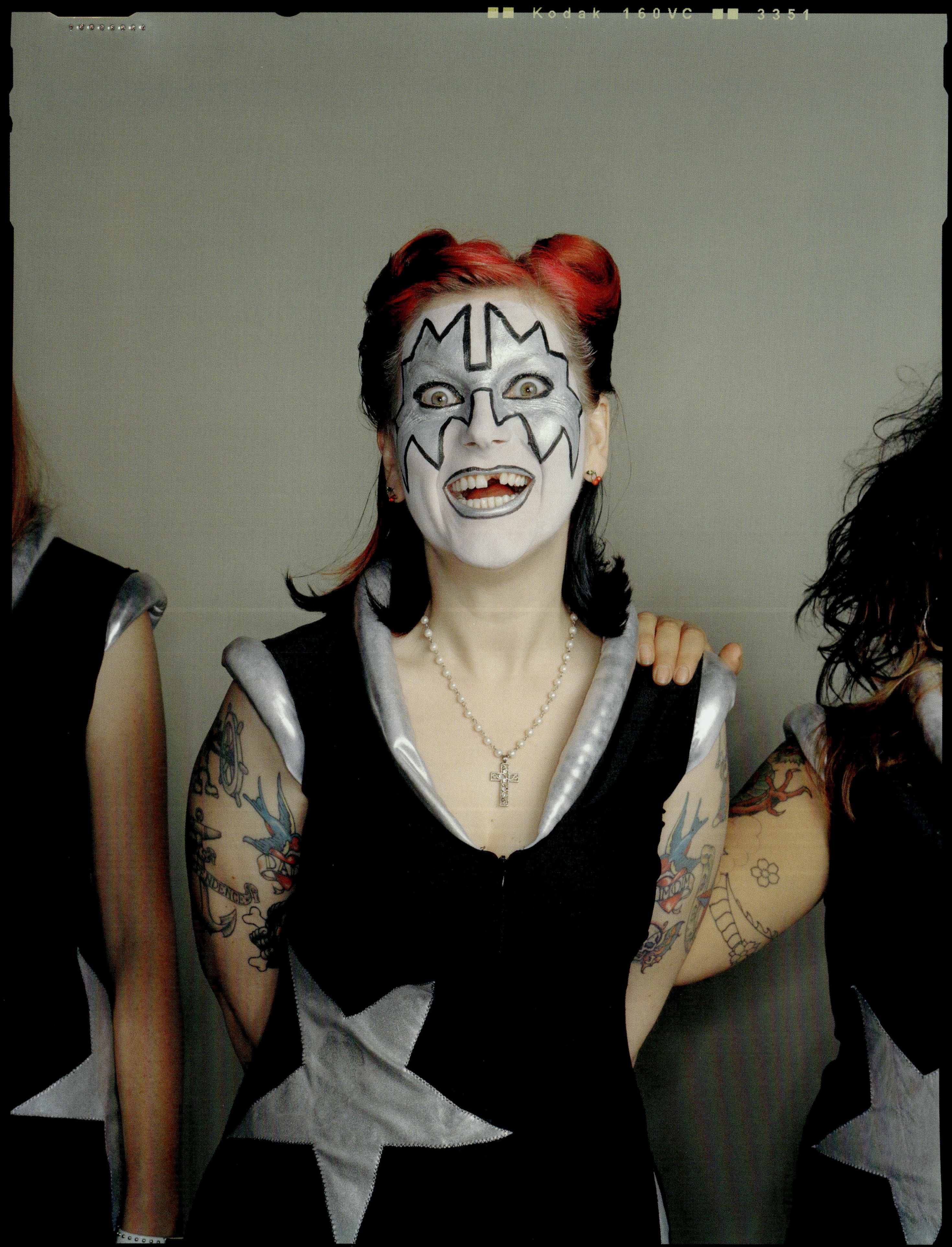
Kodak 160VC 3351

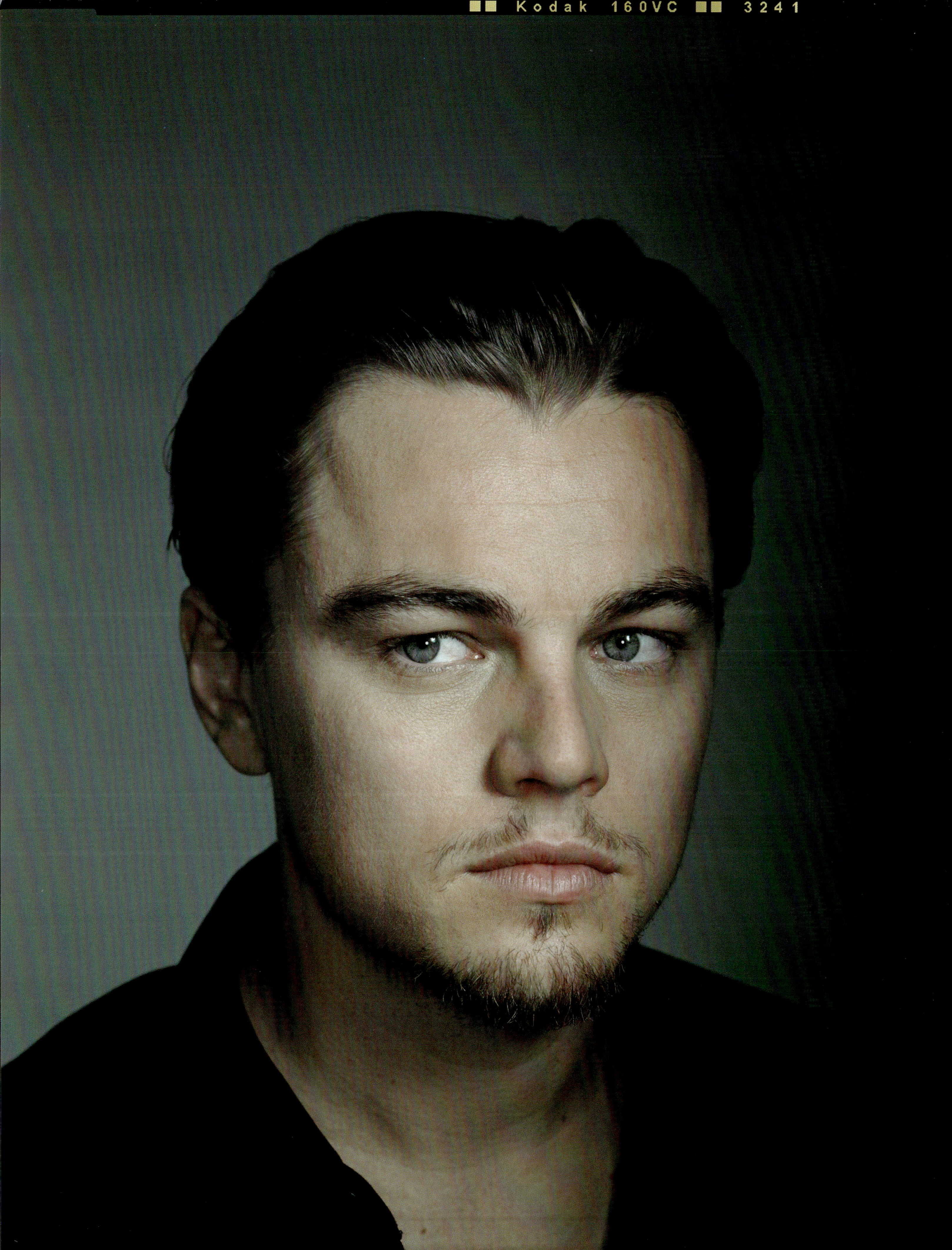
Kodak 160VC 3241

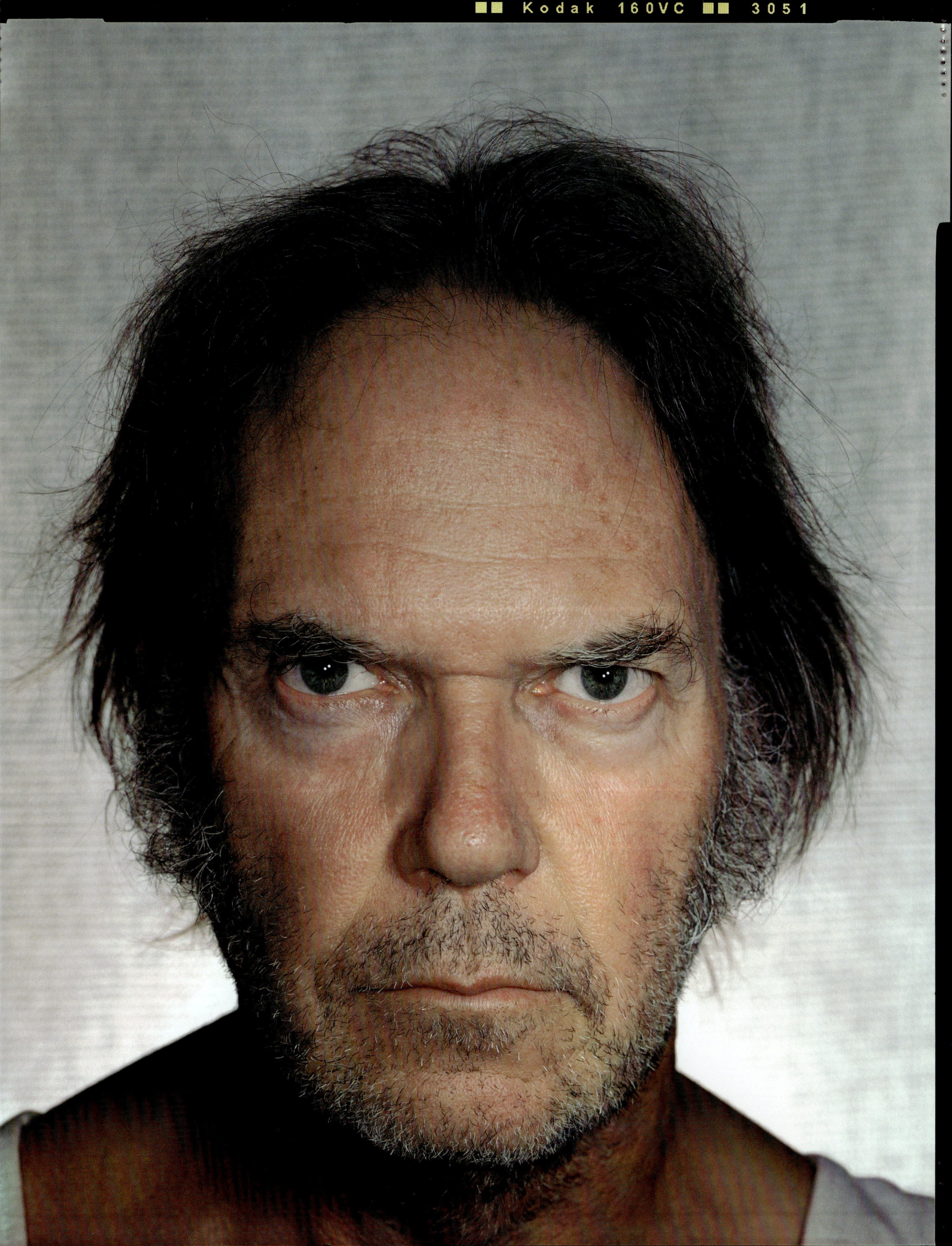

Kodak 160VC 3051

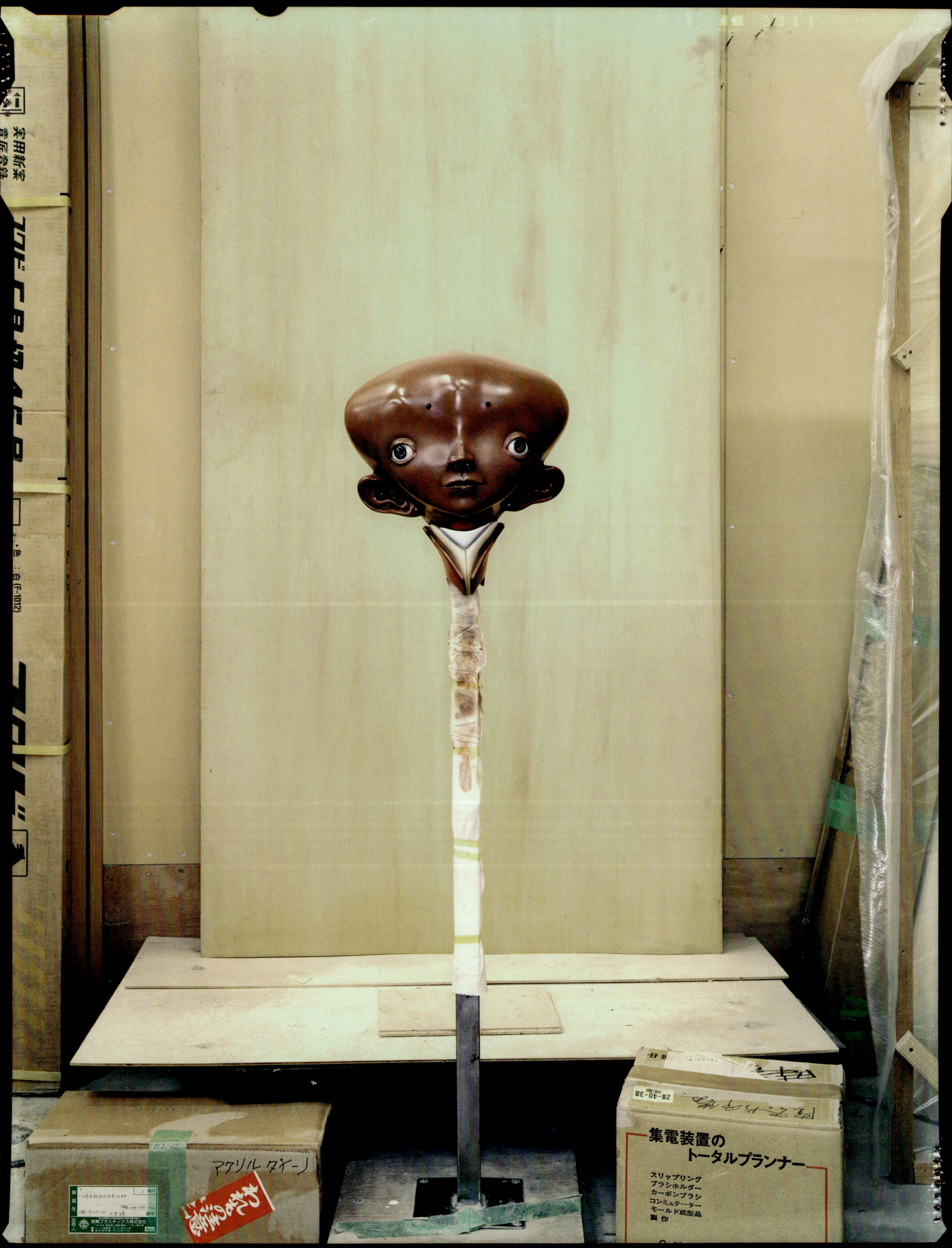

集電装置の
トータルプランナー
スリップリング
ブラシホルダー
カーボンブラシ
コンミュテーター
モールド成型品
製作
28-40-38

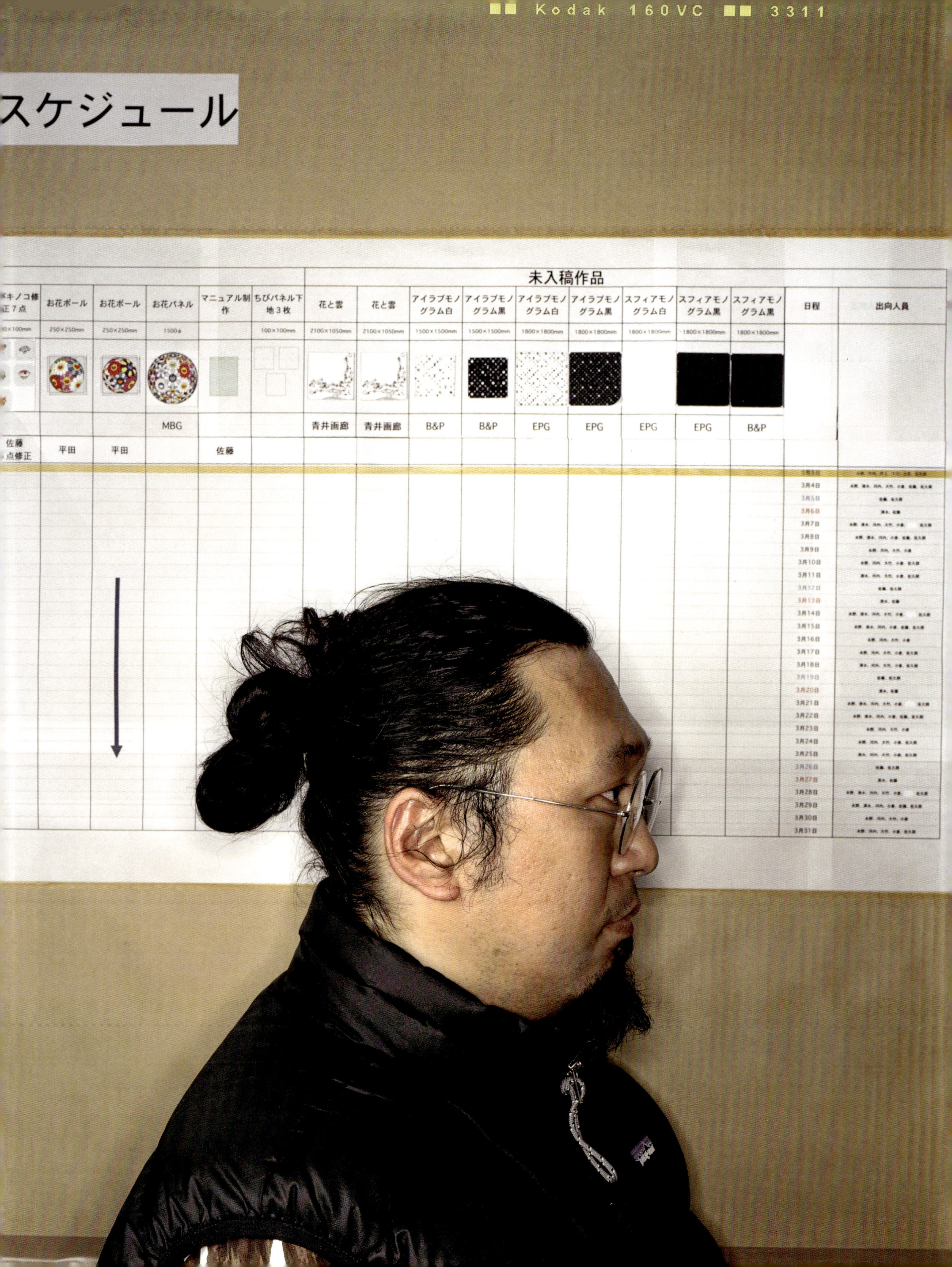

Kodak 160VC 3311

スケジュール

						未入稿作品										
キノコ修正7点	お花ボール	お花ボール	お花パネル	マニュアル制作	ちびパネル下地3枚	花と雲	花と雲	アイラブモノグラム白	アイラブモノグラム黒	アイラブモノグラム白	アイラブモノグラム黒	スフィアモノグラム白	スフィアモノグラム黒	スフィアモノグラム黒	日程	出向人員
0×100mm	250×250mm	250×250mm	1500φ		100×100mm	2100×1050mm	2100×1050mm	1500×1500mm	1500×1500mm	1800×1800mm	1800×1800mm	1800×1800mm	1800×1800mm	1800×1800mm		
			MBG			青井画廊	青井画廊	B&P	B&P	EPG	EPG	EPG	EPG	B&P		
佐藤 点修正	平田	平田		佐藤												
															3月3日	
															3月4日	
															3月5日	
															3月6日	
															3月7日	
															3月8日	
															3月9日	
															3月10日	
															3月11日	
															3月12日	
															3月13日	
															3月14日	
															3月15日	
															3月16日	
															3月17日	
															3月18日	
															3月19日	
															3月20日	
															3月21日	
															3月22日	
															3月23日	
															3月24日	
															3月25日	
															3月26日	
															3月27日	
															3月28日	
															3月29日	
															3月30日	
															3月31日	

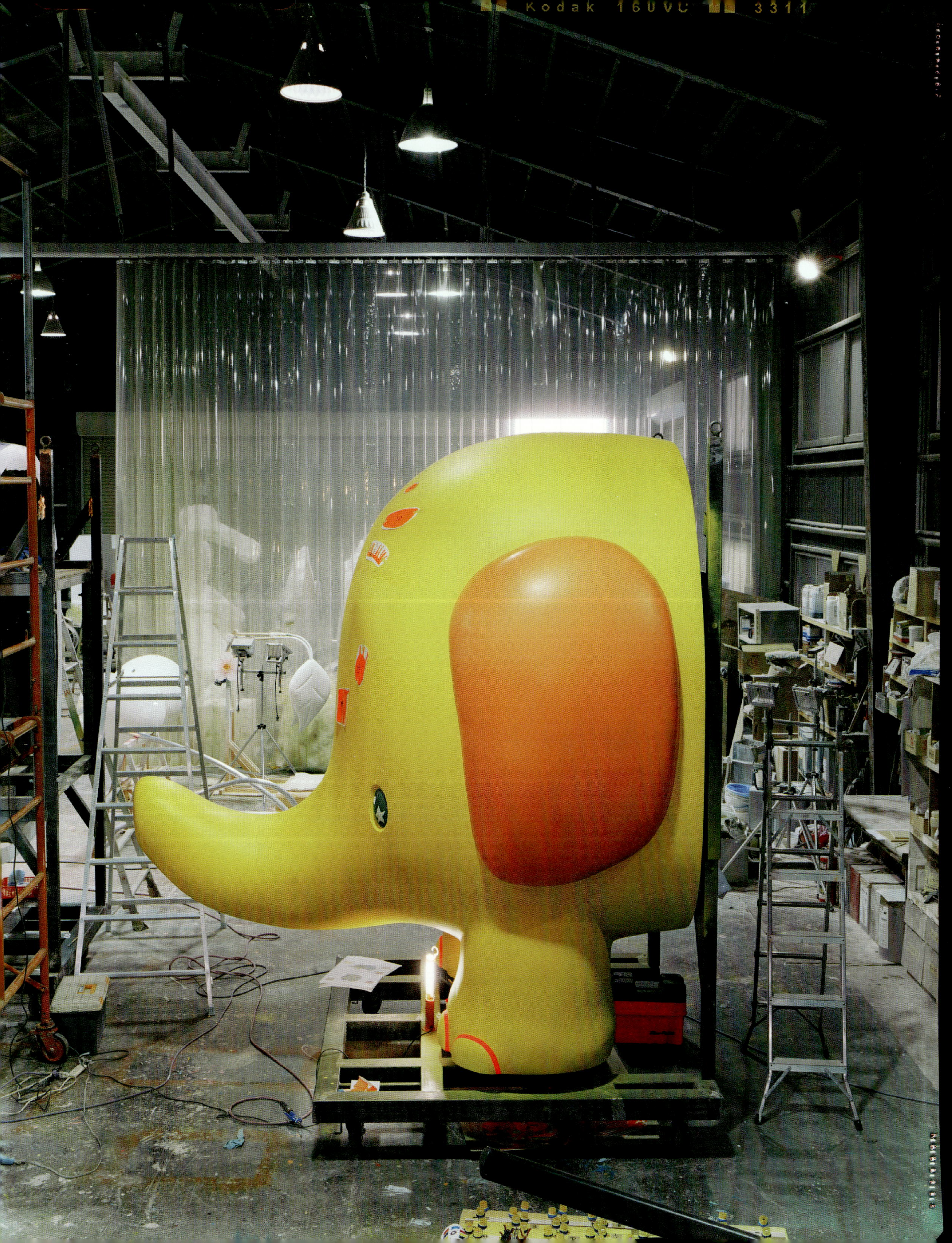
Kodak 160VC
3311

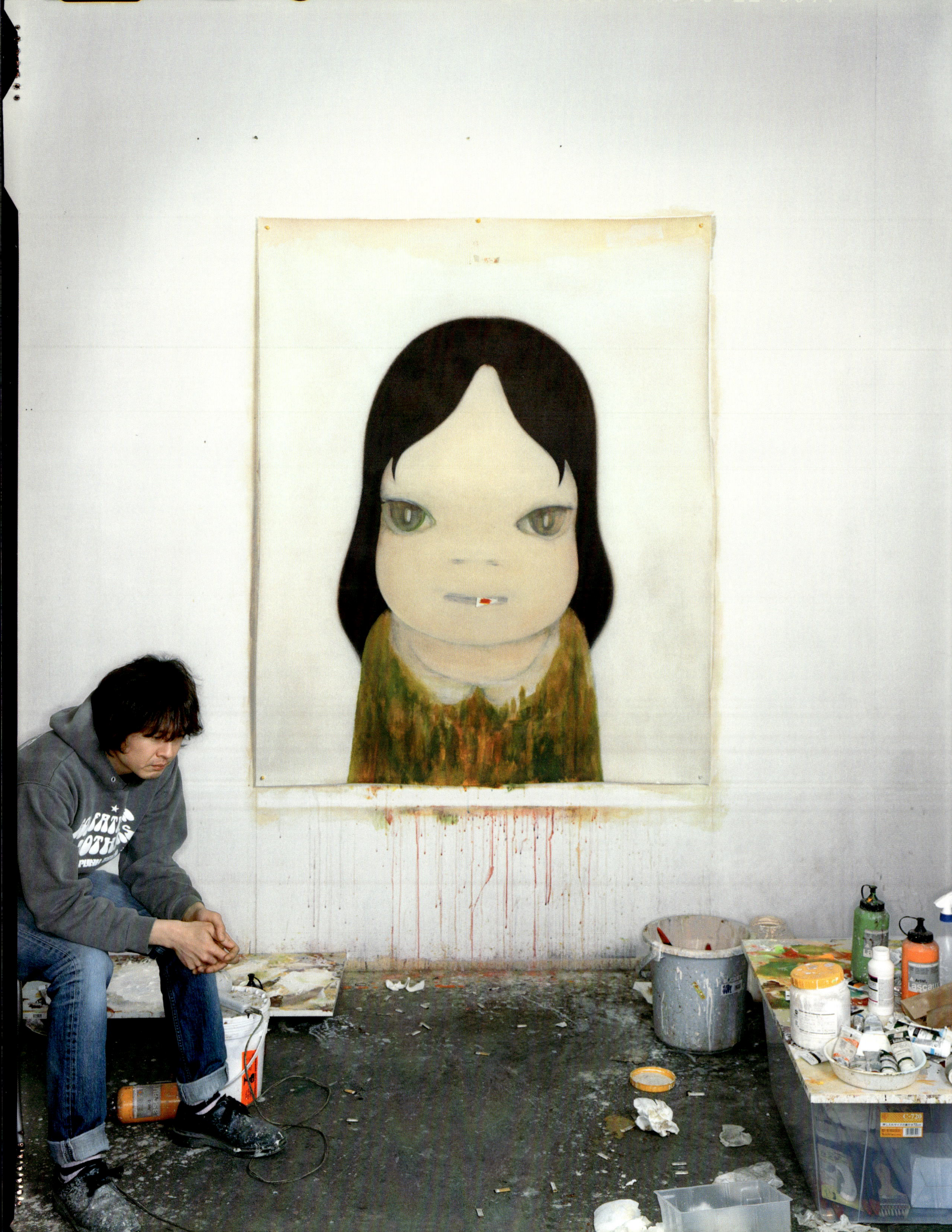

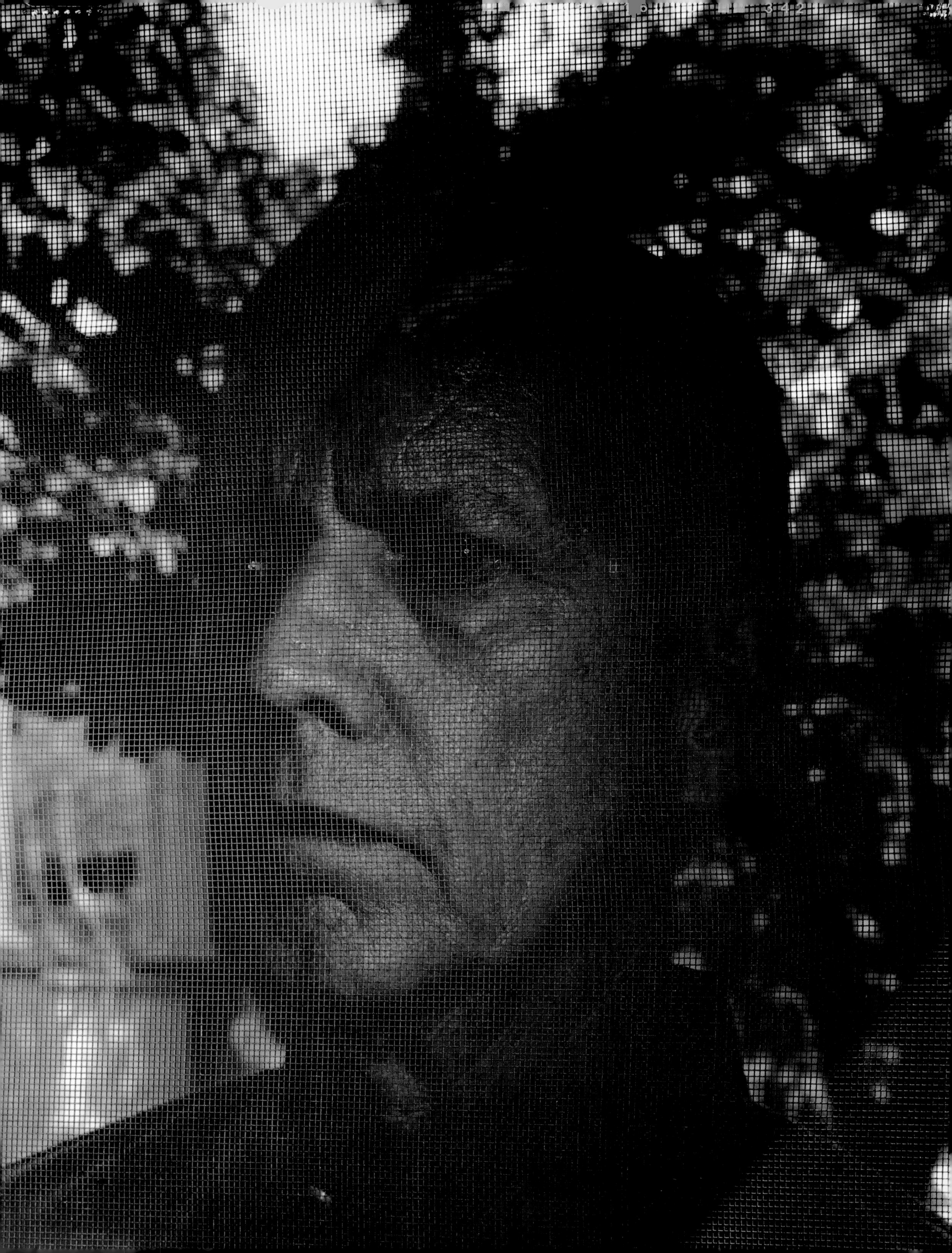

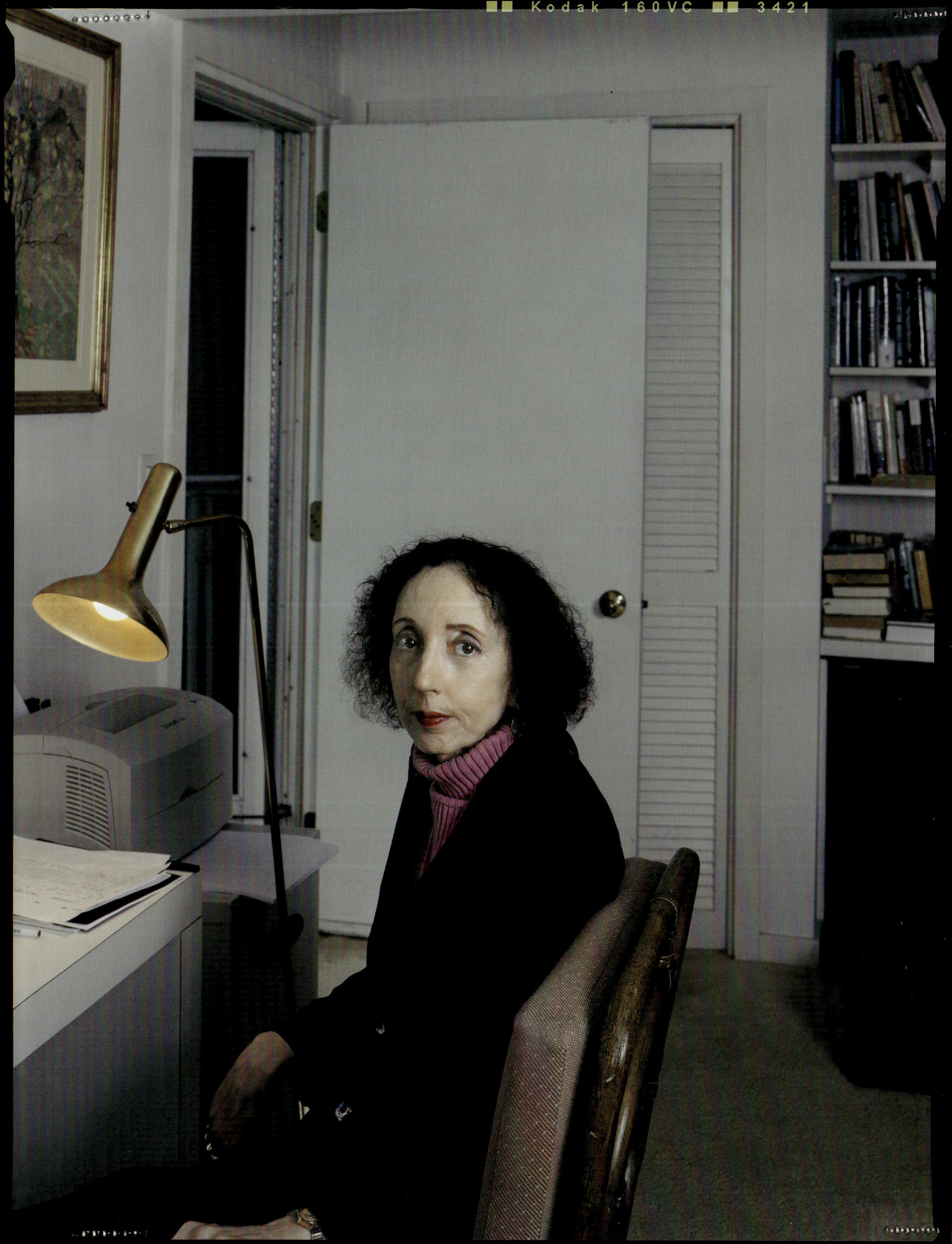
Kodak 160VC 3421

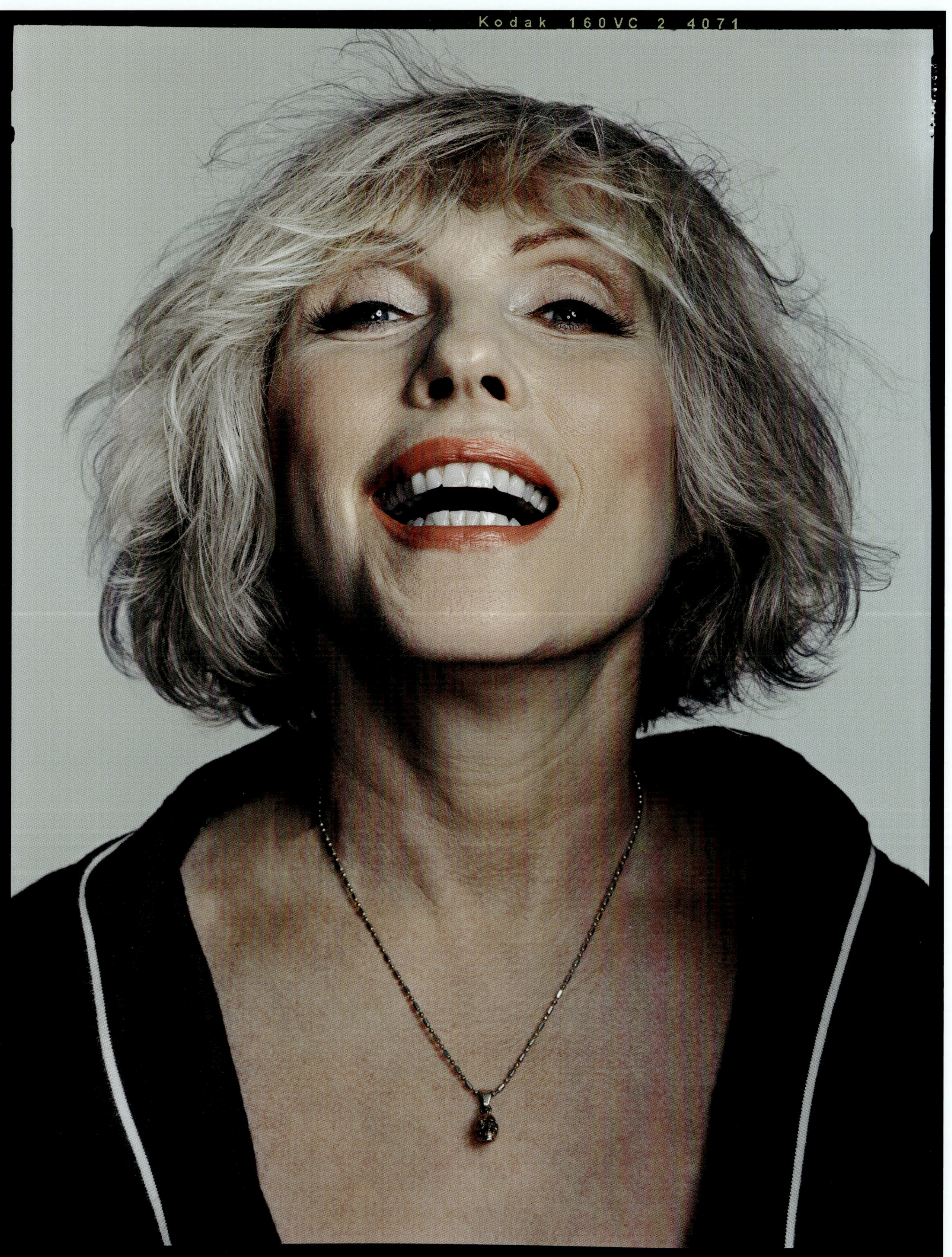
Kodak 160VC 2 4071

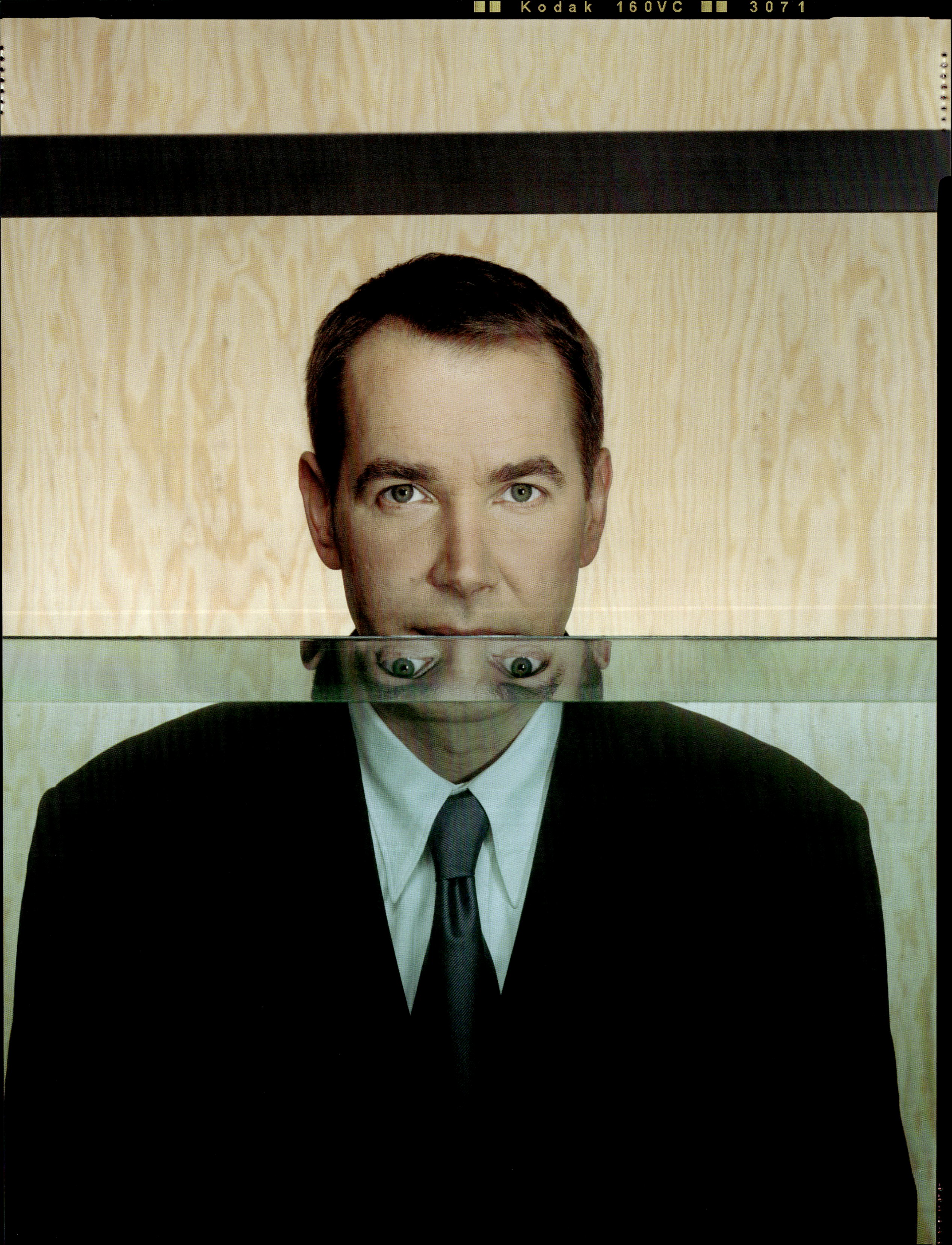

Kodak 160VC 3071

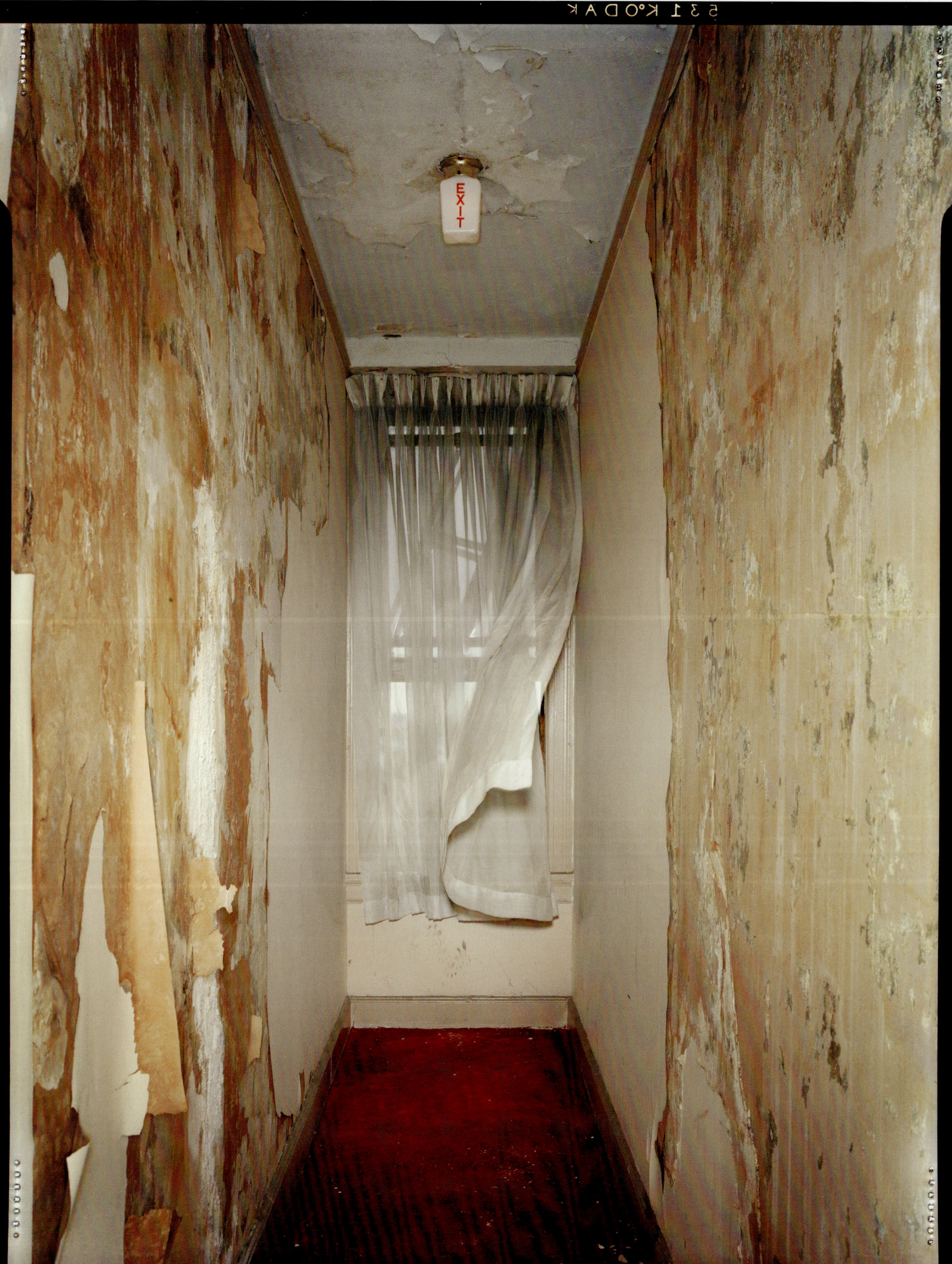
EXIT

Kodak 160VC 3381

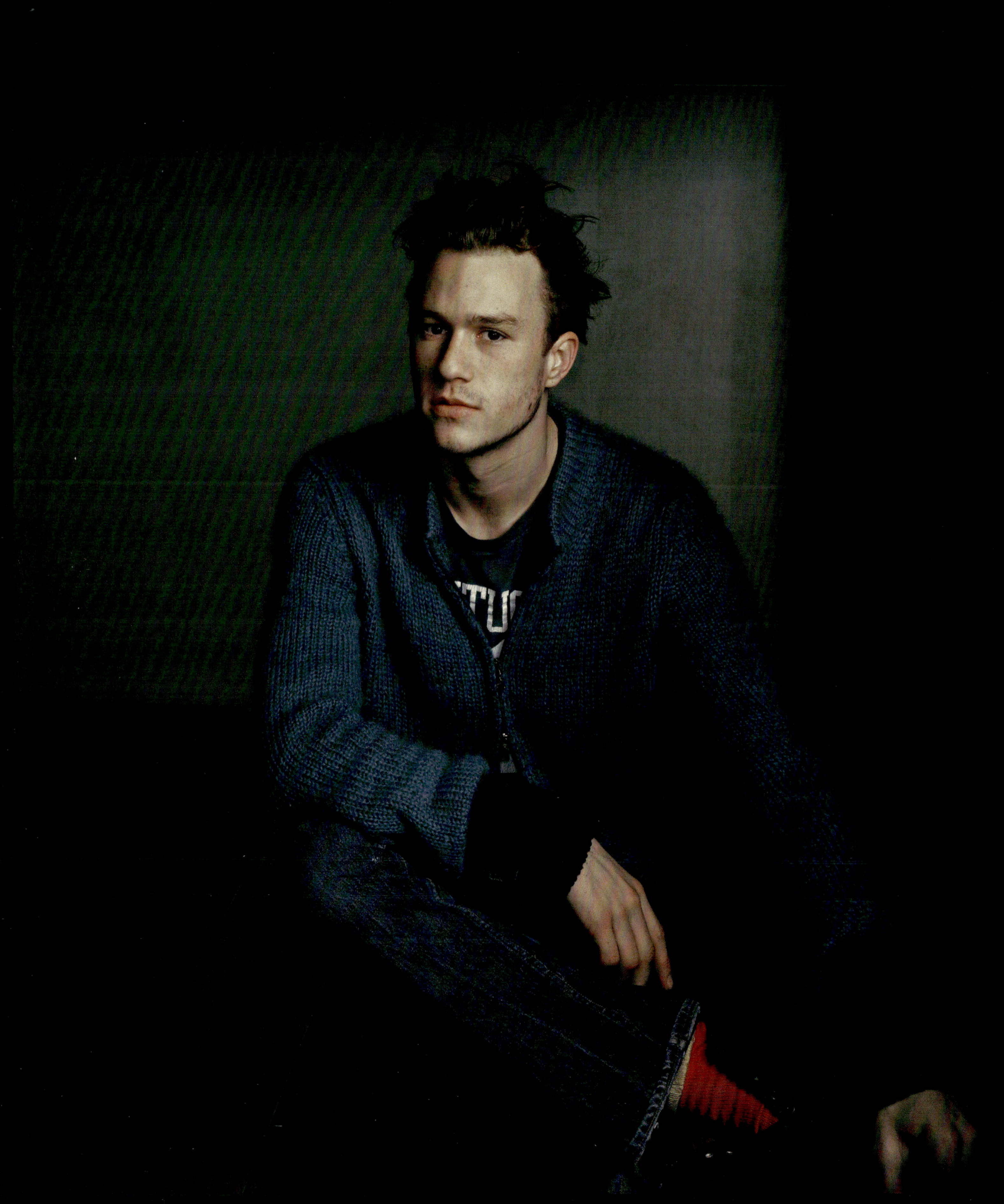

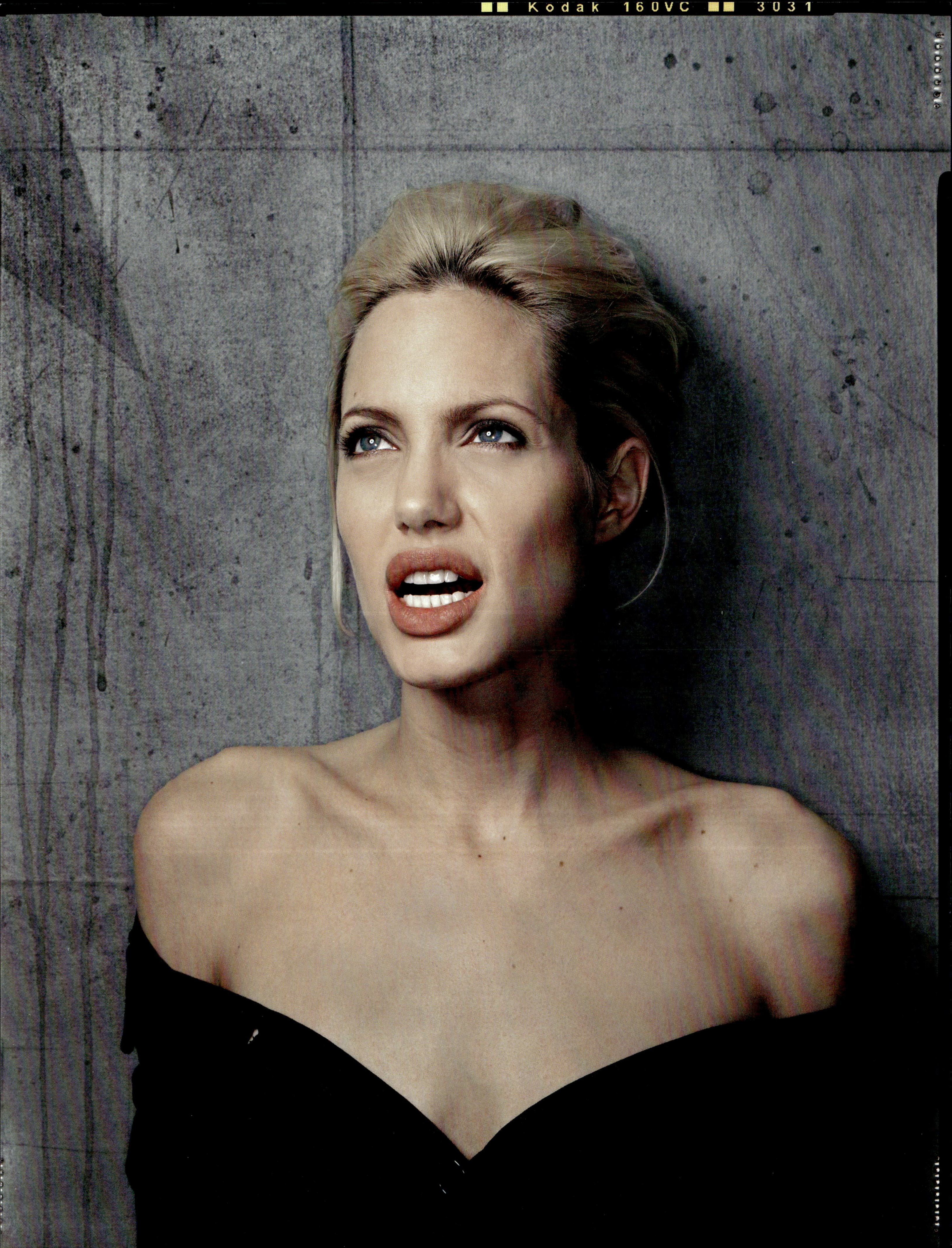
Kodak 160VC 3031

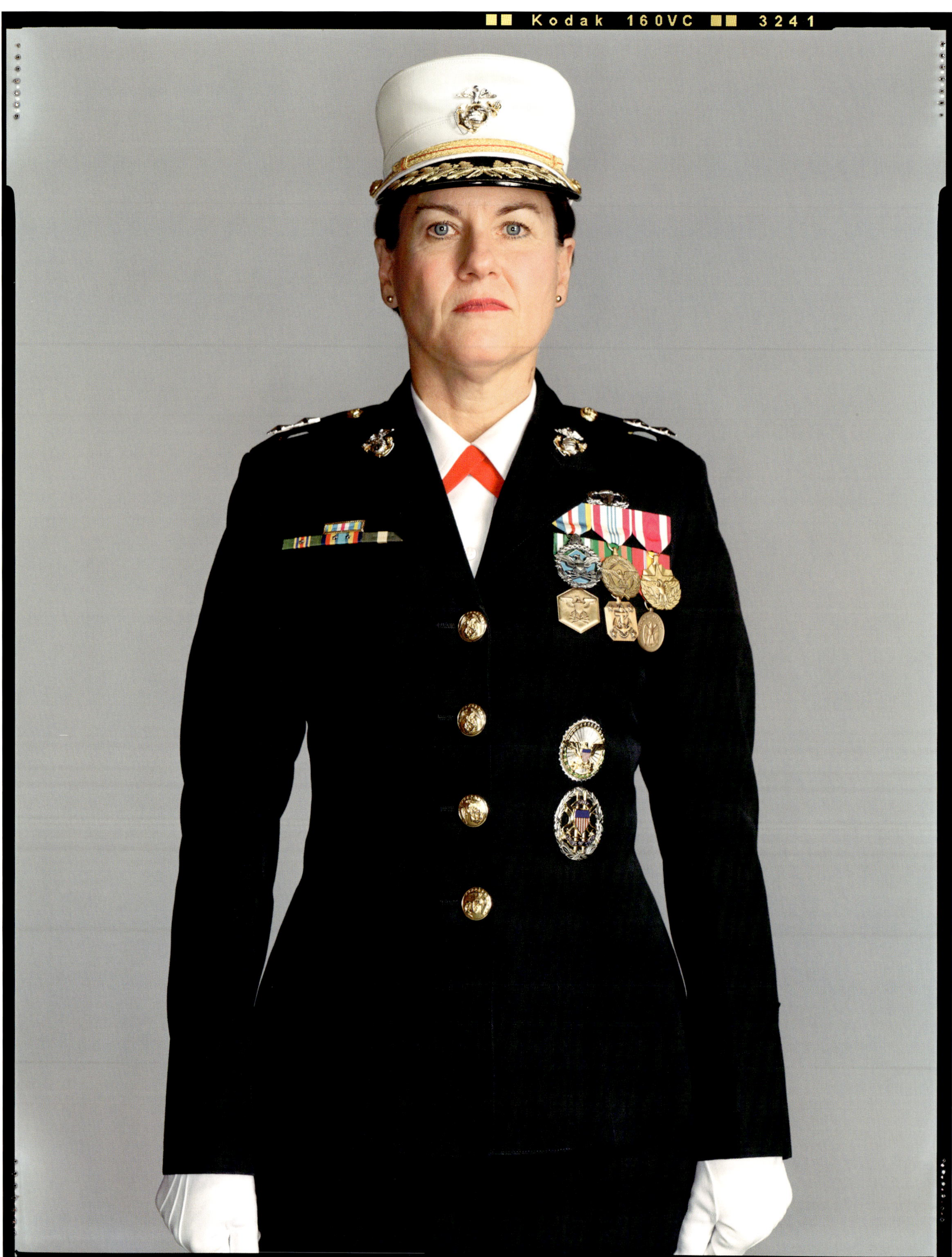
Kodak 160VC 3241

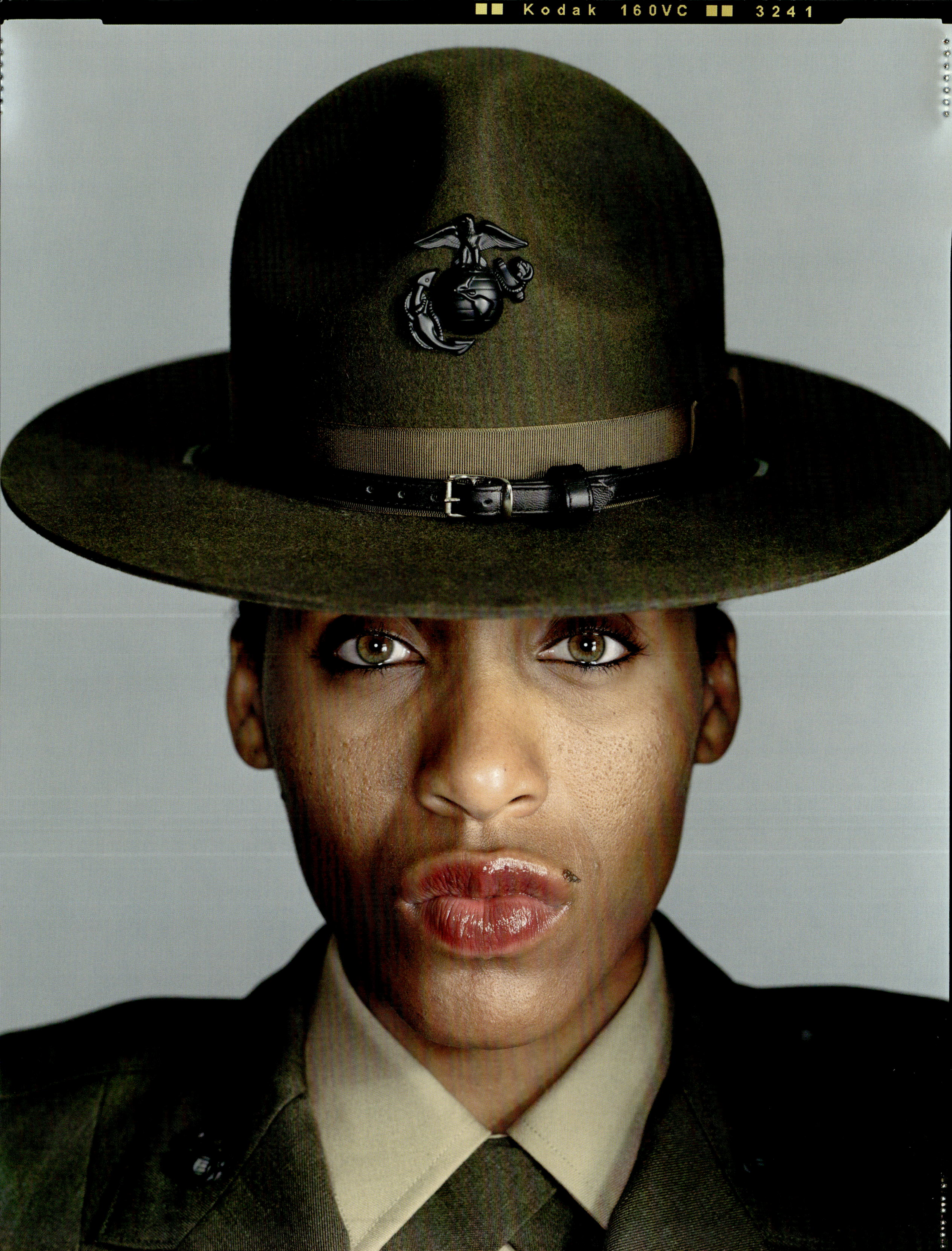

Kodak 160VC 3241

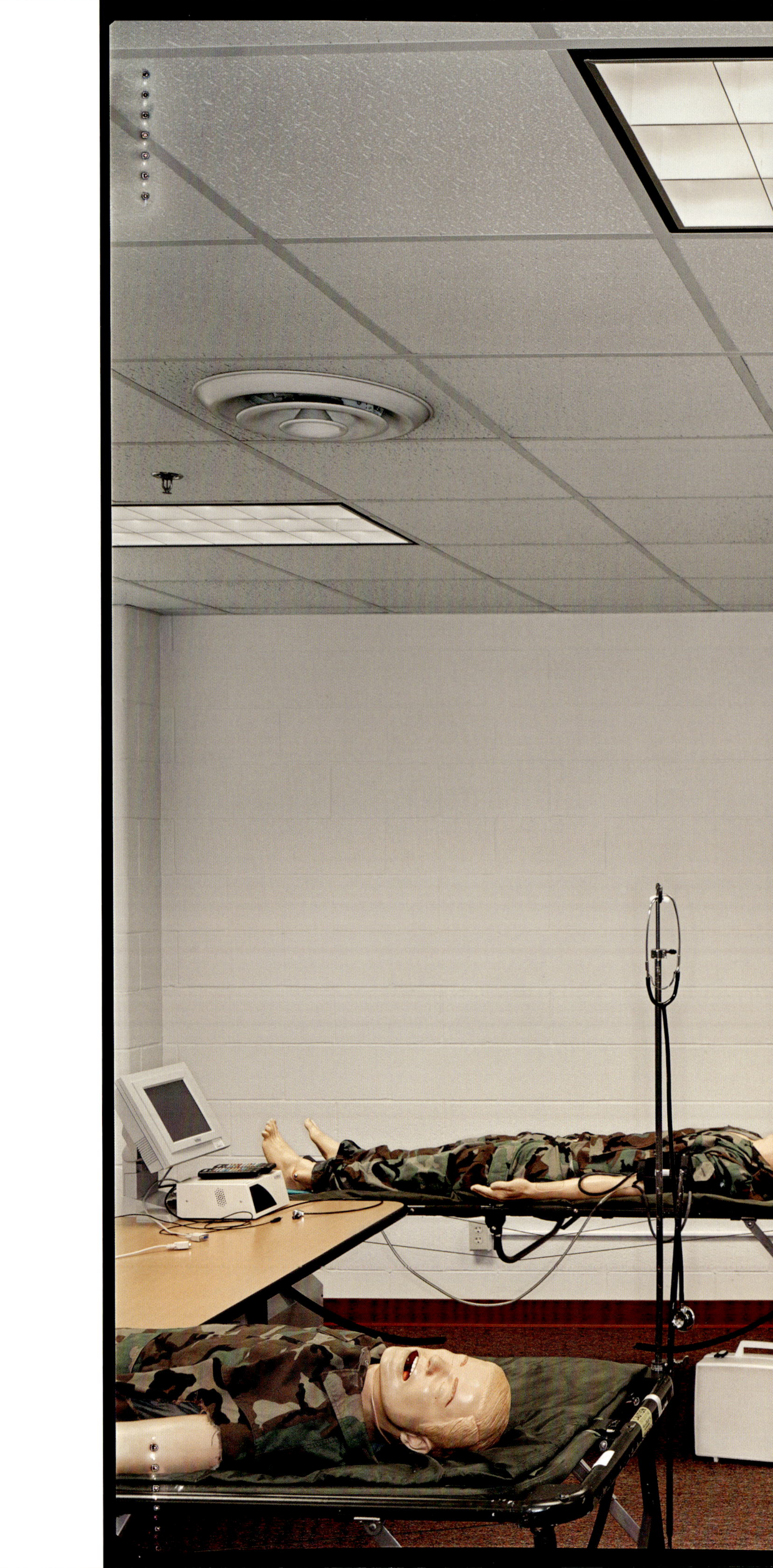

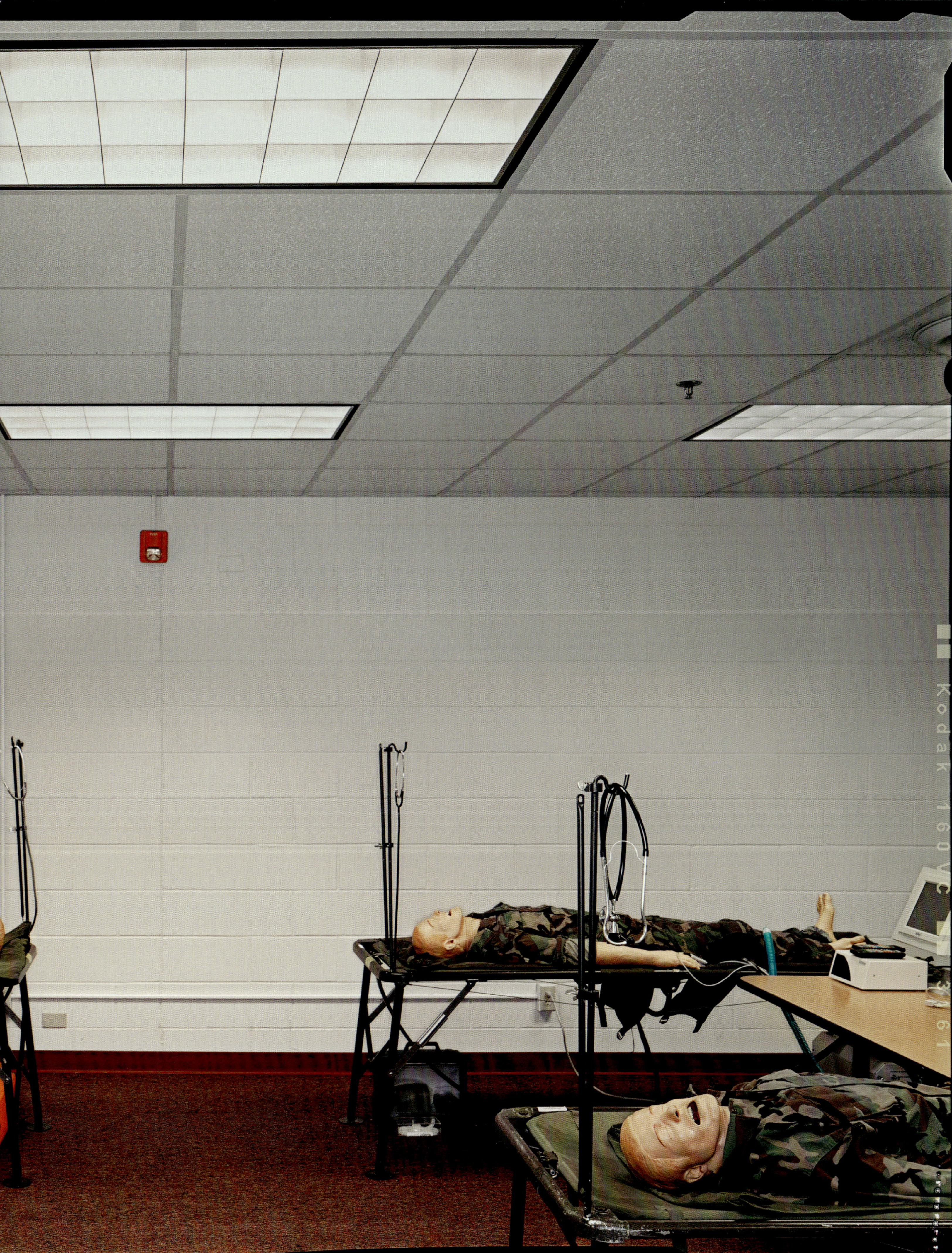

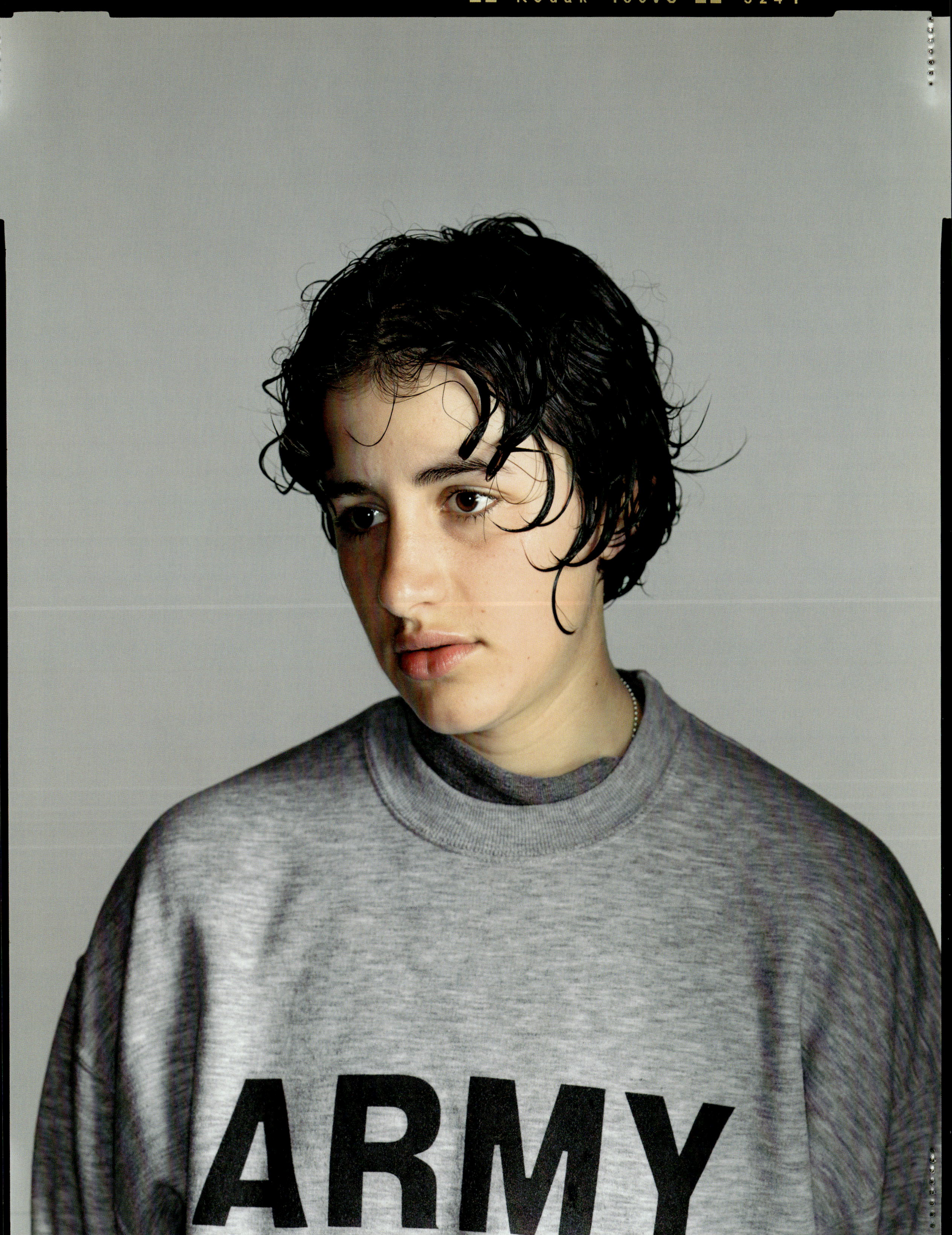
Kodak 160VC
3241
ARMY

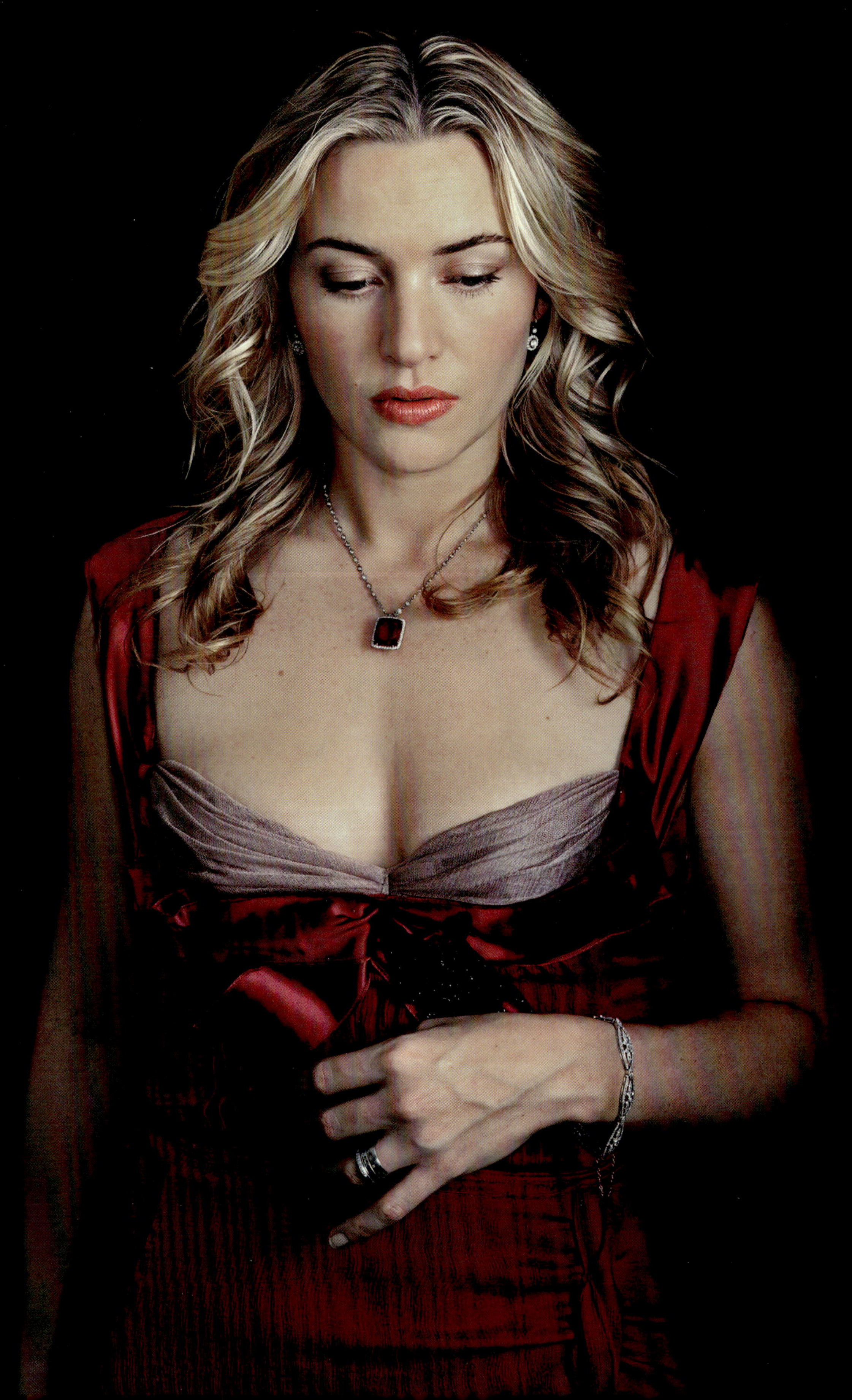
Kodak 160VC 3291

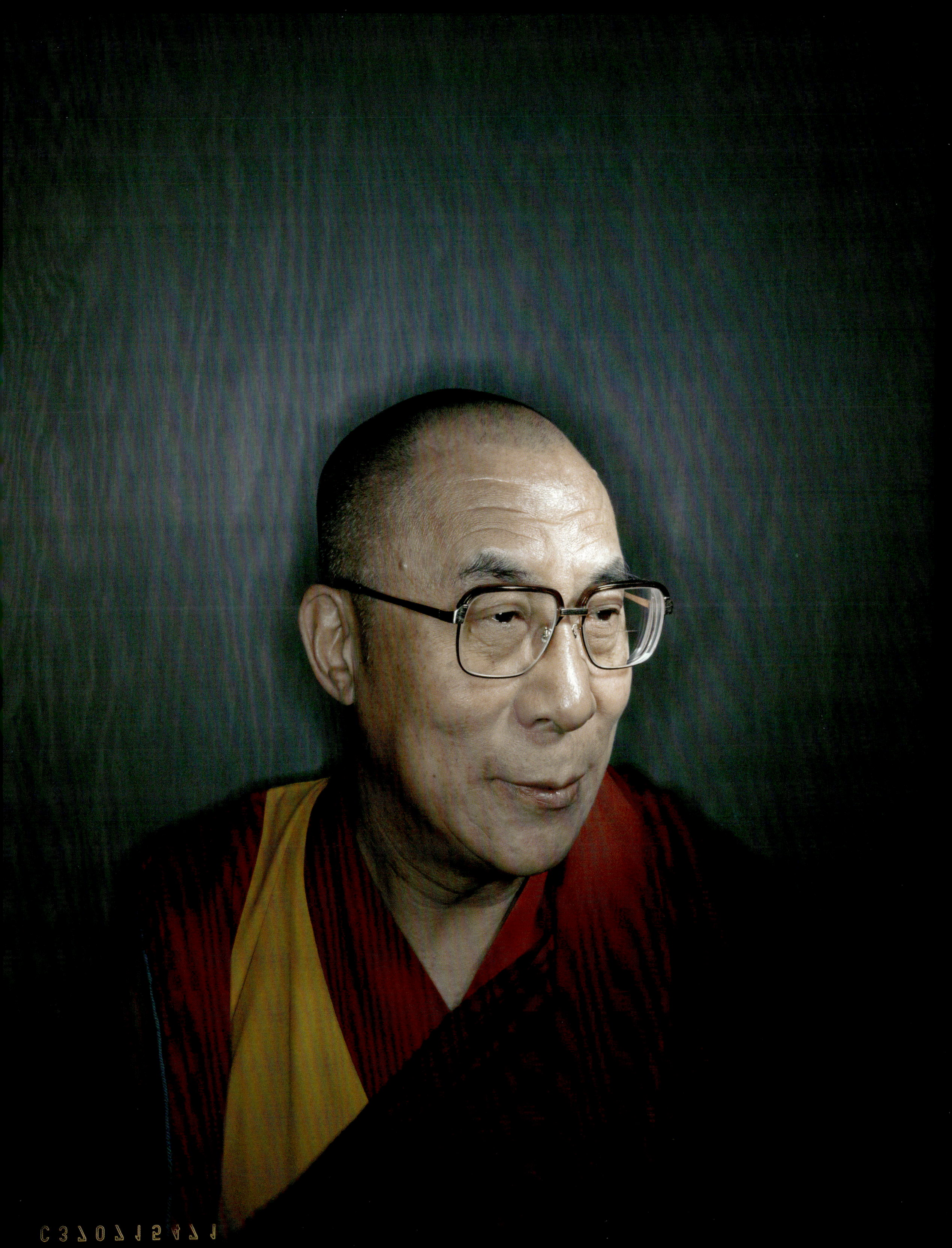

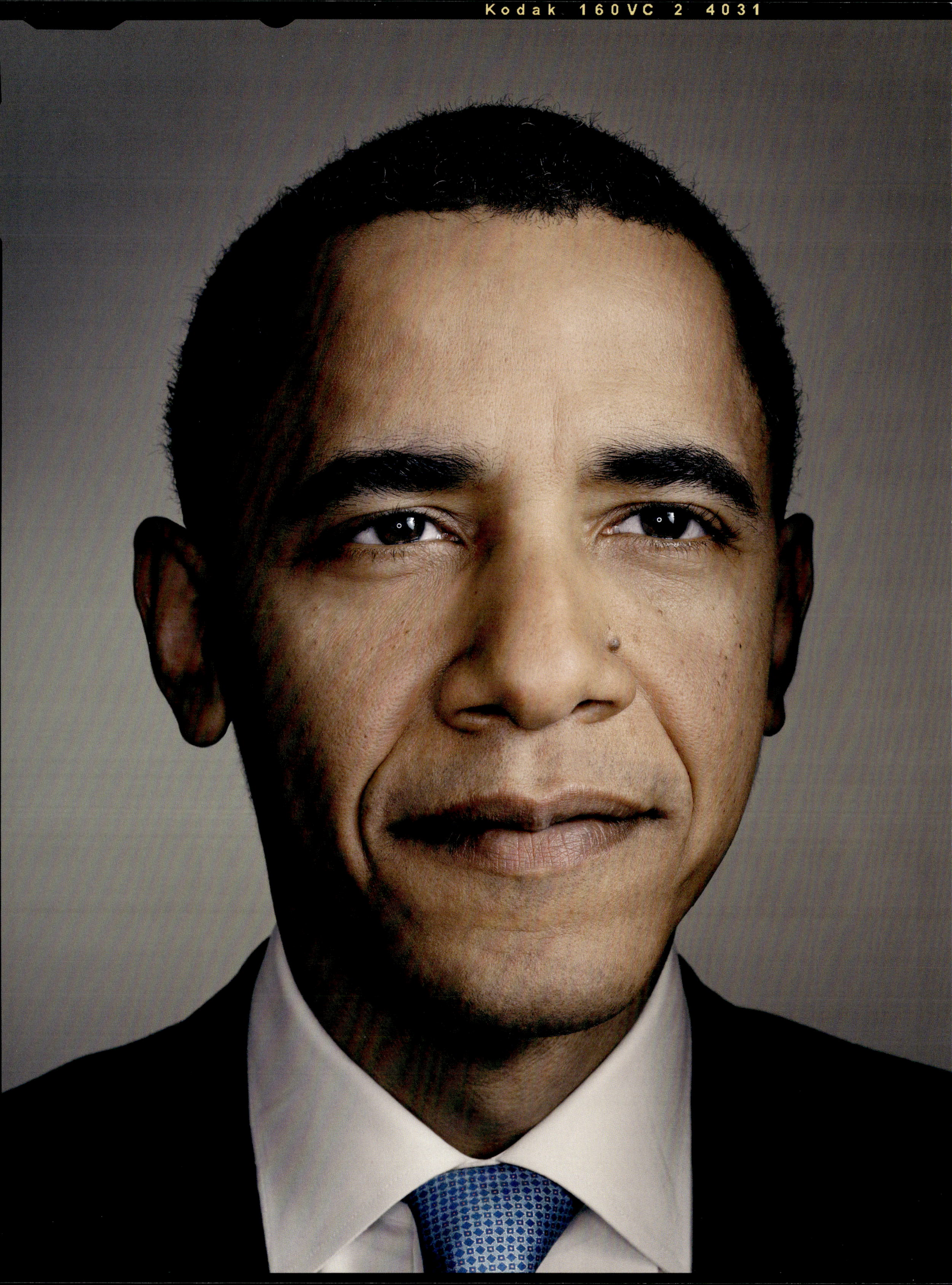

Kodak 160VC 2 4031

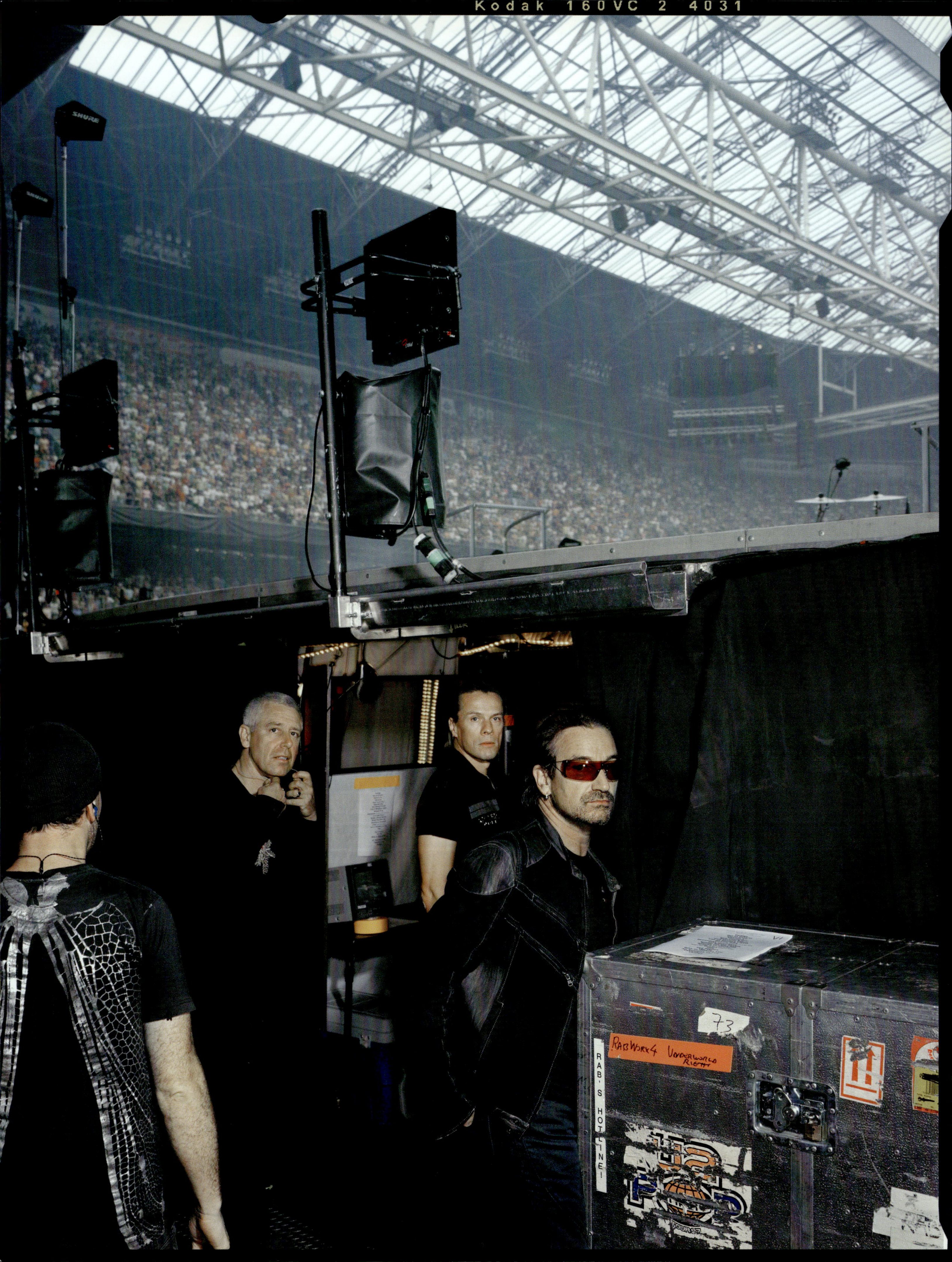

Kodak 160VC 2 4031
SHURE
73
RAB'S HOT LINE!

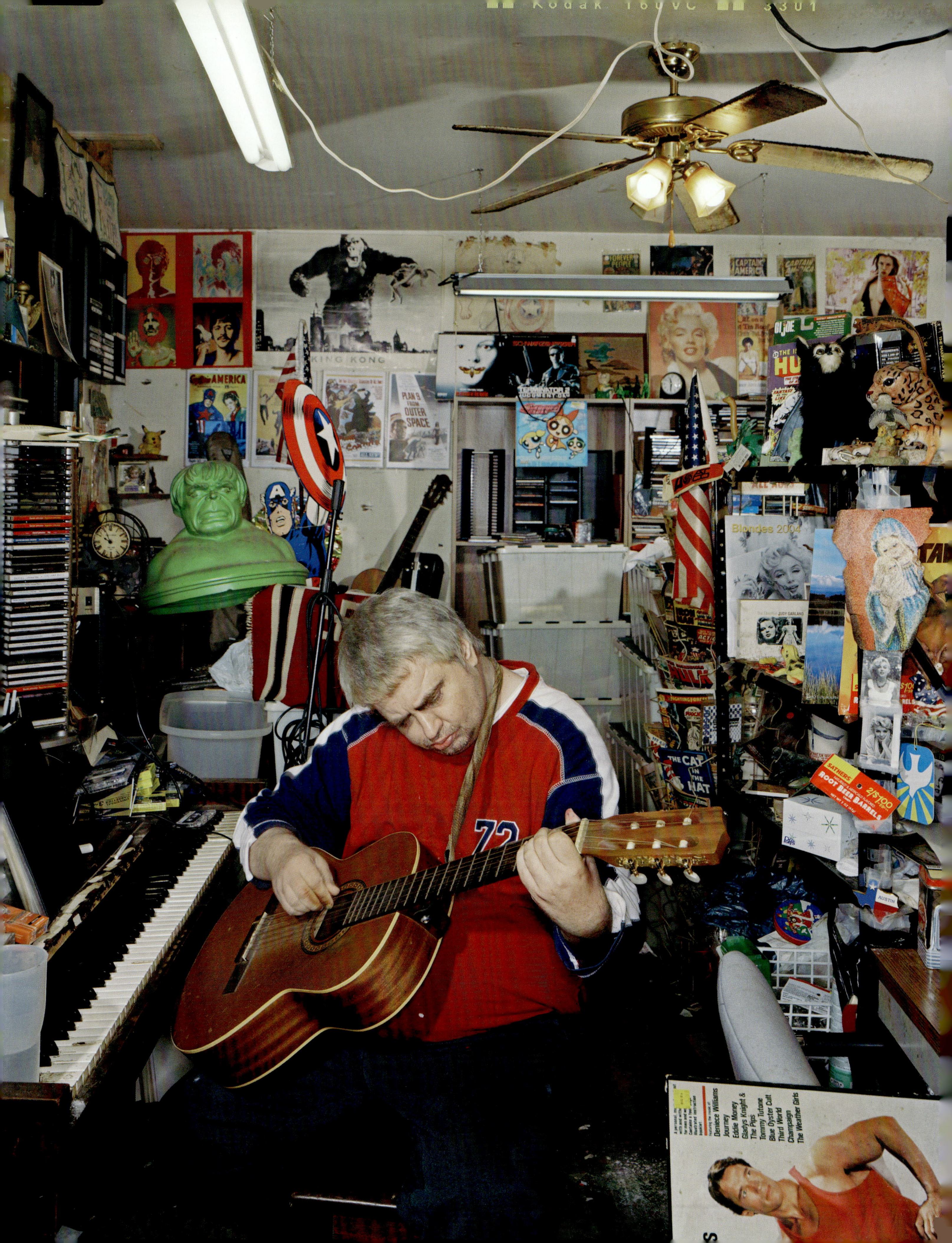

KING KONG
PLAN 9 FROM OUTER SPACE
TERMINATOR 3 JUDGMENT DAY
Blondes 2004
THE CAT IN THE HAT
ROOT BEER BARRELS
AUSTIN
Deniece Williams
Journey
Eddie Money
Gladys Knight &
The Pips
Tommy Tutone
Blue Oyster Cult
Third World
Champaign
The Weather Girls

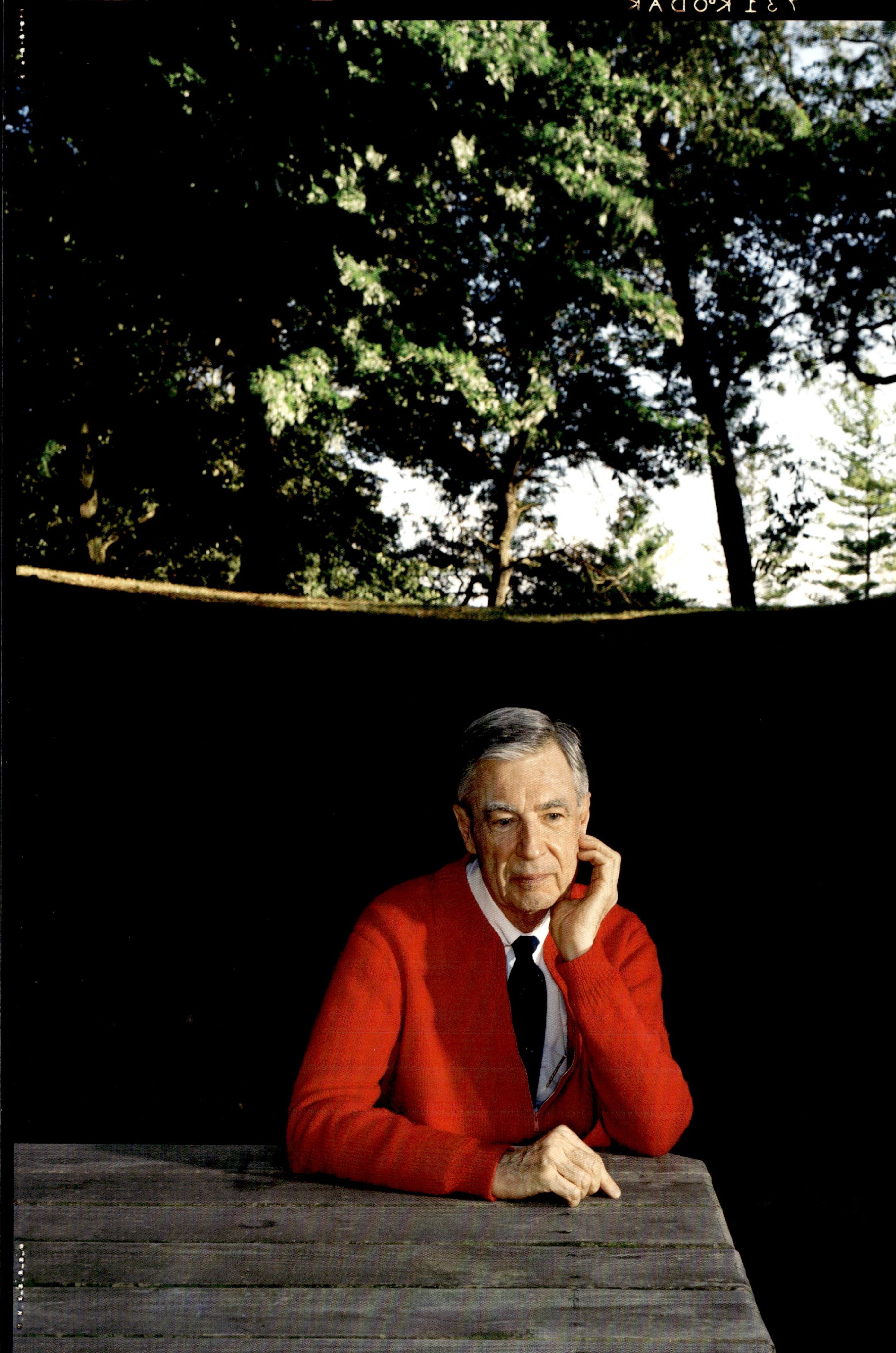

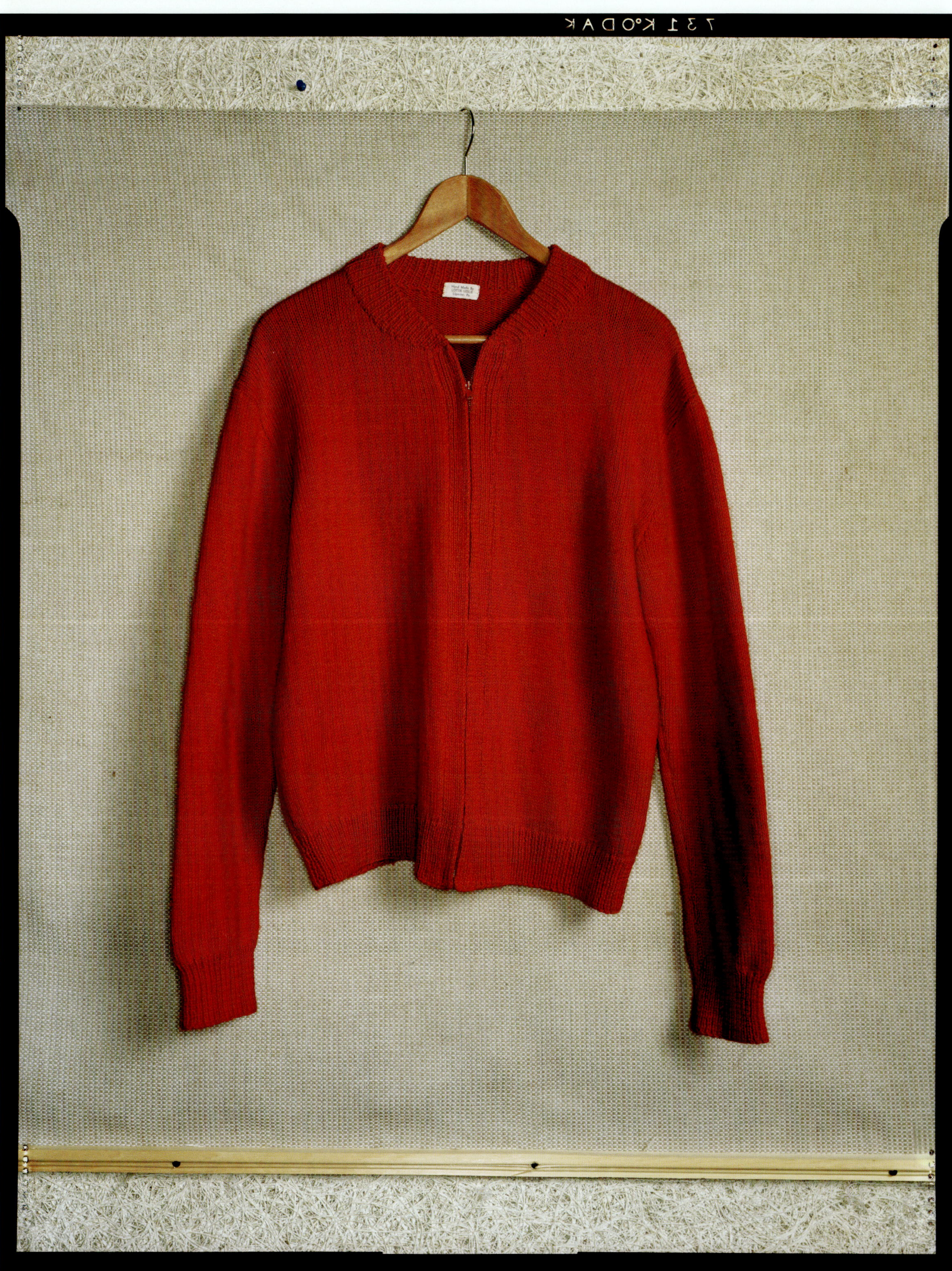

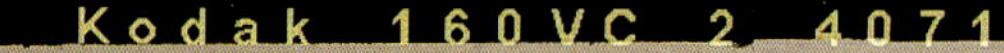
Kodak 160VC 2 4071

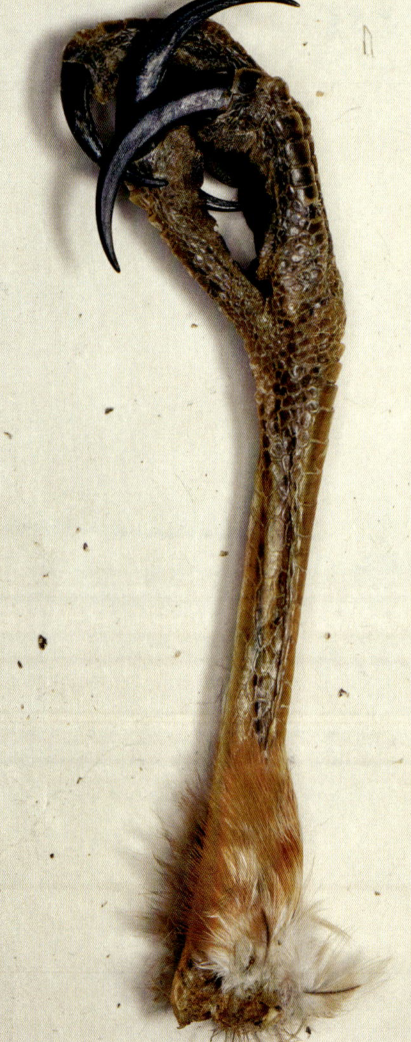
created.
STK3
PRINTED IN U S A
015
EVIDENCE IDENTIFICATION TAG
SEIZURE TAG NO
607734
ITEM NO.
1
DATE:
10/12/2006
FILE NO.

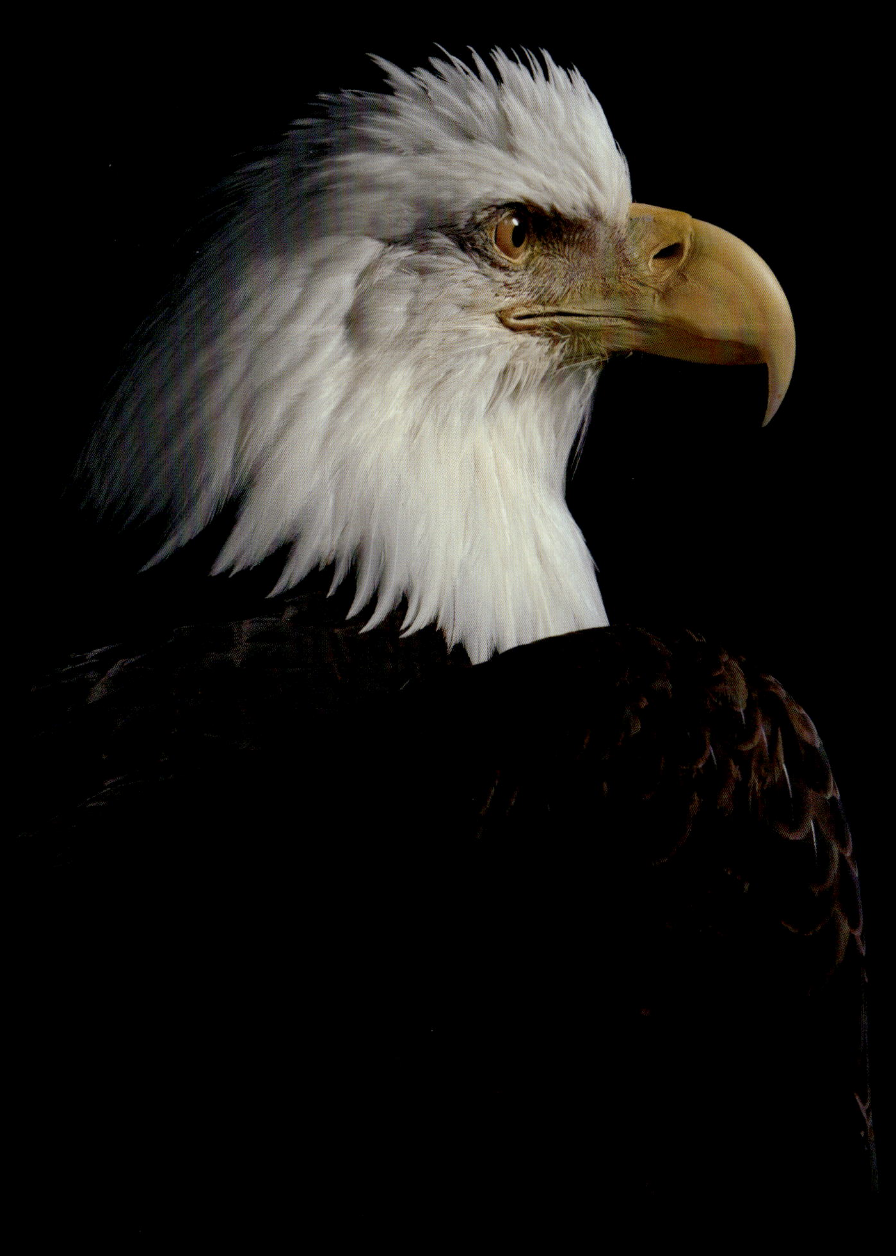
Kodak 160VC 2 4031

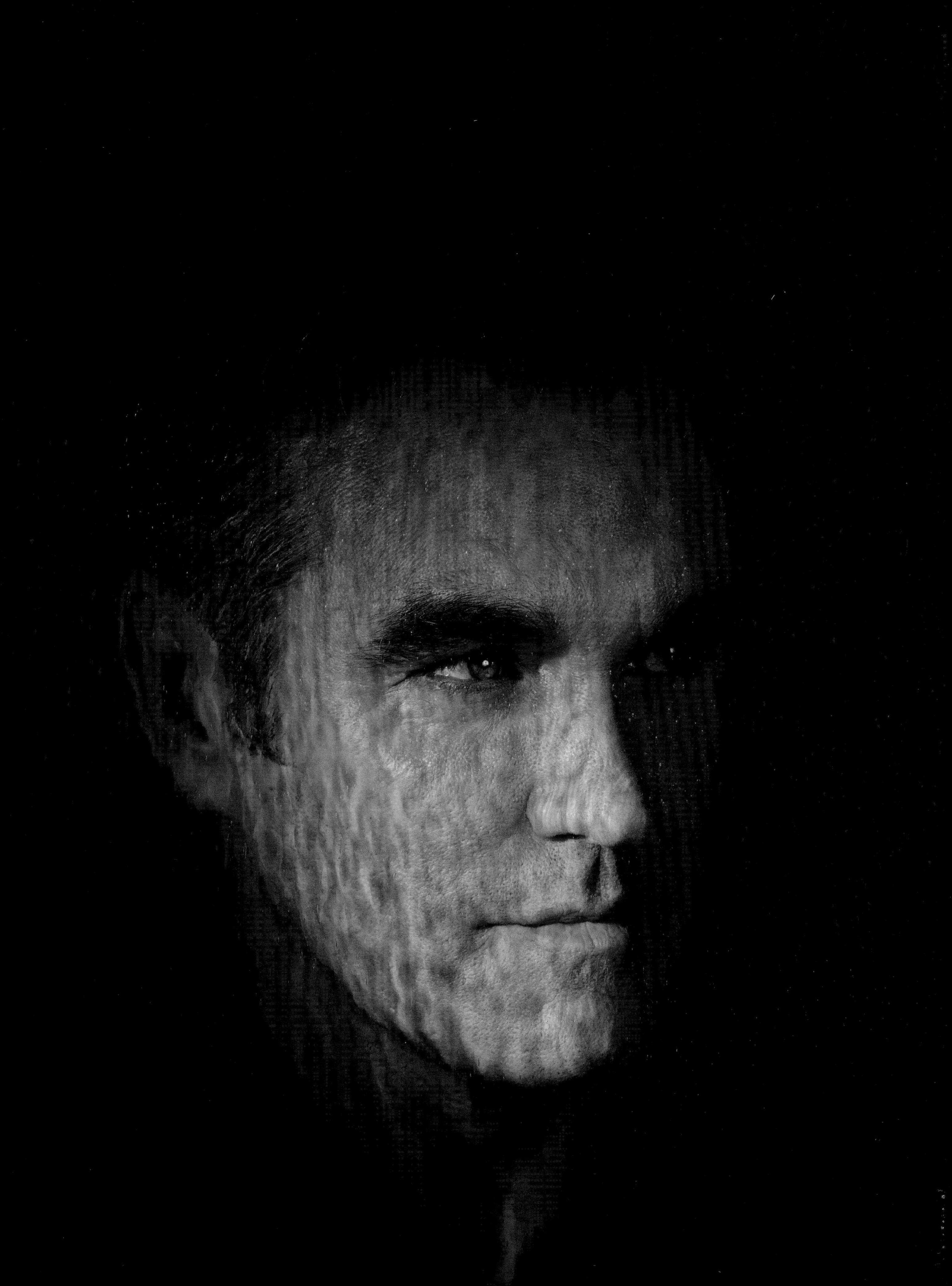

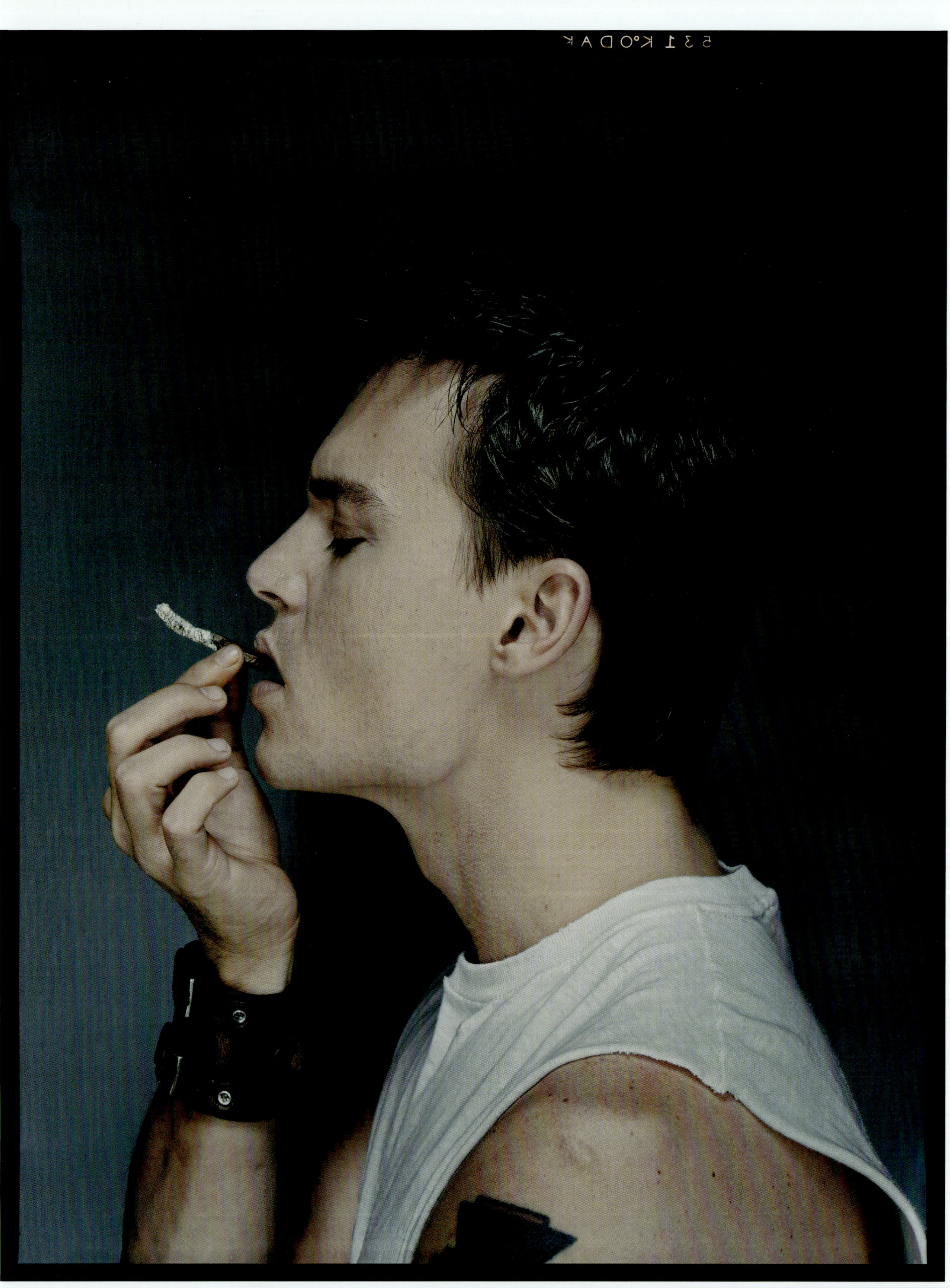

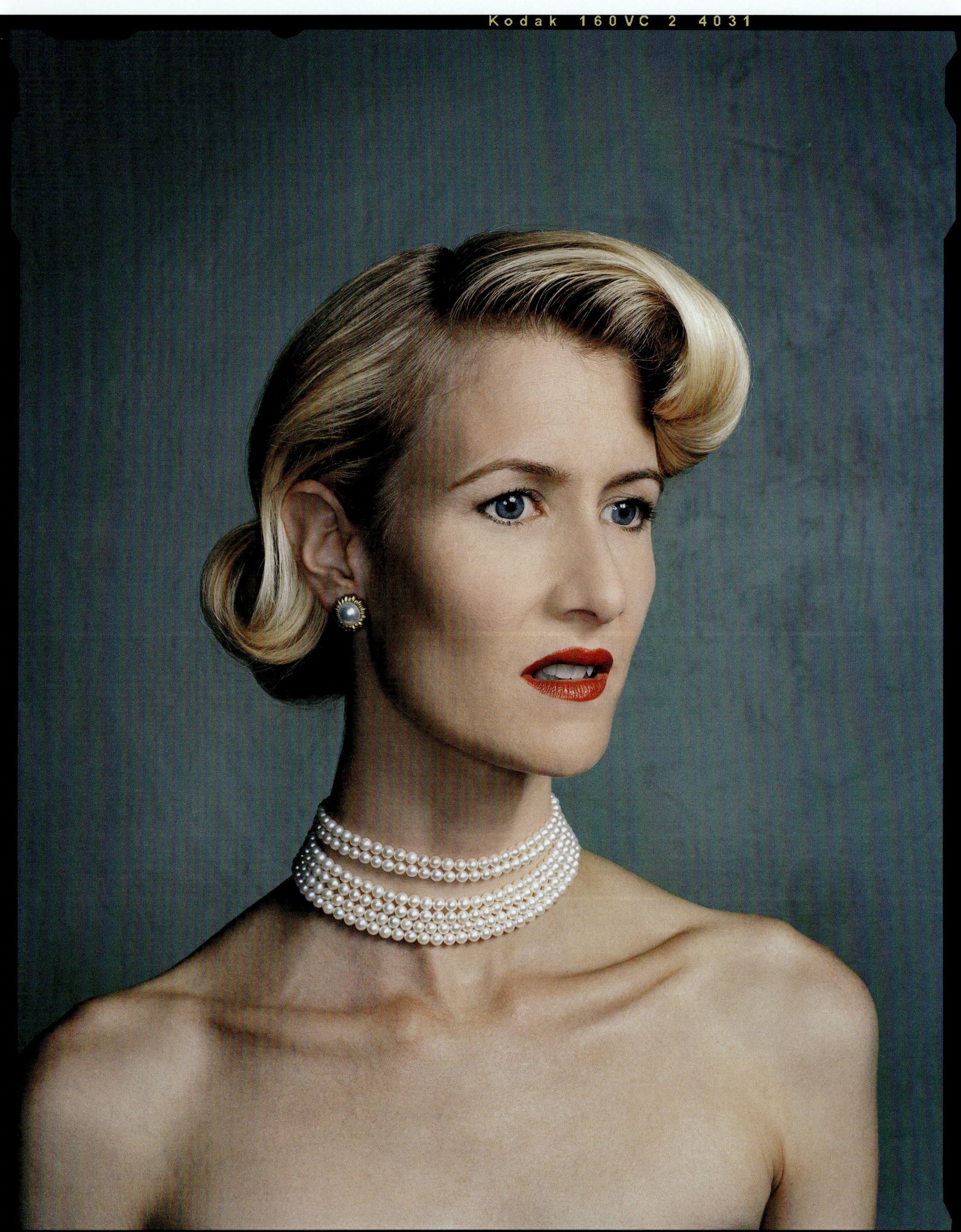
Kodak 160VC 2 4031

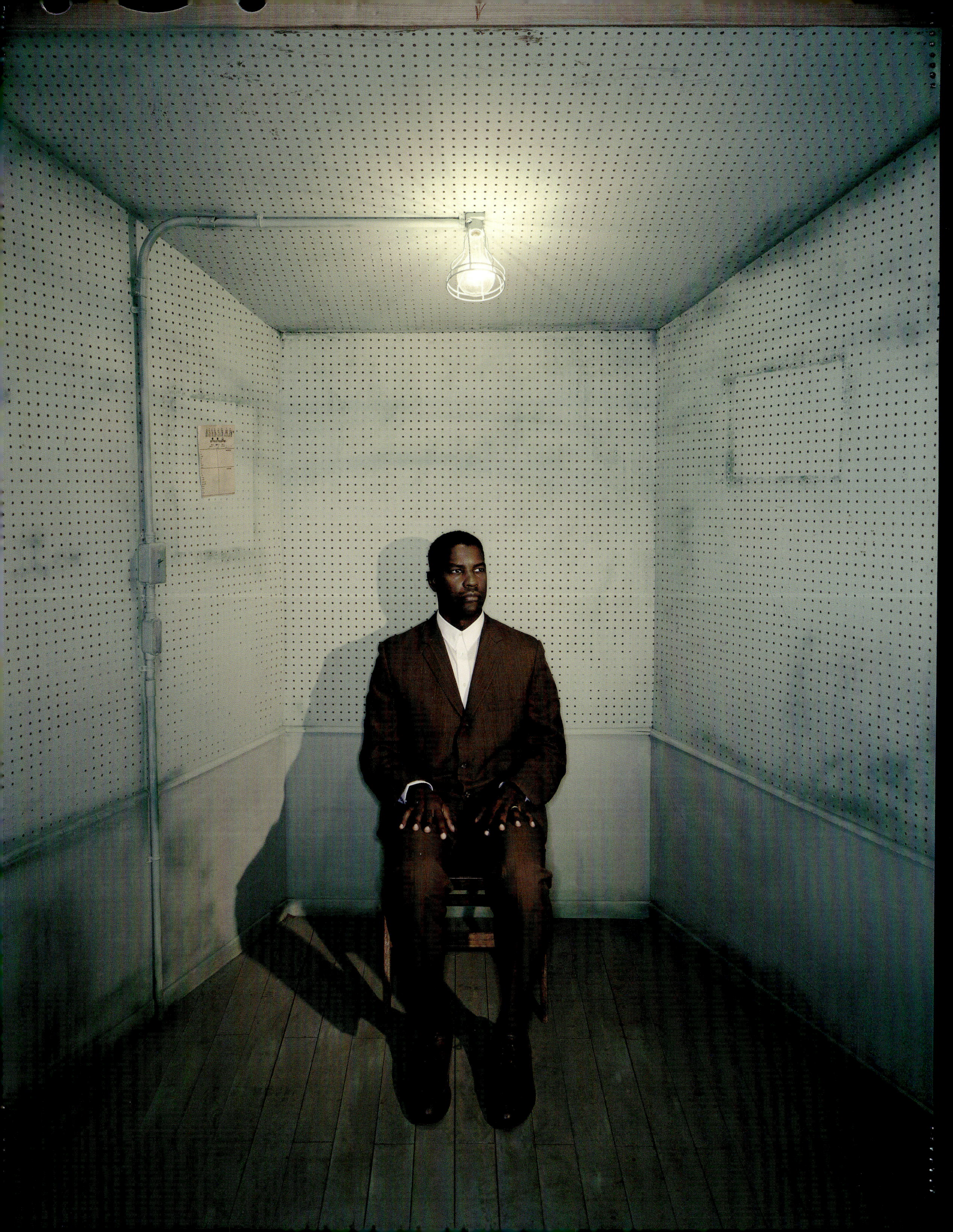

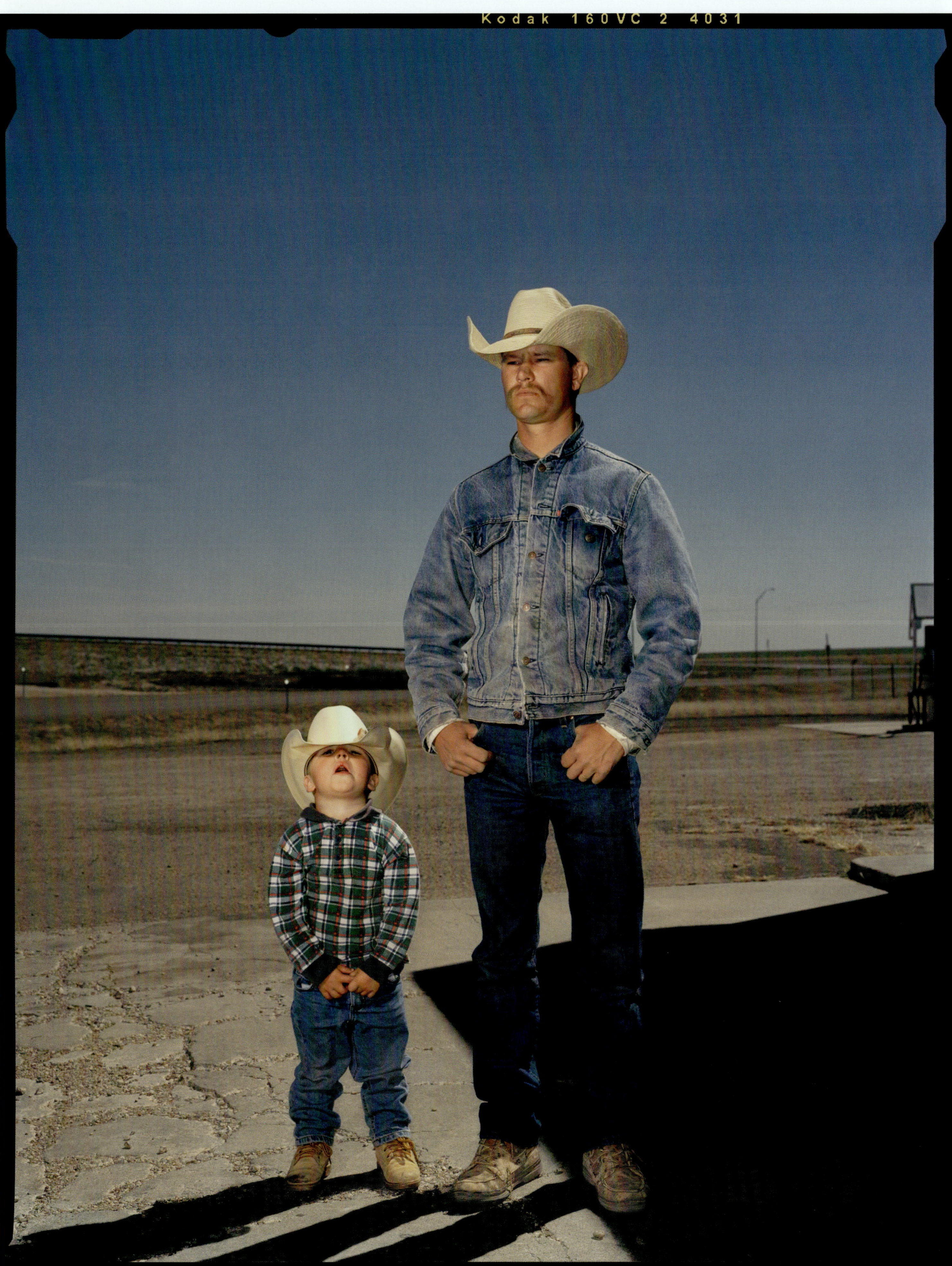
Kodak 160VC 2 4031

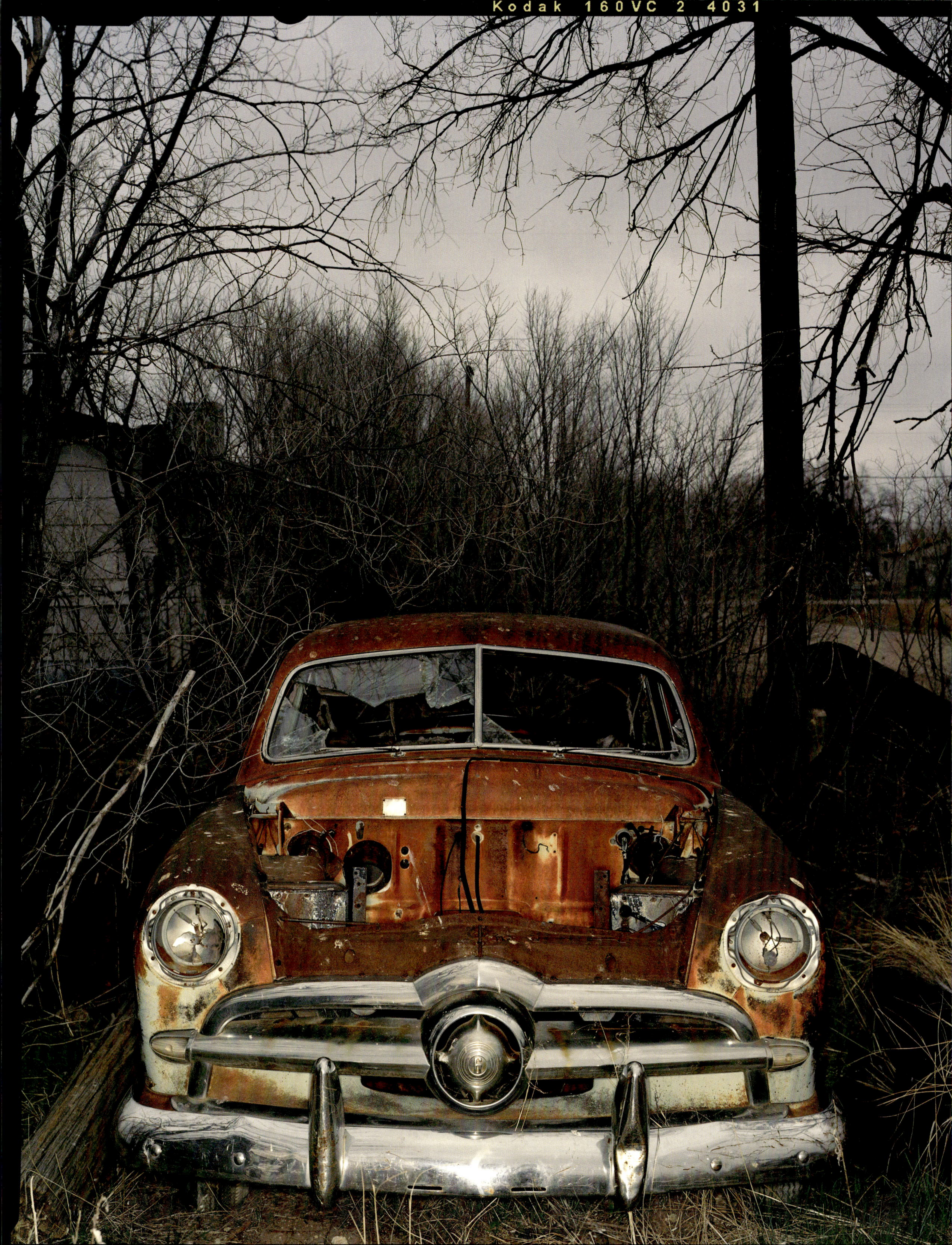
Kodak 160VC 2 4031

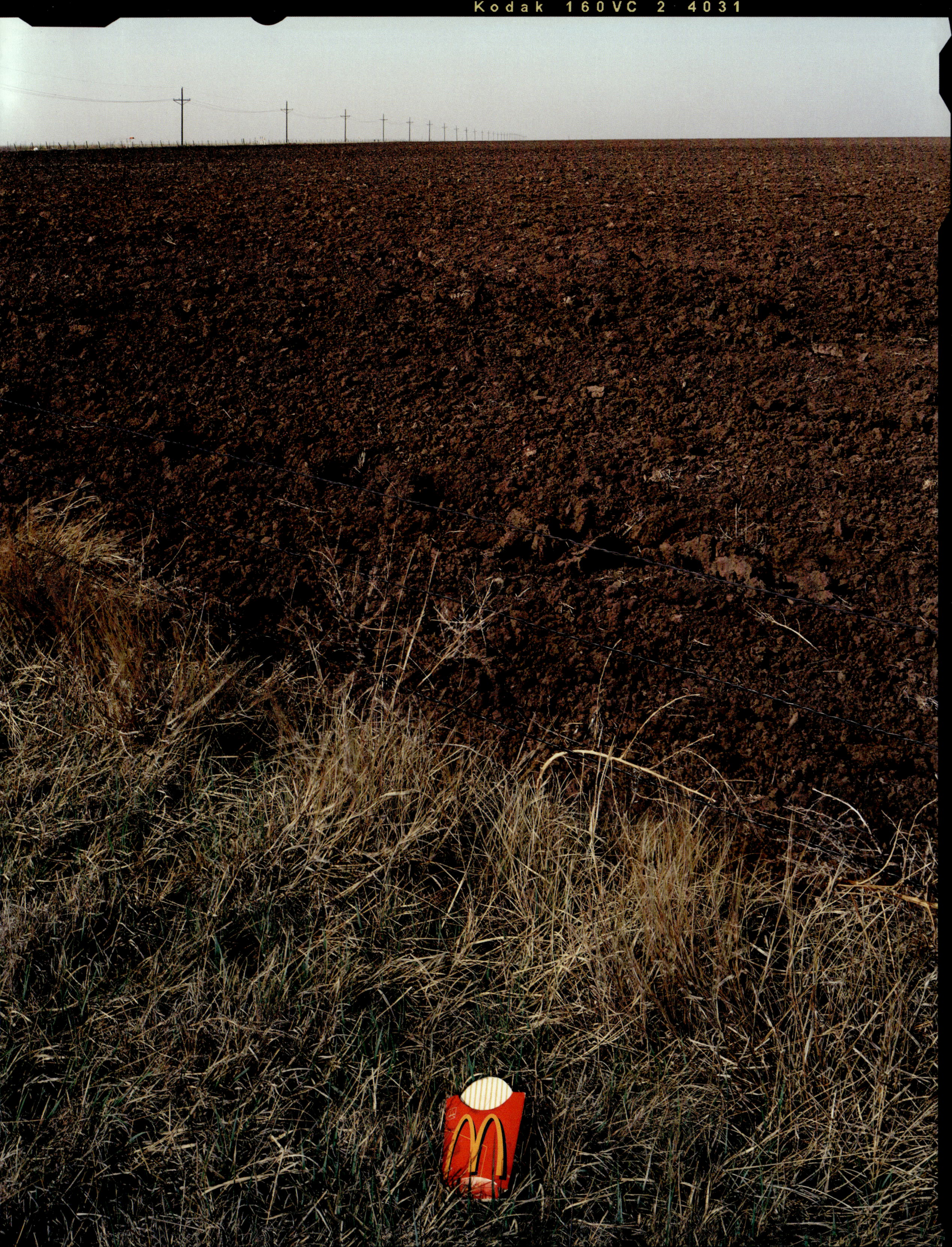
Kodak 160VC 2 4031

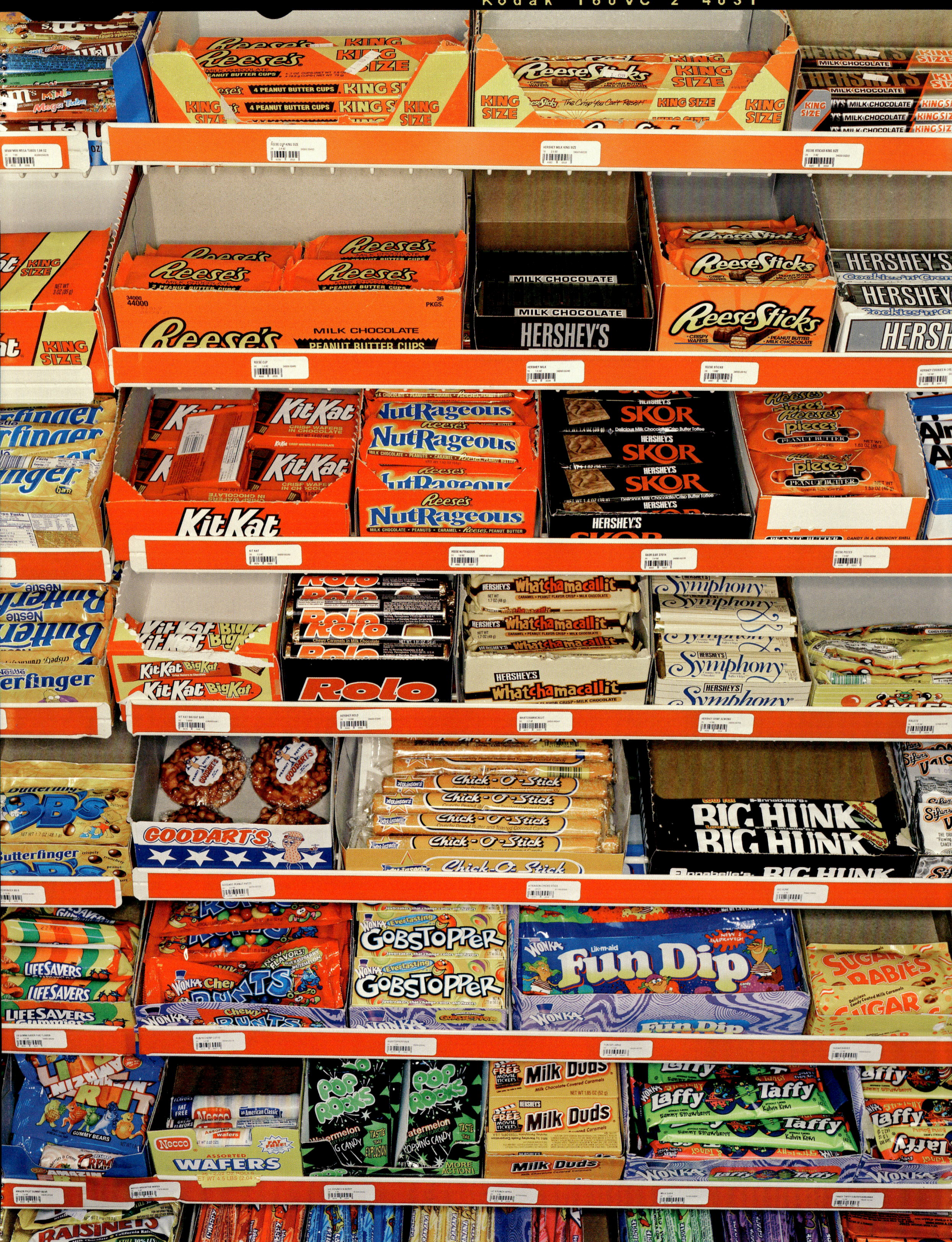
Kodak 160VC 2 4031
Reese's
KING SIZE
4 PEANUT BUTTER CUPS
ReeseSticks
HERSHEY'S MILK CHOCOLATE
MILK CHOCOLATE
HERSHEY'S
Reese's
MILK CHOCOLATE
PEANUT BUTTER CUPS
ReeseSticks
KitKat
NutRageous
SKOR
Reese's pieces
Butterfinger
KitKat BigKat
Rolo
Whatchamacallit
Symphony
GOODART'S
Chick-O-Stick
BIG HUNK
LIFESAVERS
GOBSTOPPER
Fun Dip
SUGAR BABIES
Milk Duds
Taffy
Necco
WAFERS
POP ROCKS
RAISINETS

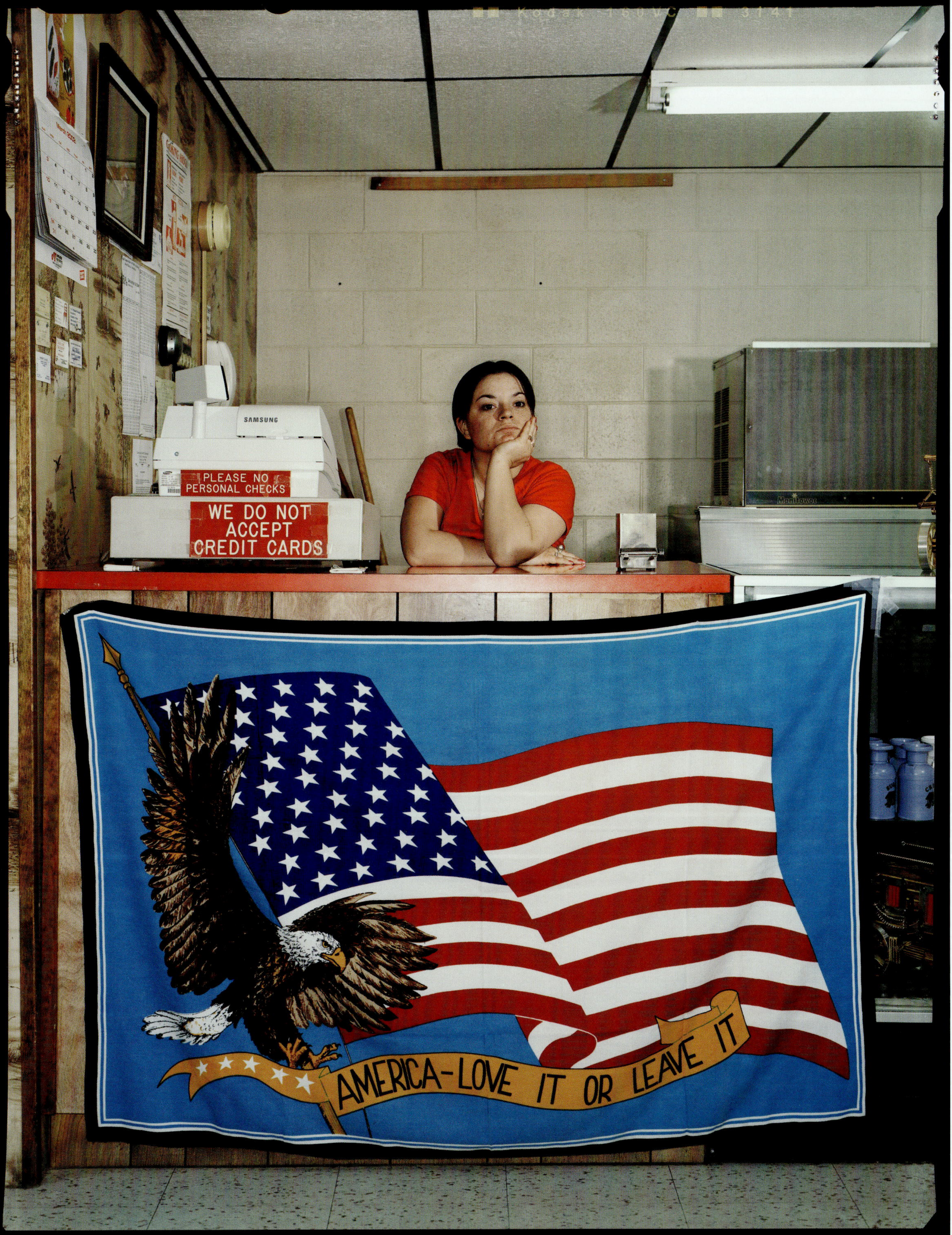
SAMSUNG
PLEASE NO PERSONAL CHECKS
WE DO NOT ACCEPT CREDIT CARDS
AMERICA-LOVE IT OR LEAVE IT

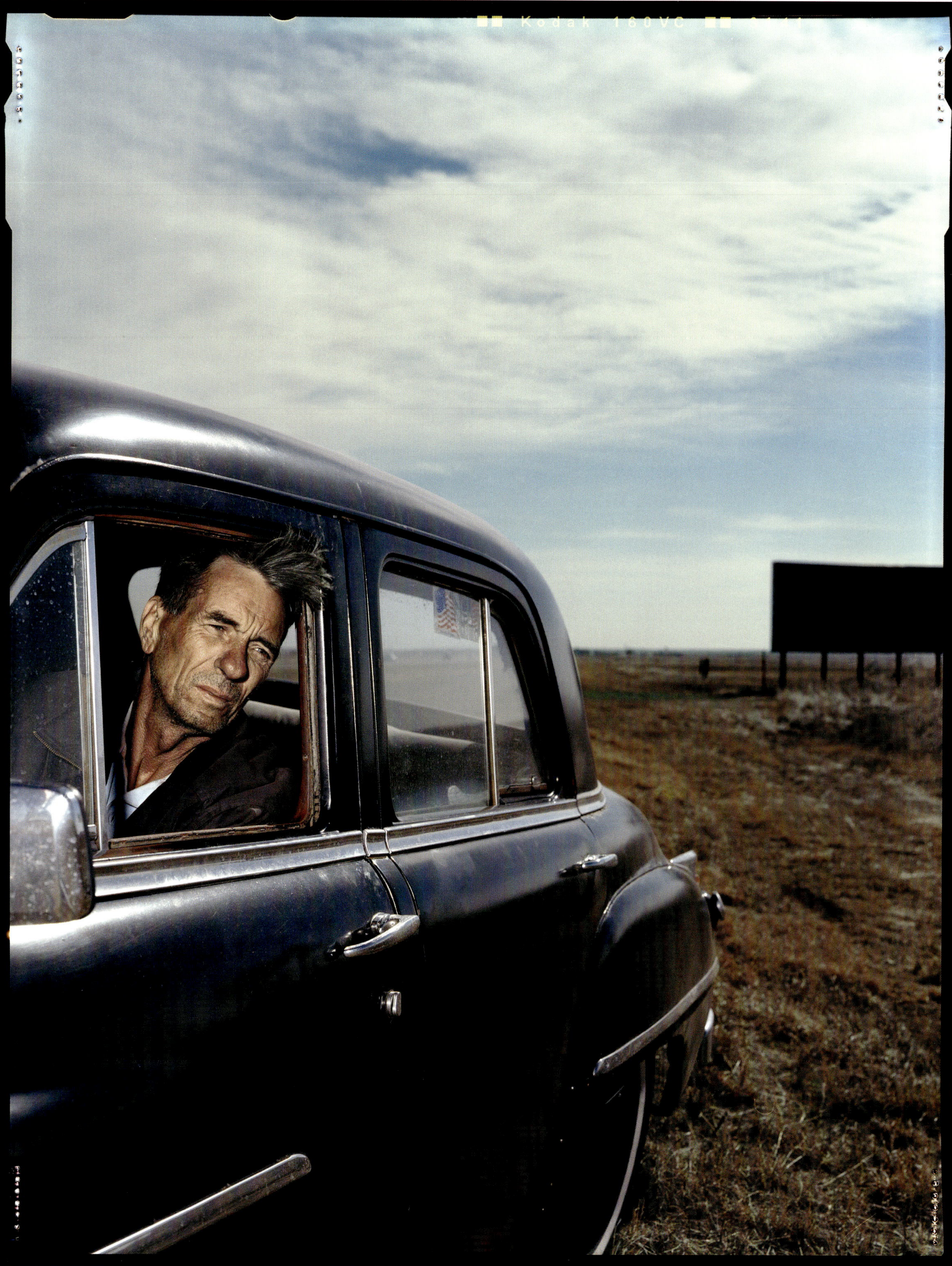
Kodak 160VC

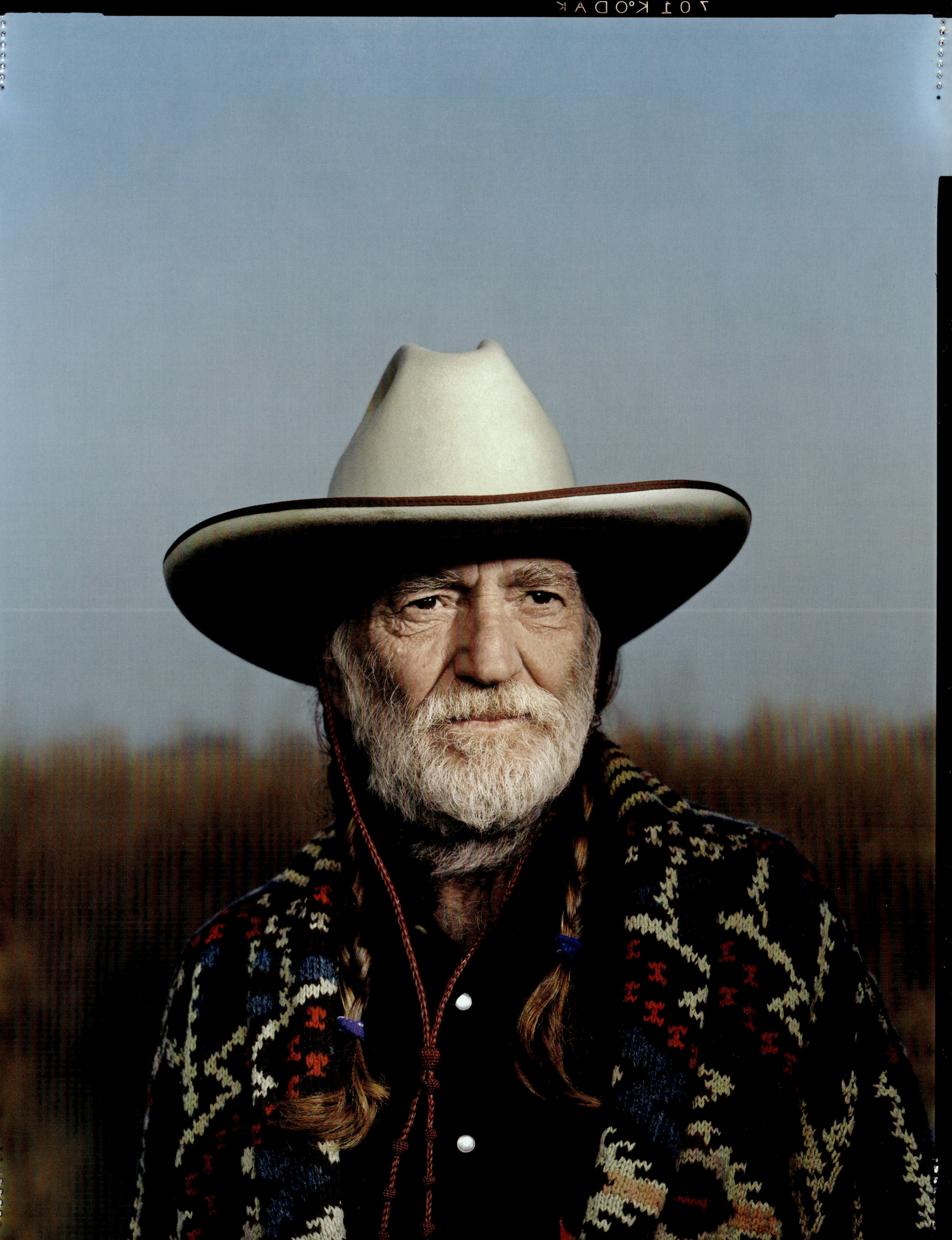

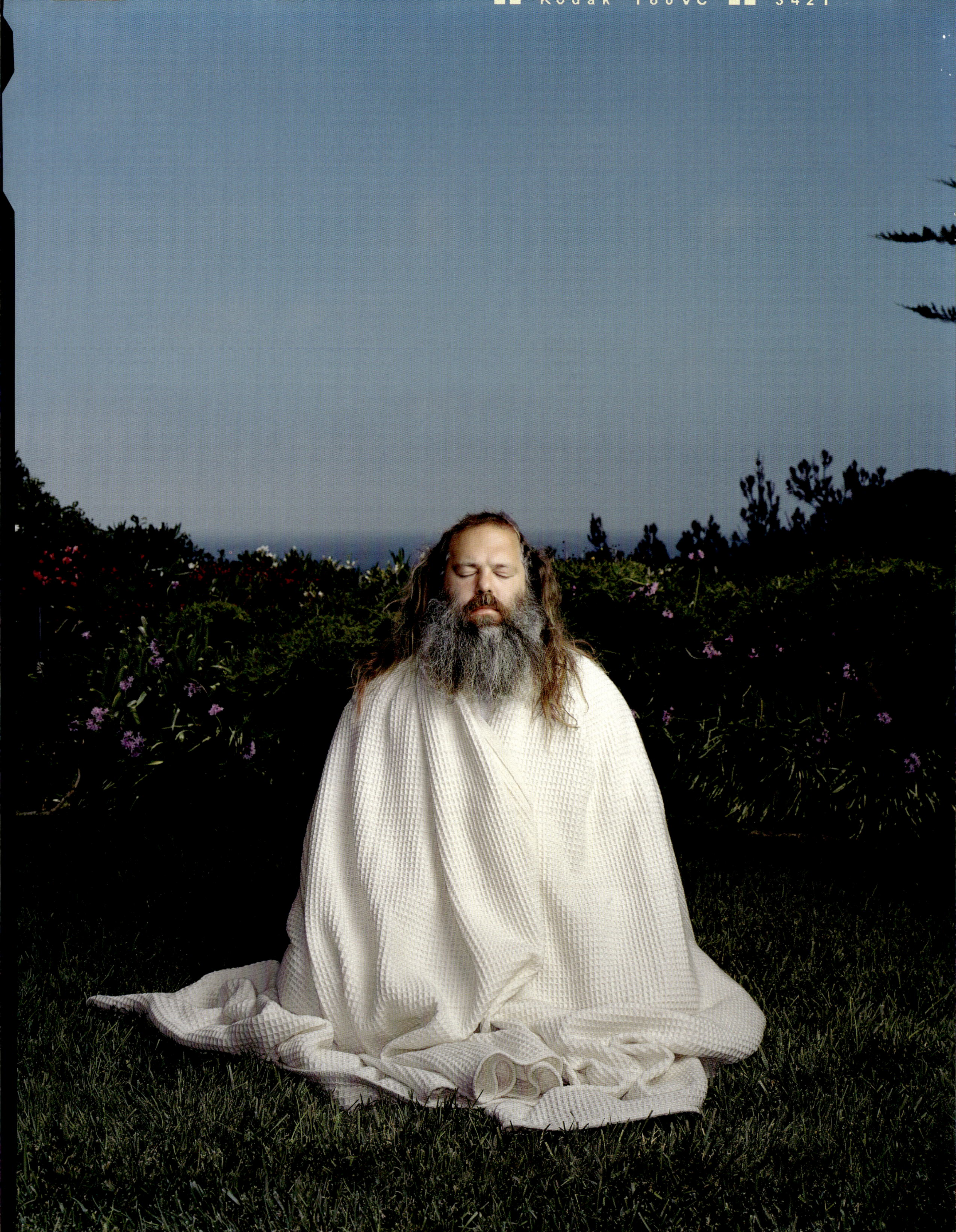

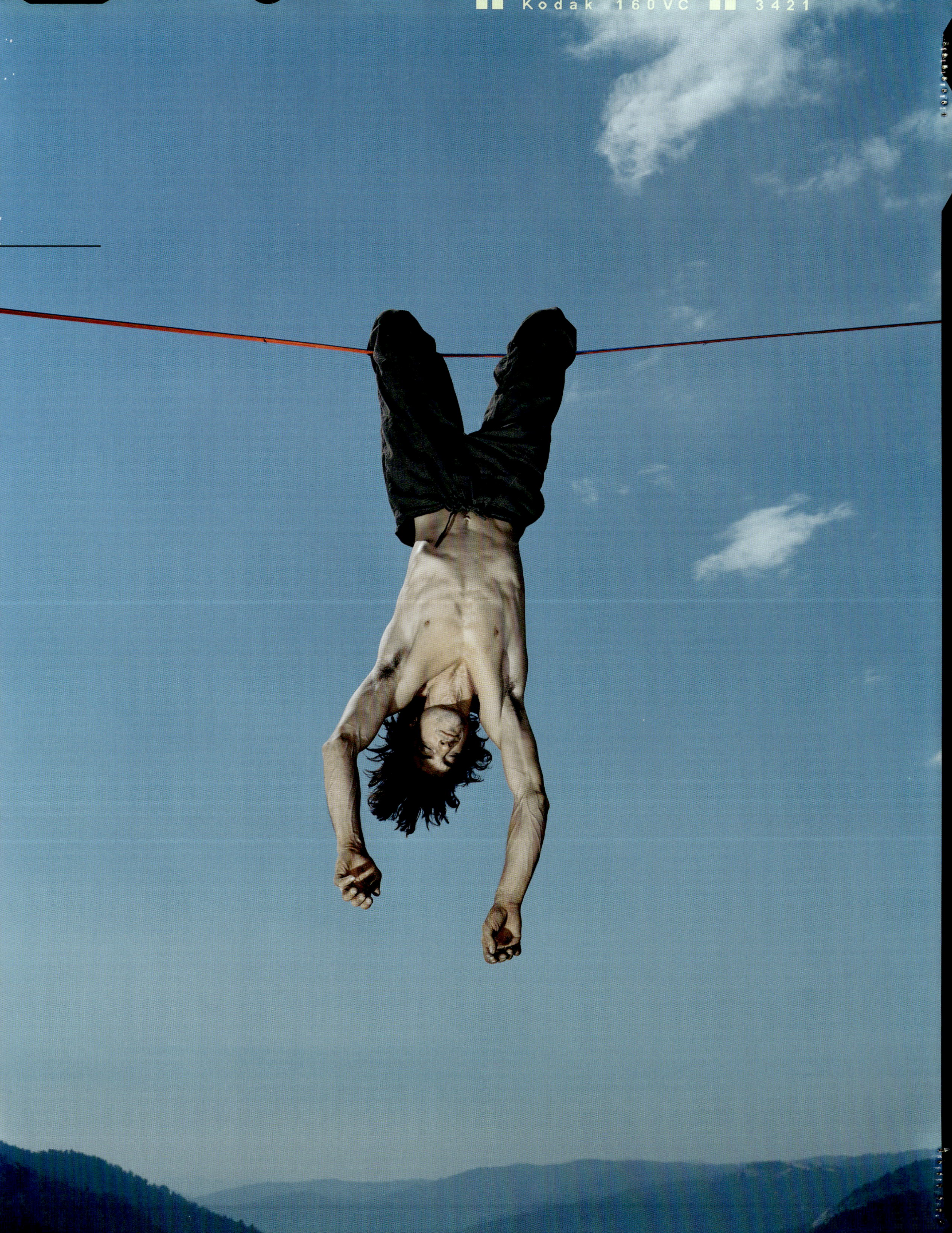
Kodak 160VC 3421

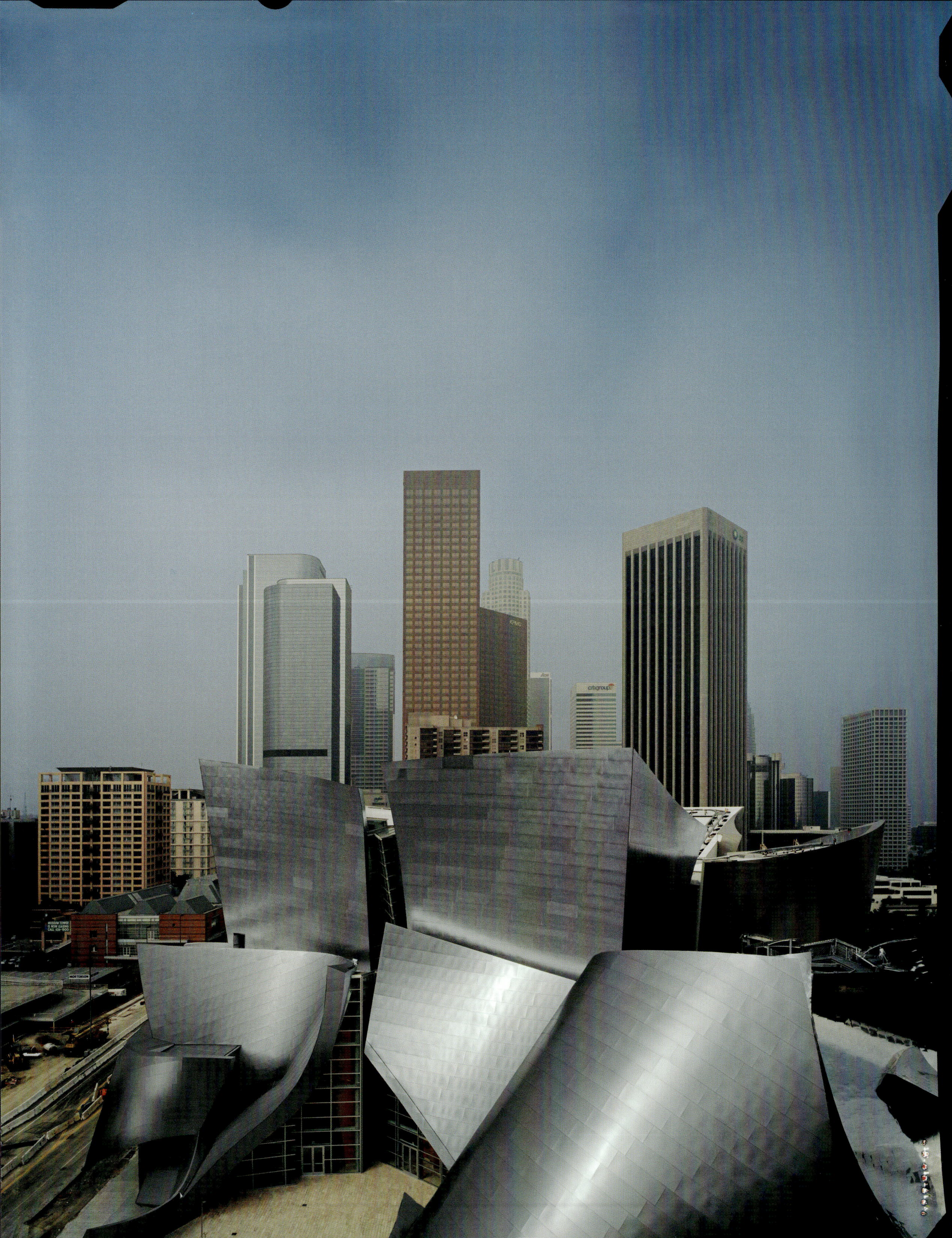

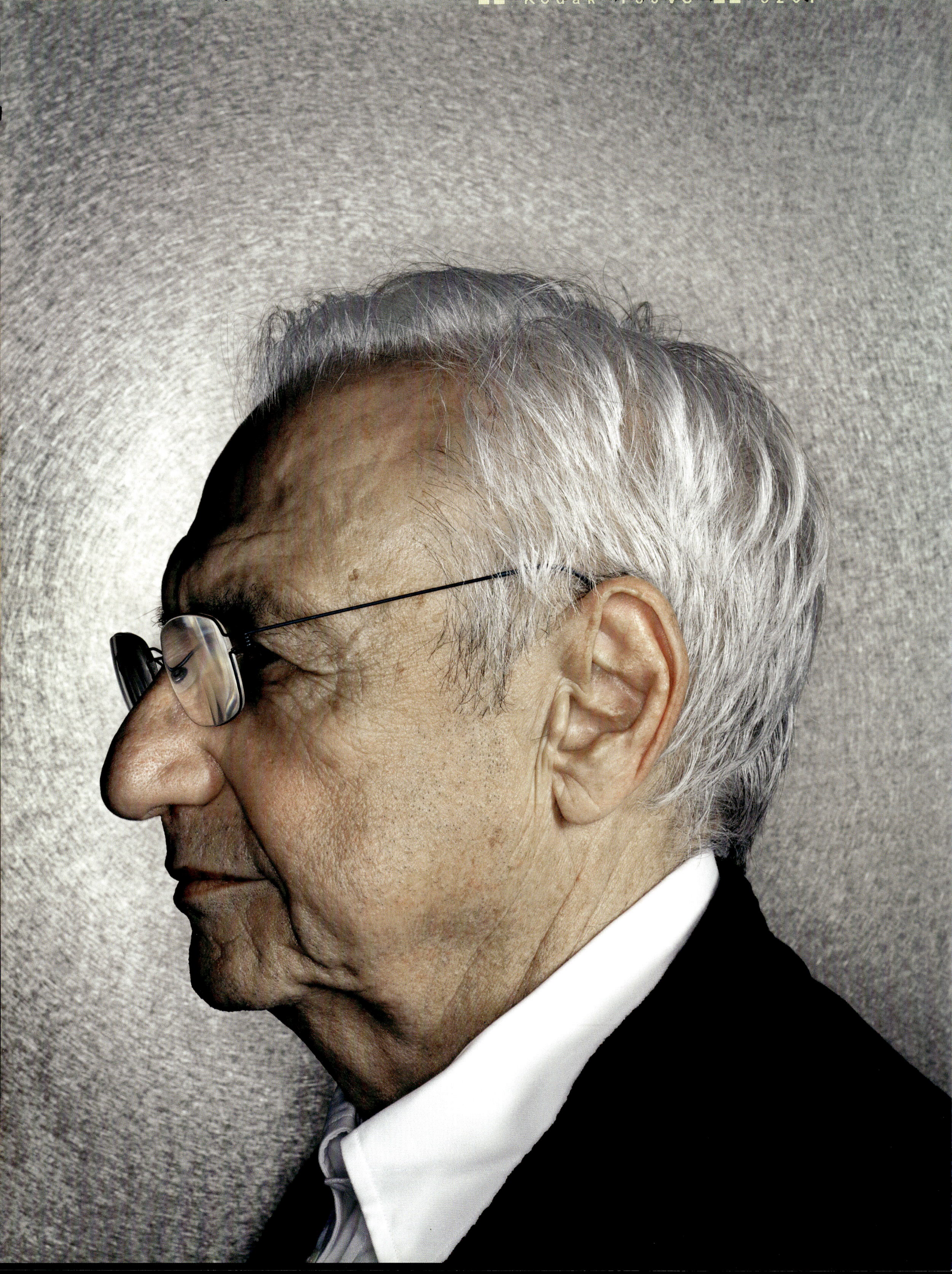

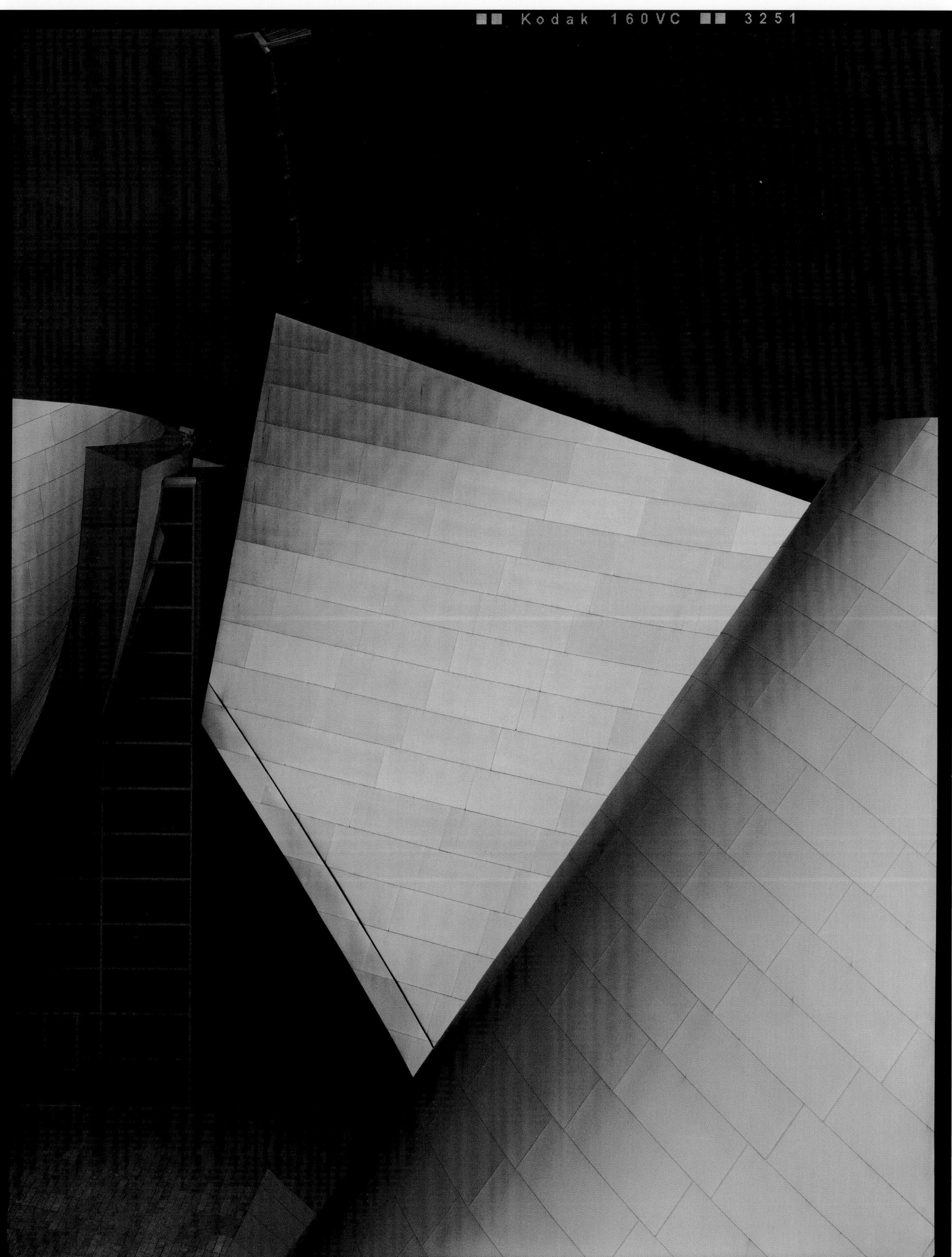
Kodak 160VC 3251

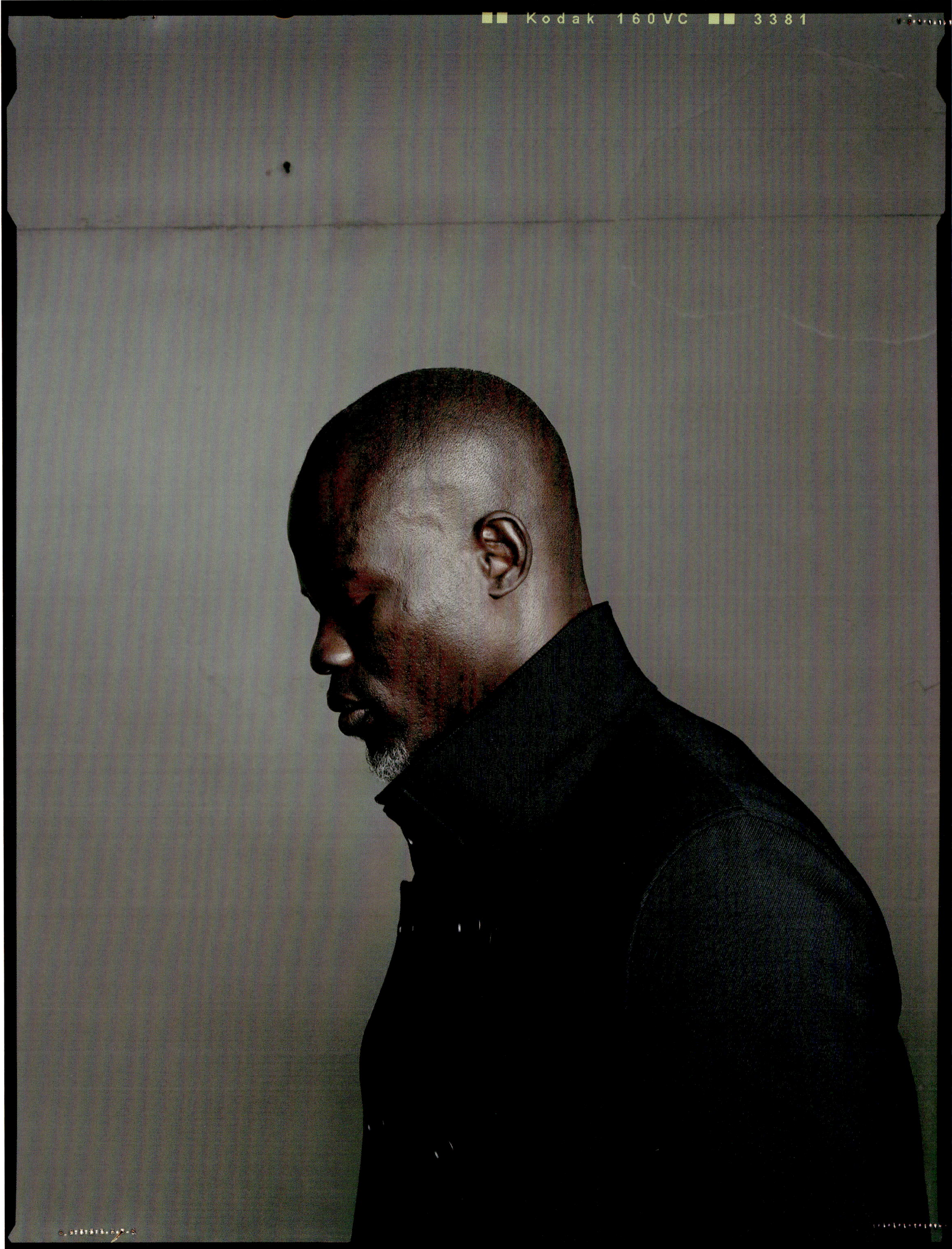
Kodak 160VC
3381

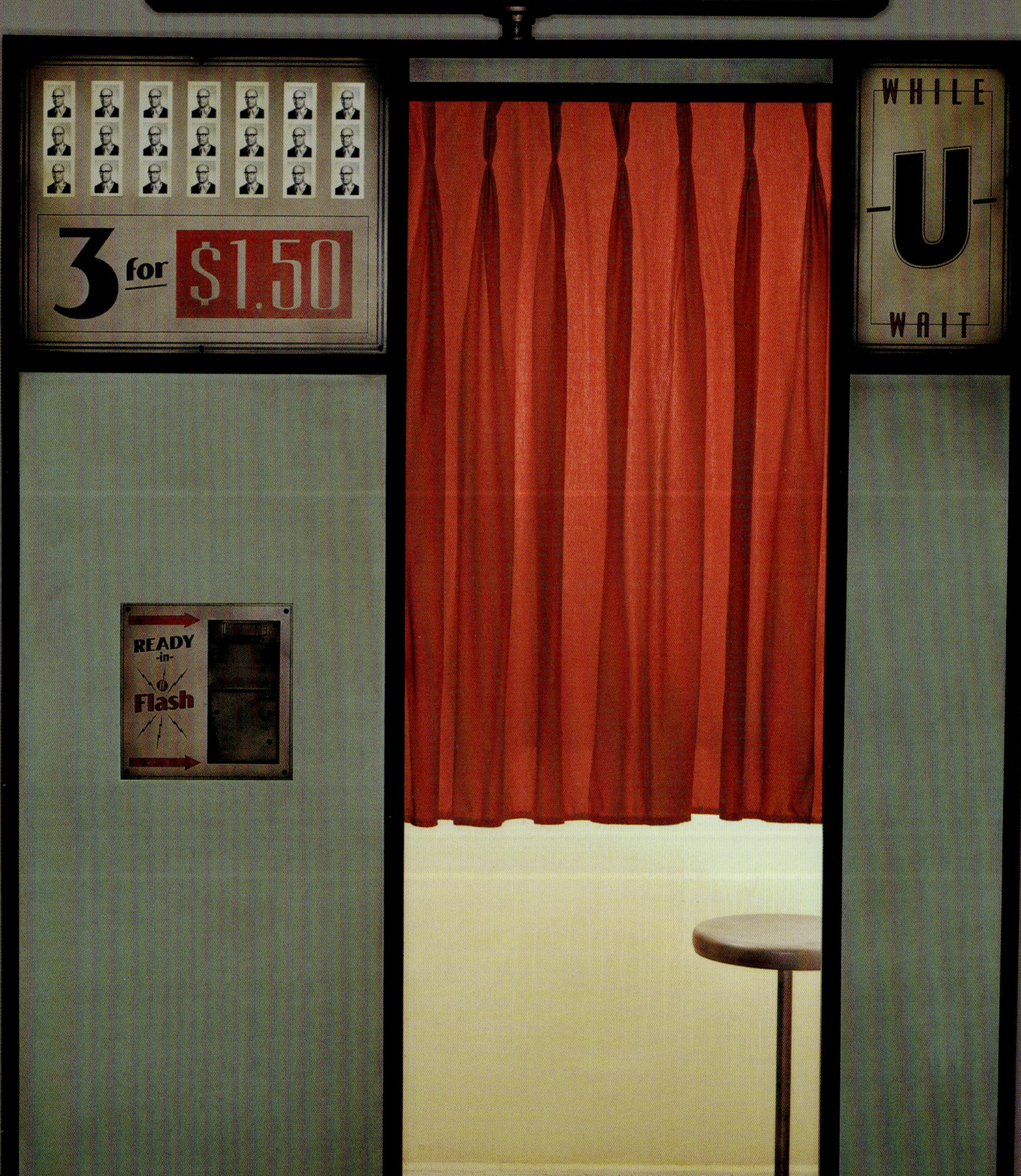
Kodak 160VC 3271
Photographs
3 for $1.50
WHILE
U
WAIT
READY
-in-
Flash

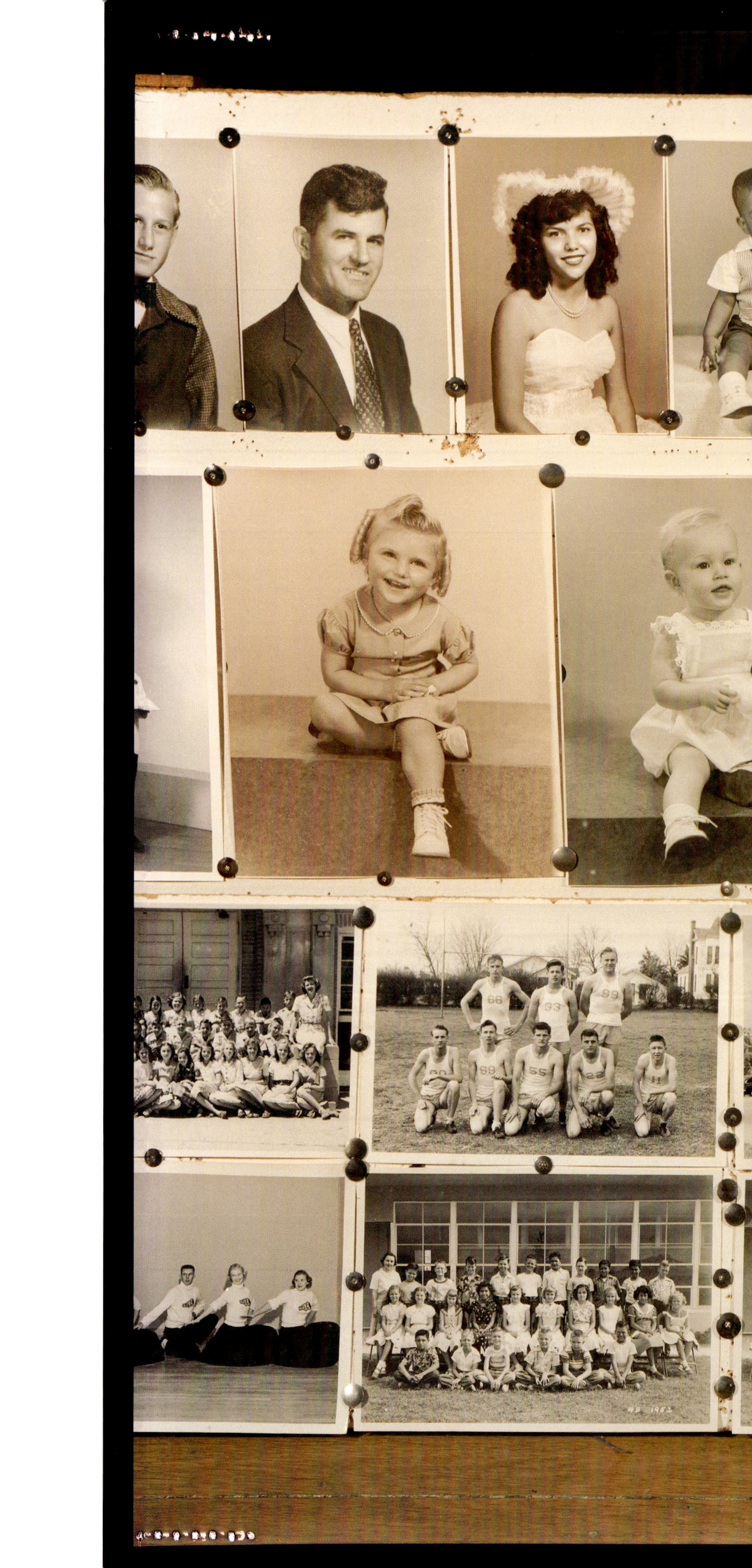

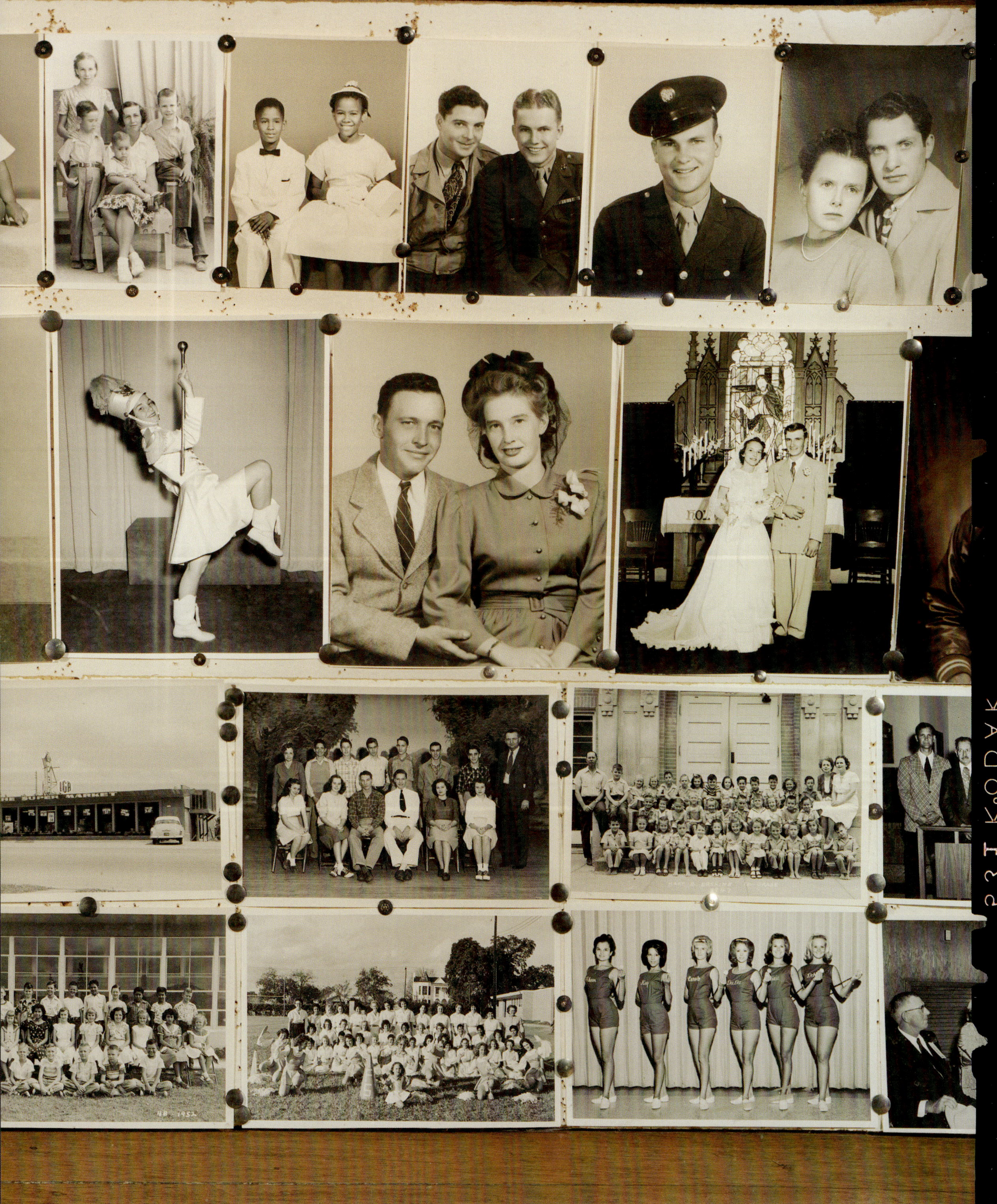

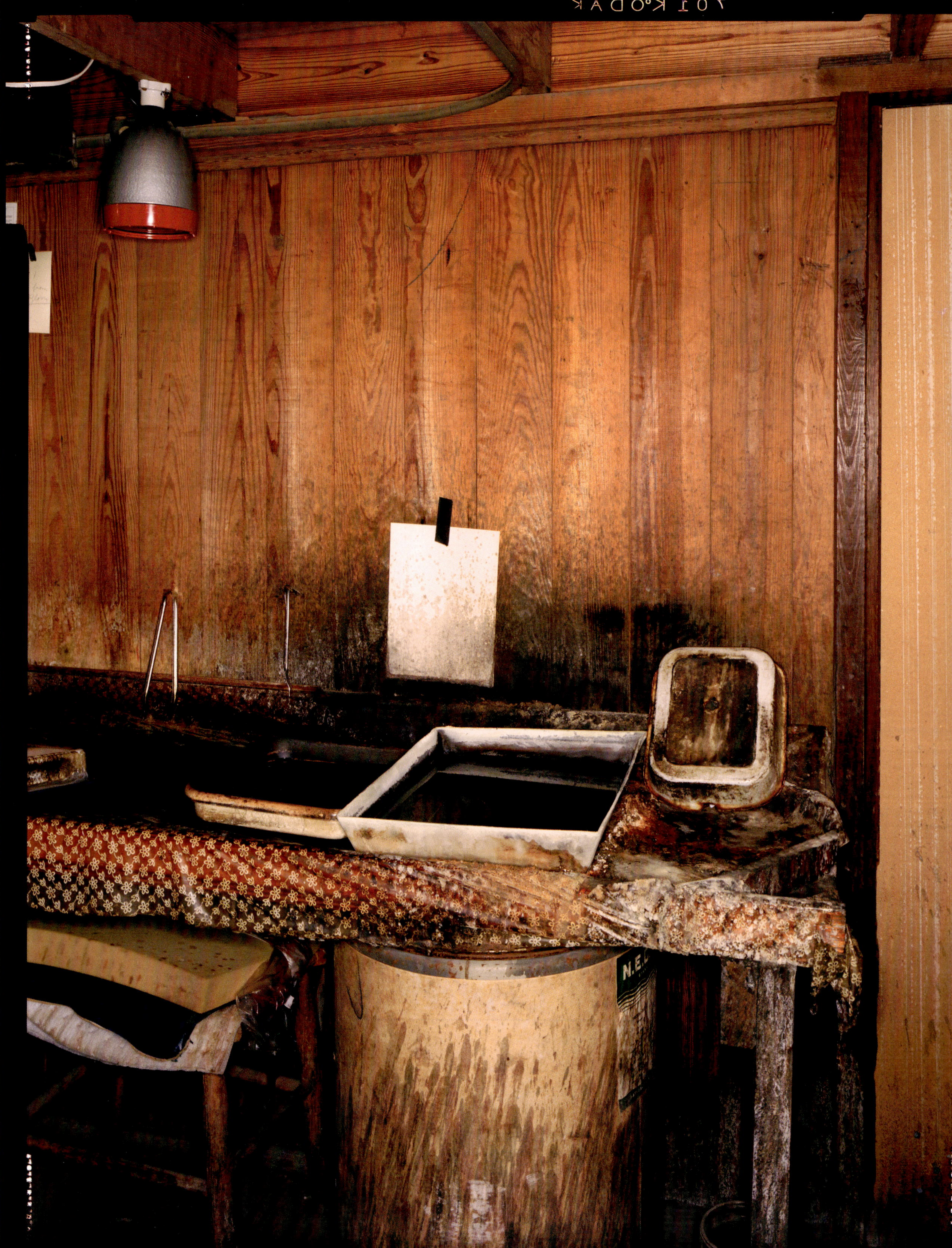

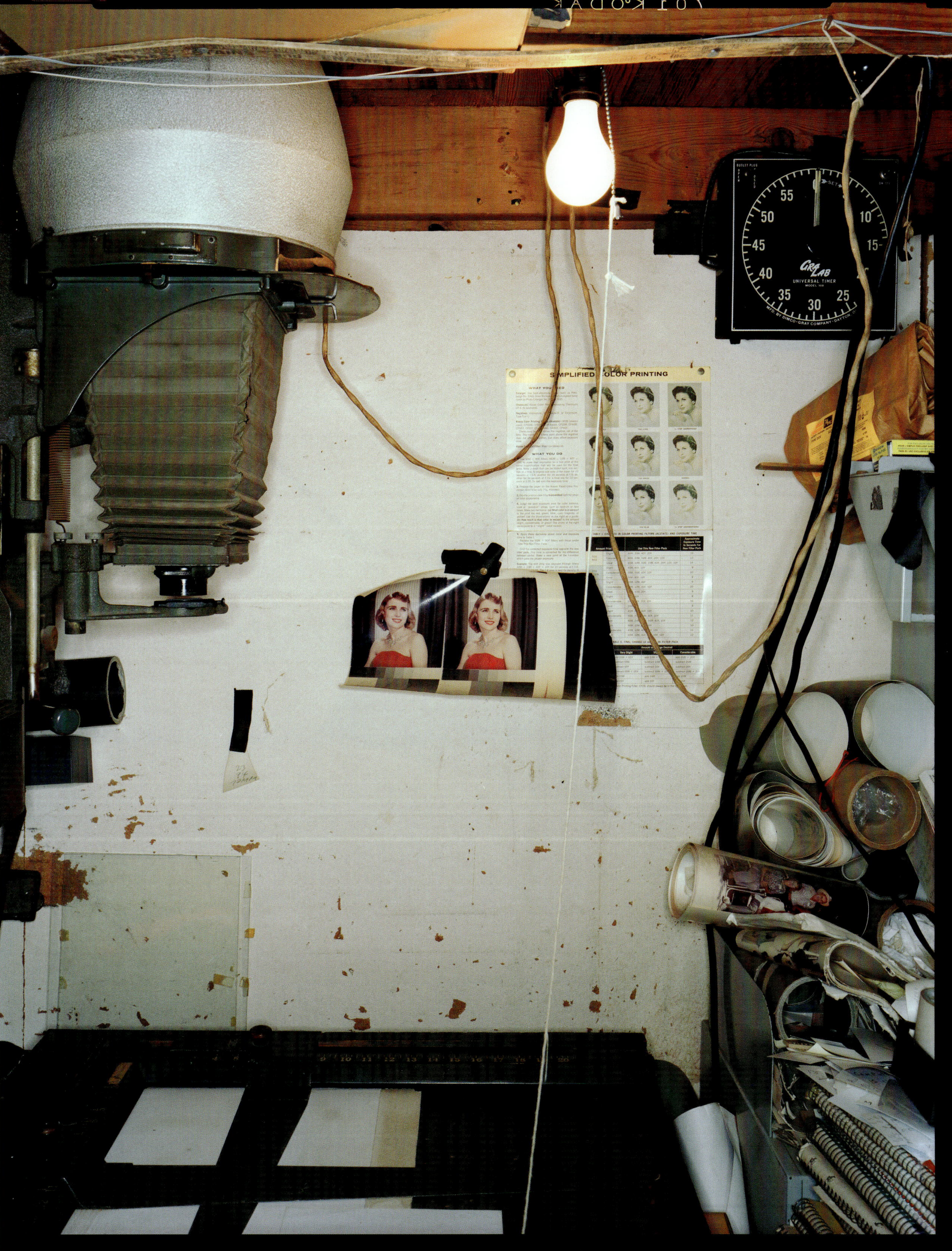
GRALAB
UNIVERSAL TIMER
WHAT YOU DO

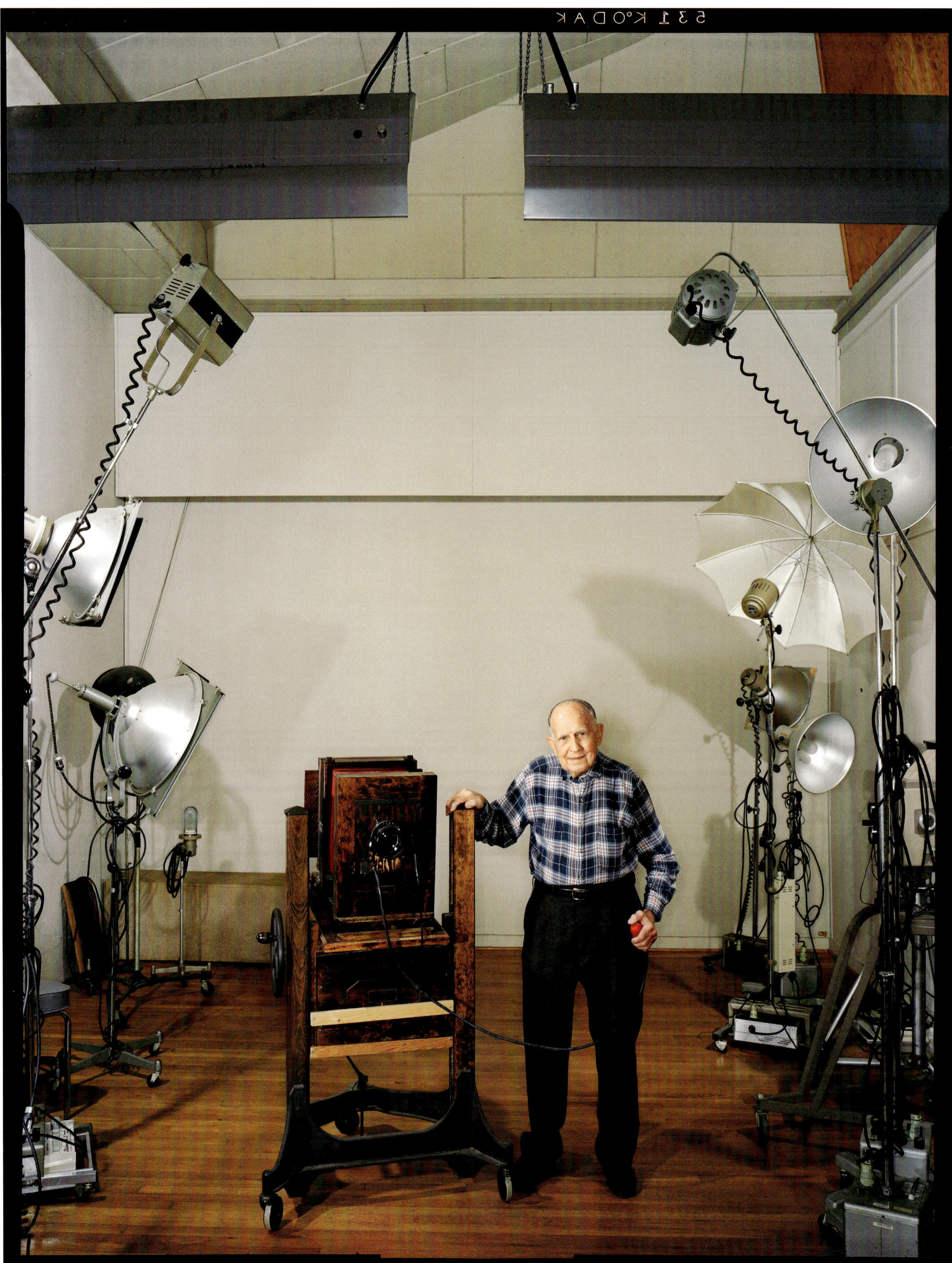

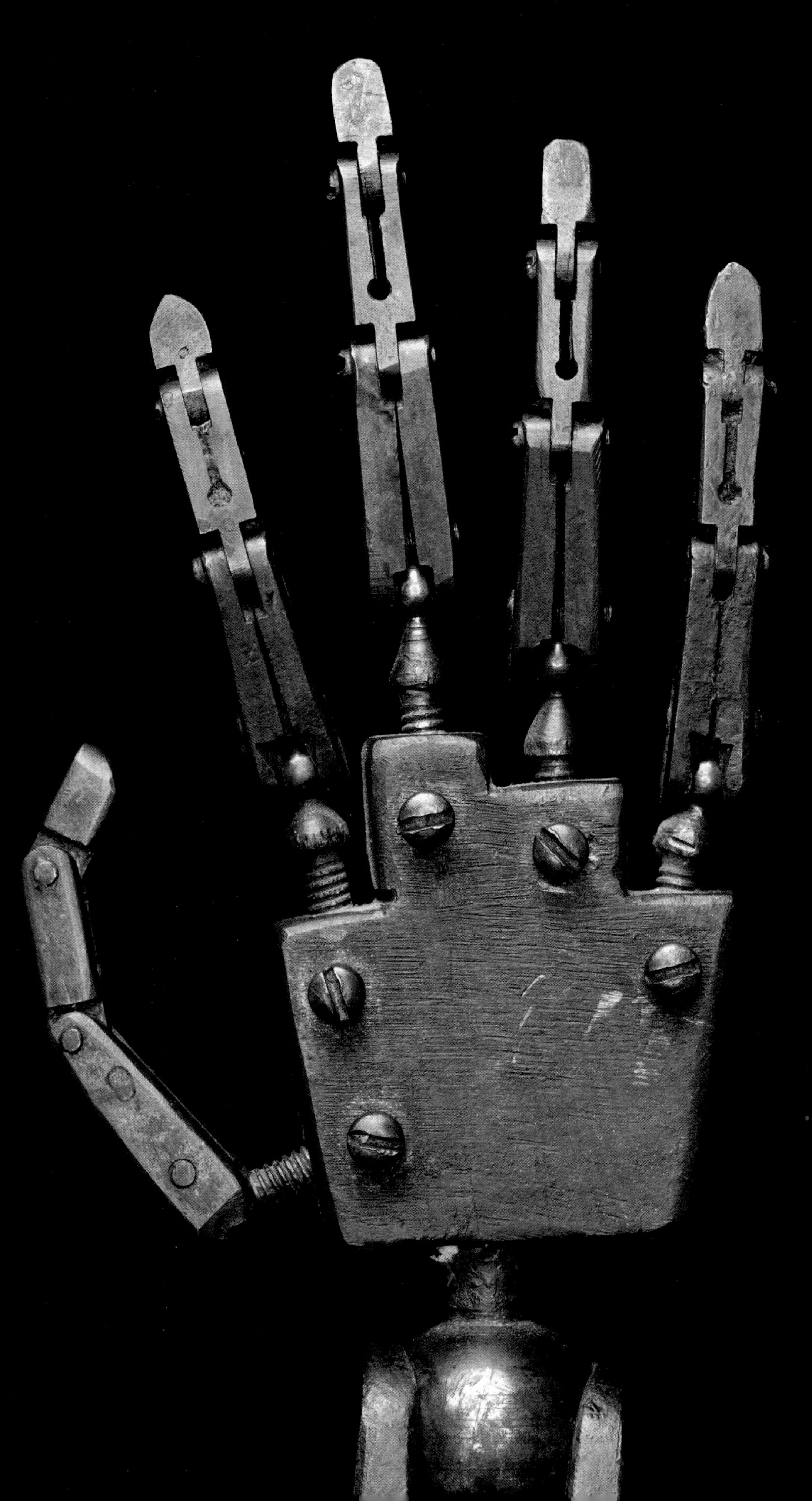
Kodak 160VC 2 4031

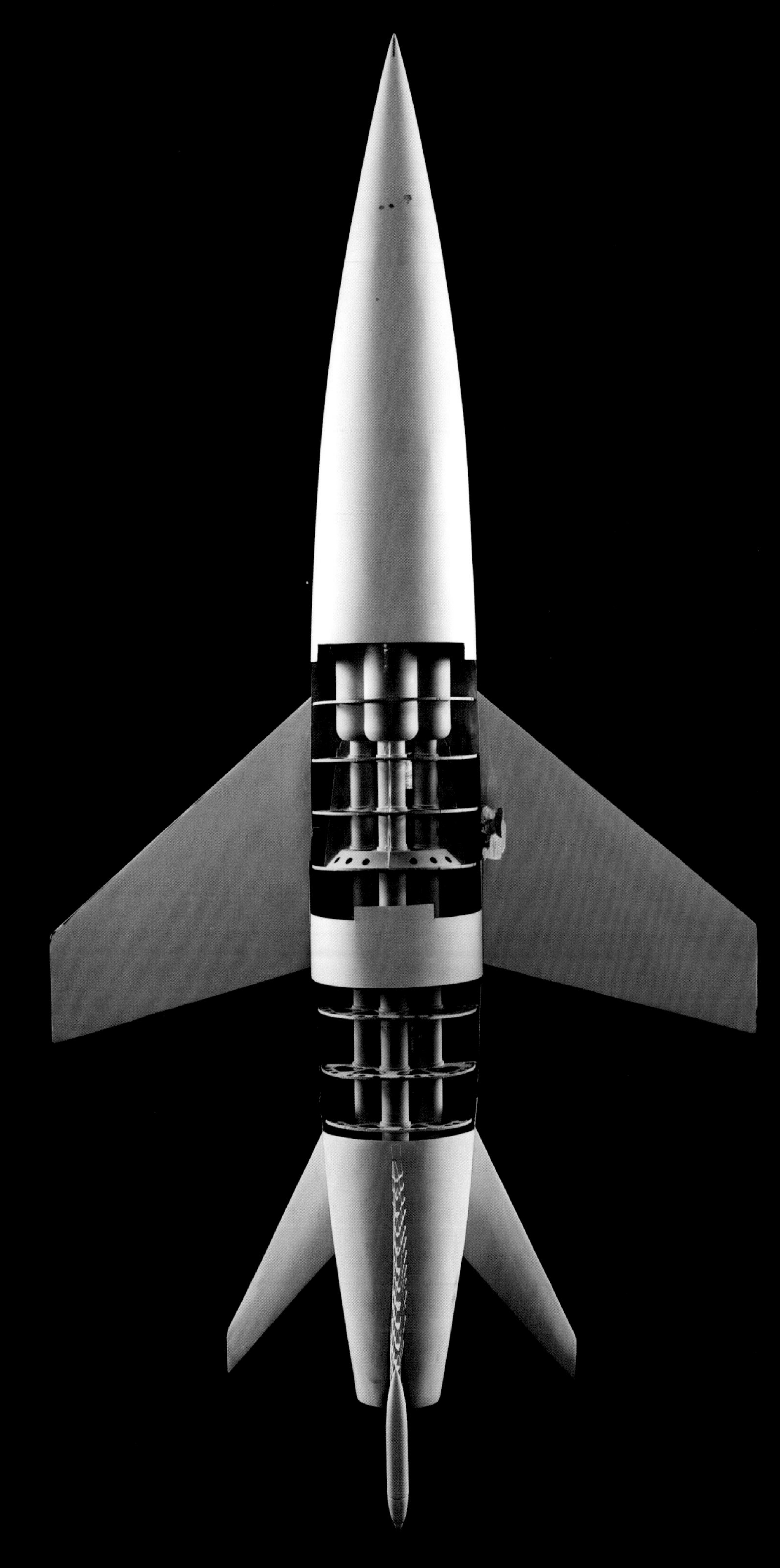

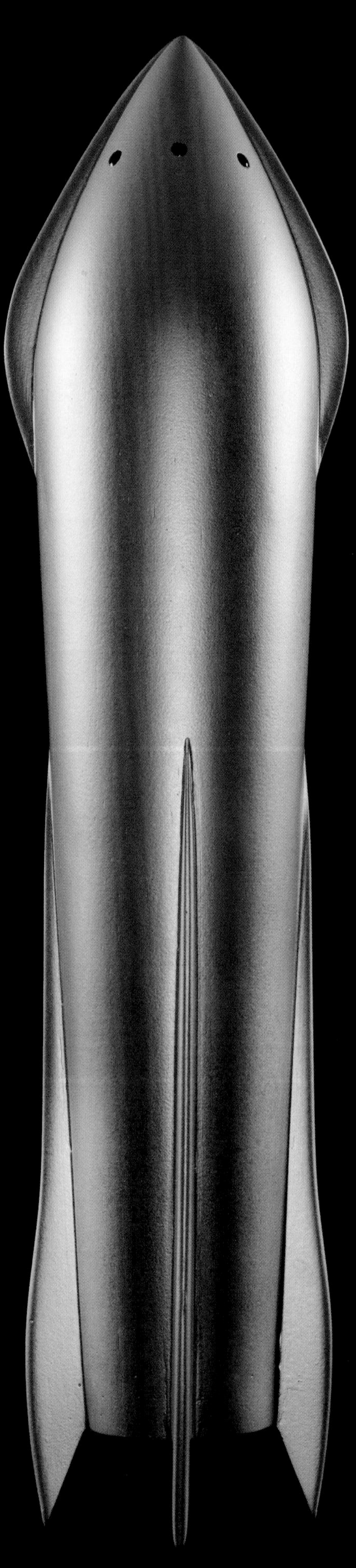
Kodak 160VC 2 4031

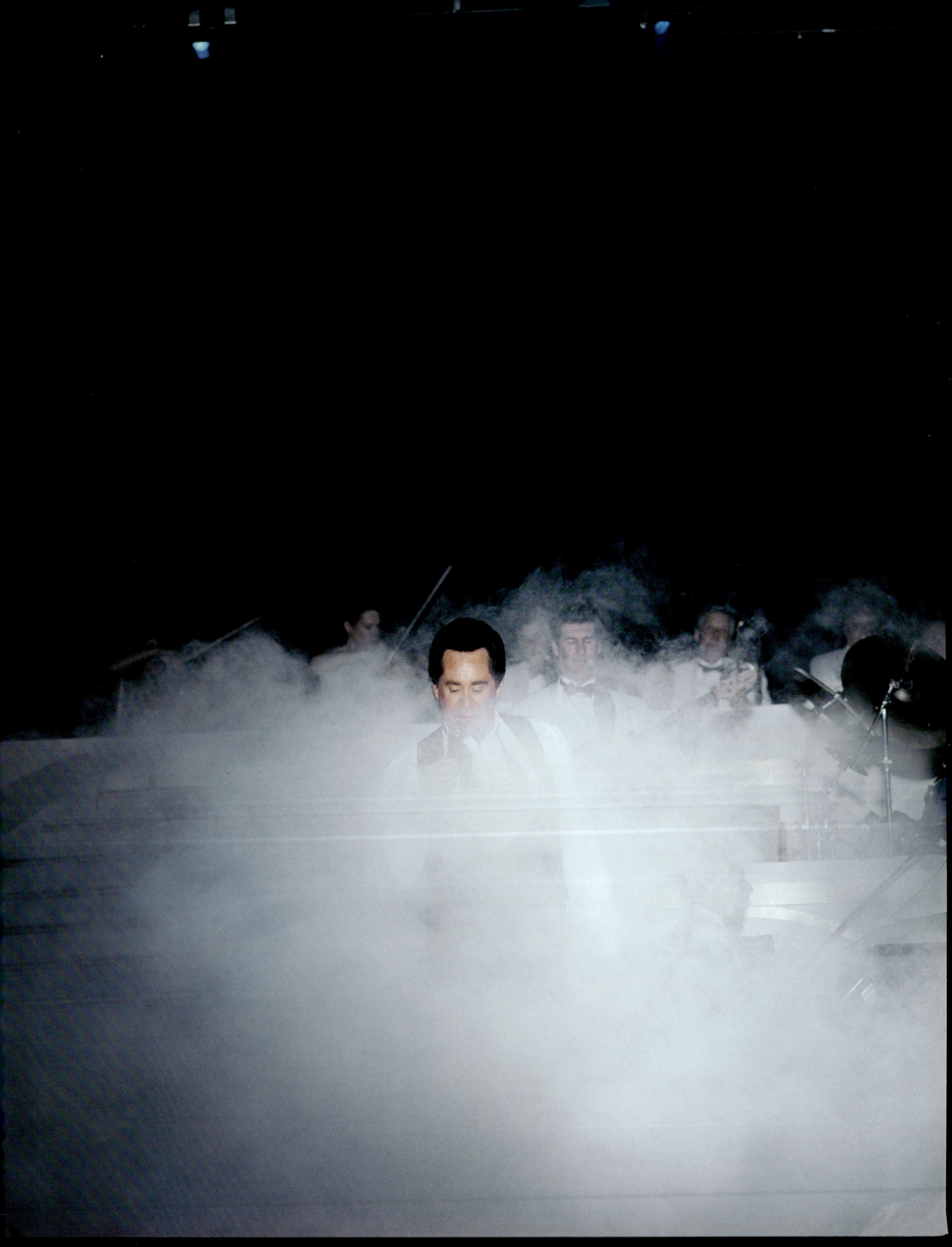

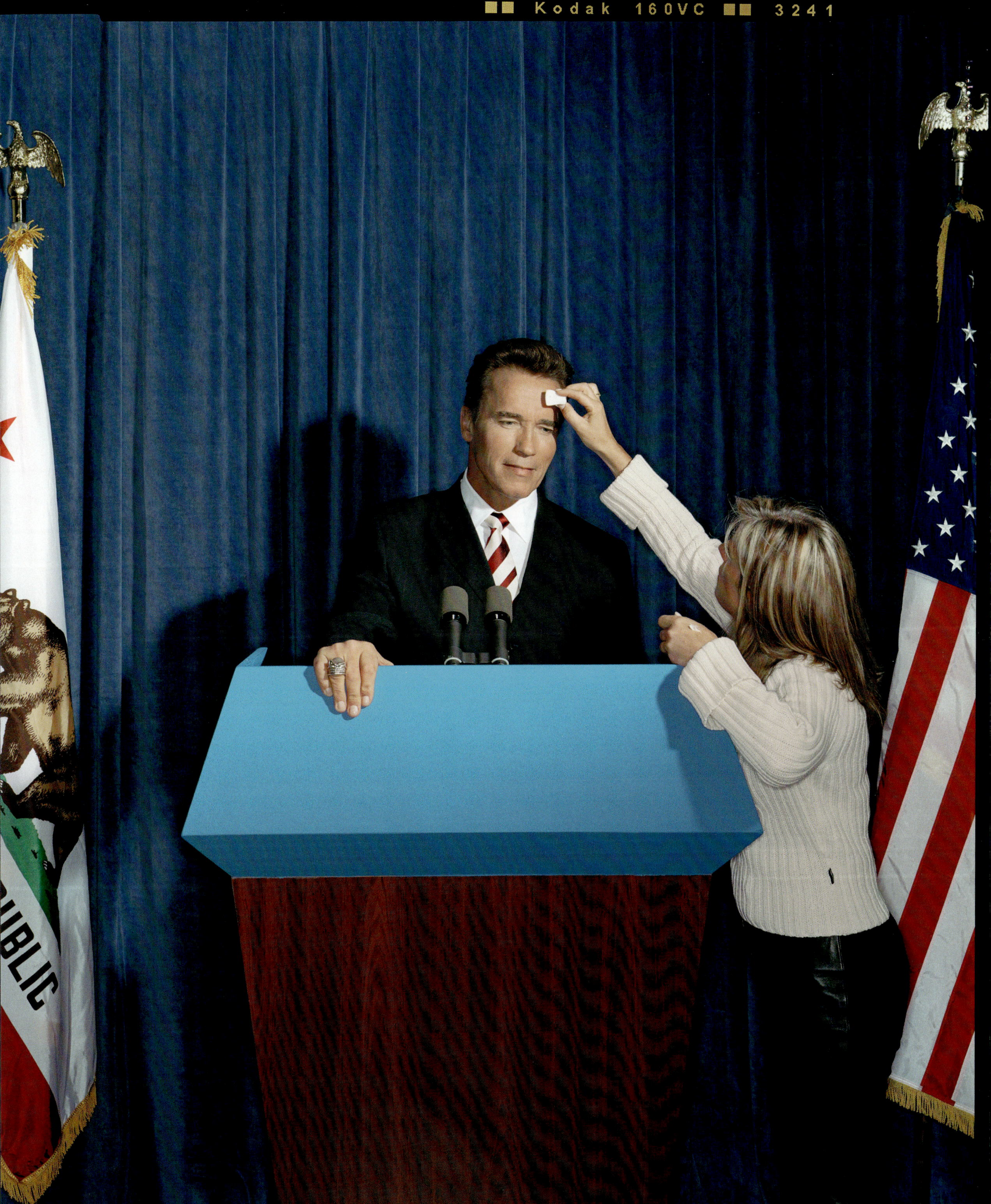
Kodak 160VC
3241

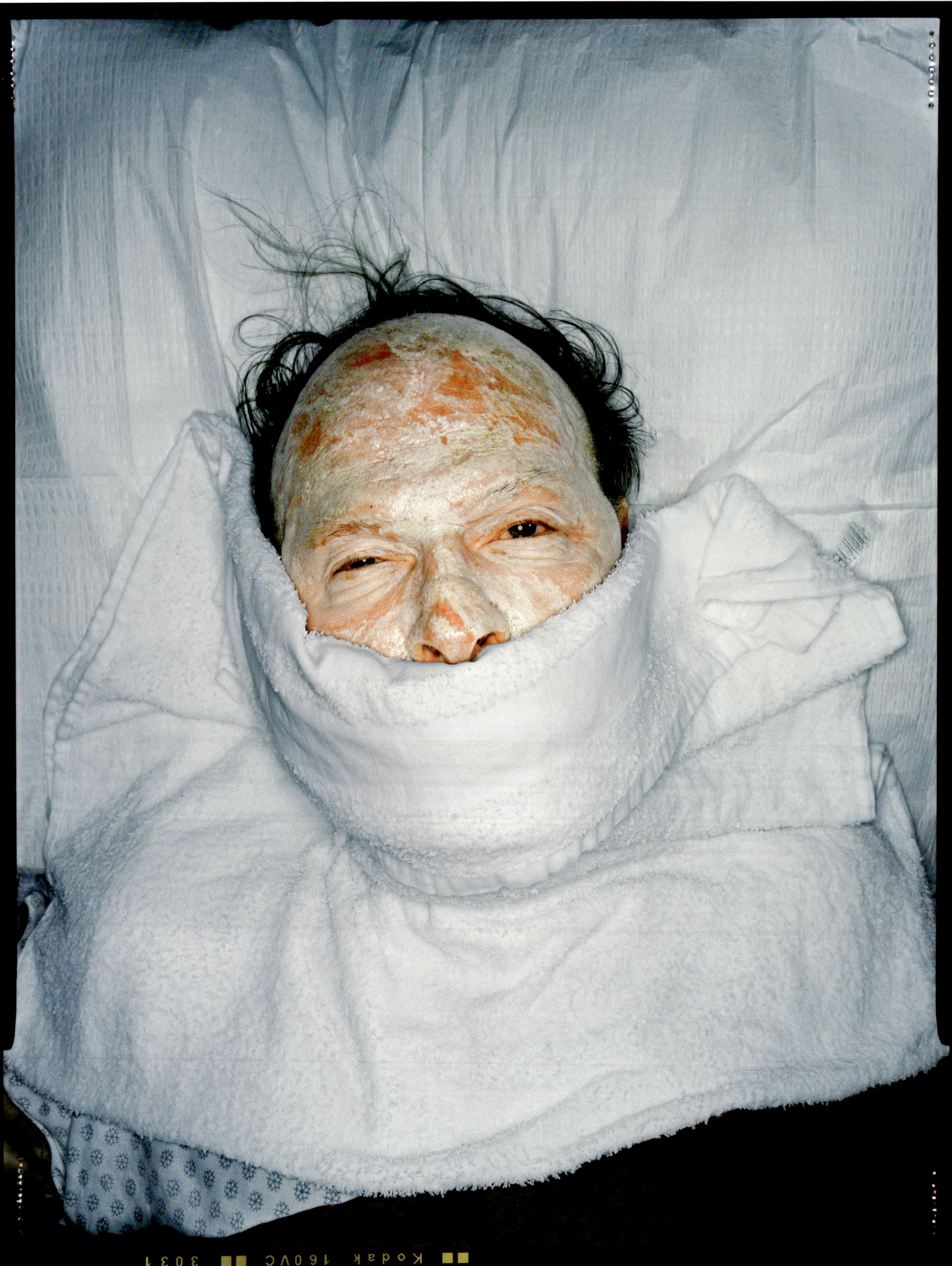
Kodak 160VC
3031

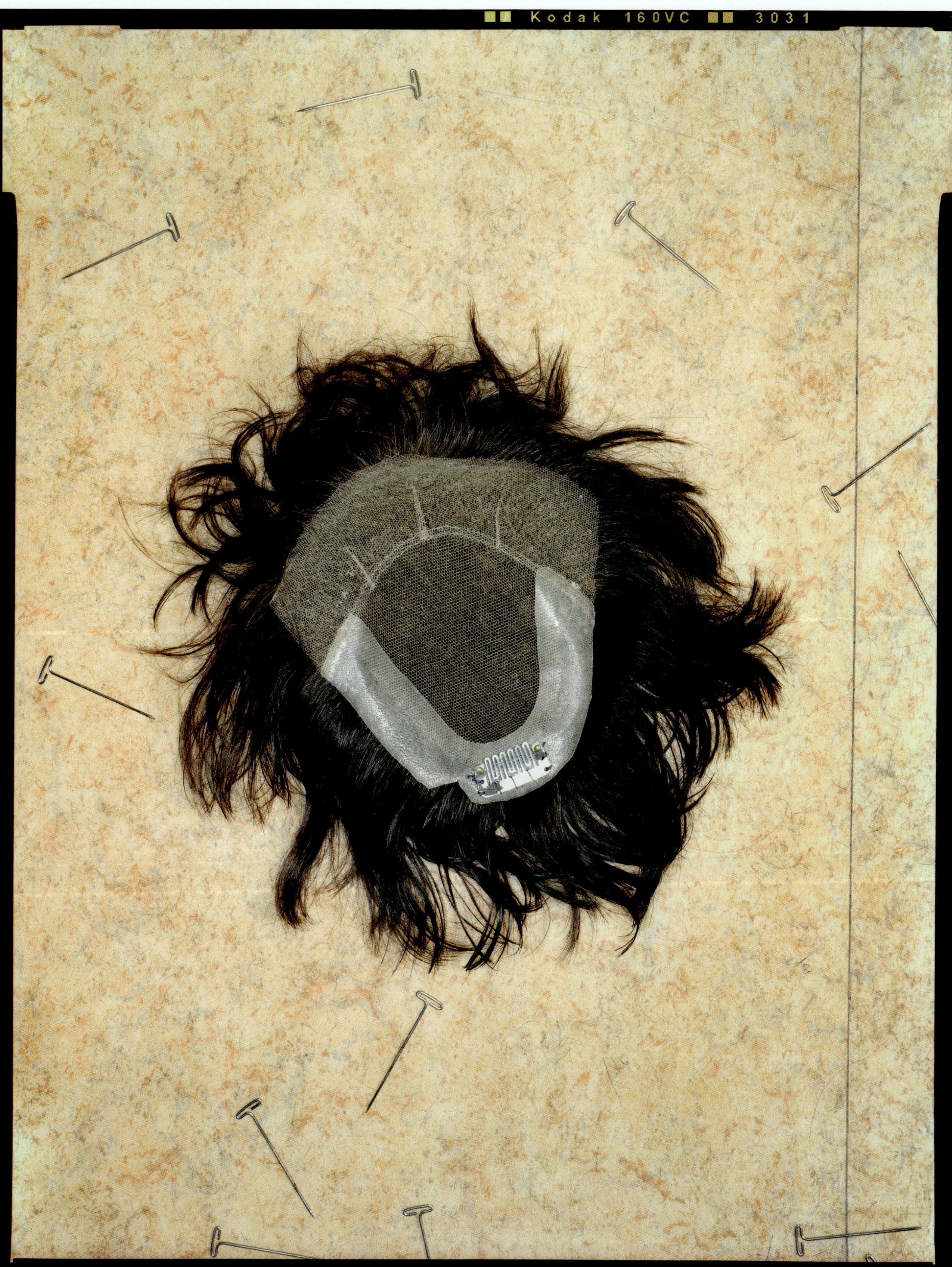
Kodak 160VC 3031

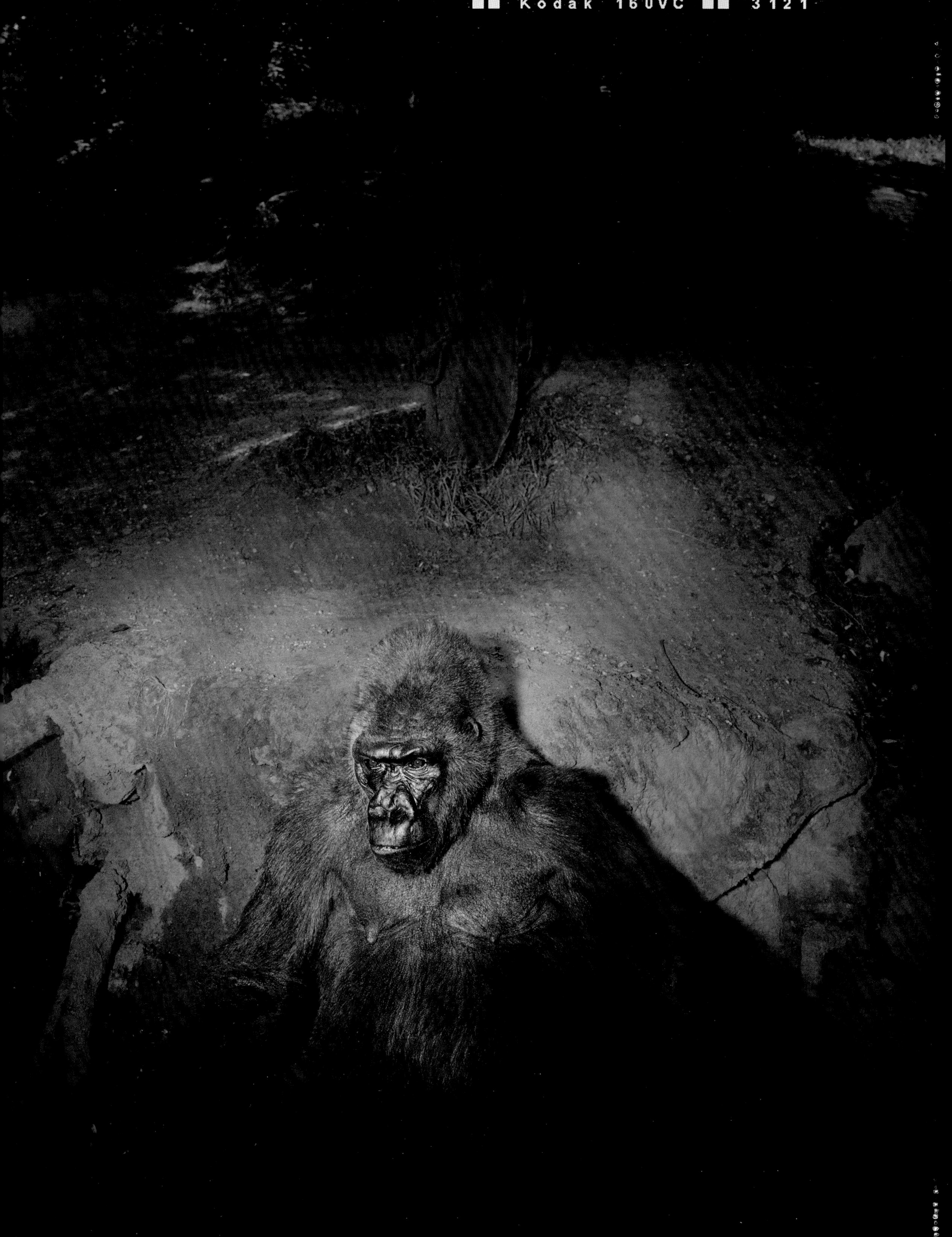
Kodak 160VC 3121

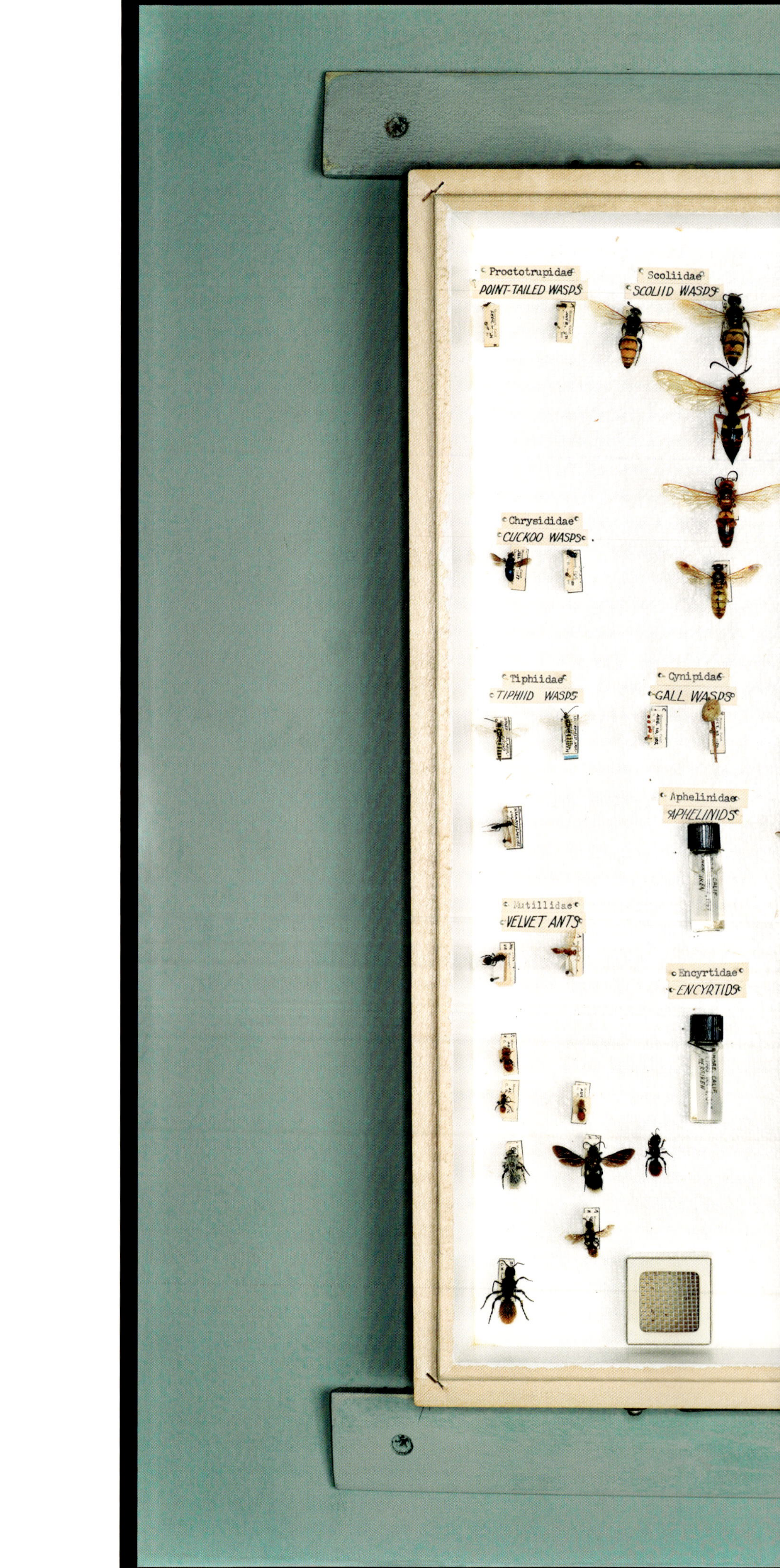
Proctotrupidae
POINT-TAILED WASPS
Scoliidae
SCOLIID WASPS
Chrysididae
CUCKOO WASPS
Tiphiidae
TIPHIID WASPS
Cynipidae
GALL WASPS
Aphelinidae
APHELINIDS
Mutillidae
VELVET ANTS
Encyrtidae
ENCYRTIDS

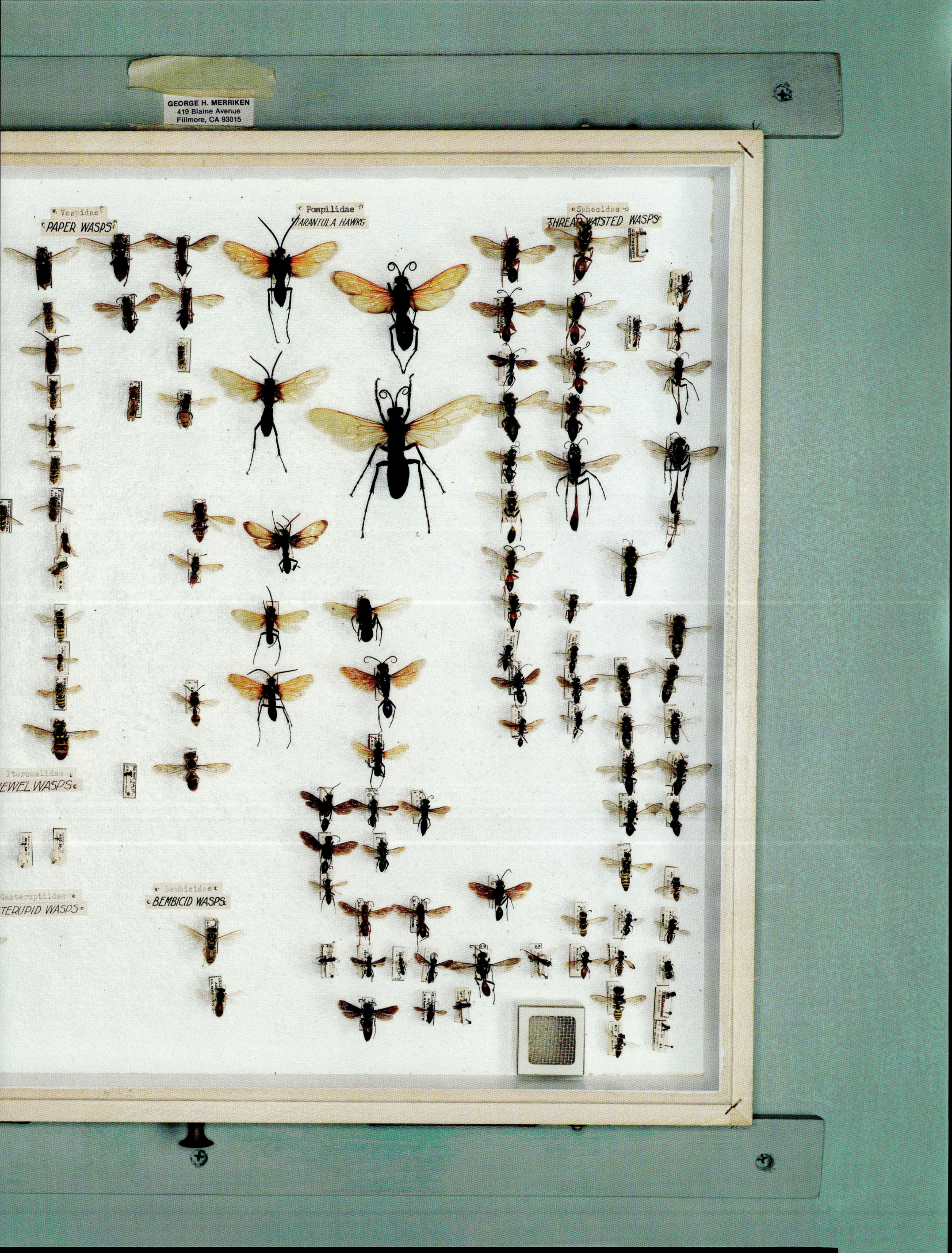

GEORGE H. MERRIKEN
419 Blaine Avenue
Fillmore, CA 93015

Vespidae
PAPER WASPS

Pompilidae
TARANTULA HAWKS

Sphecidae
THREAD WAISTED WASPS

Pteromalidae
EWEL WASPS

Gasteruptiidae
TERUPID WASPS

Bembicidae
BEMBICID WASPS

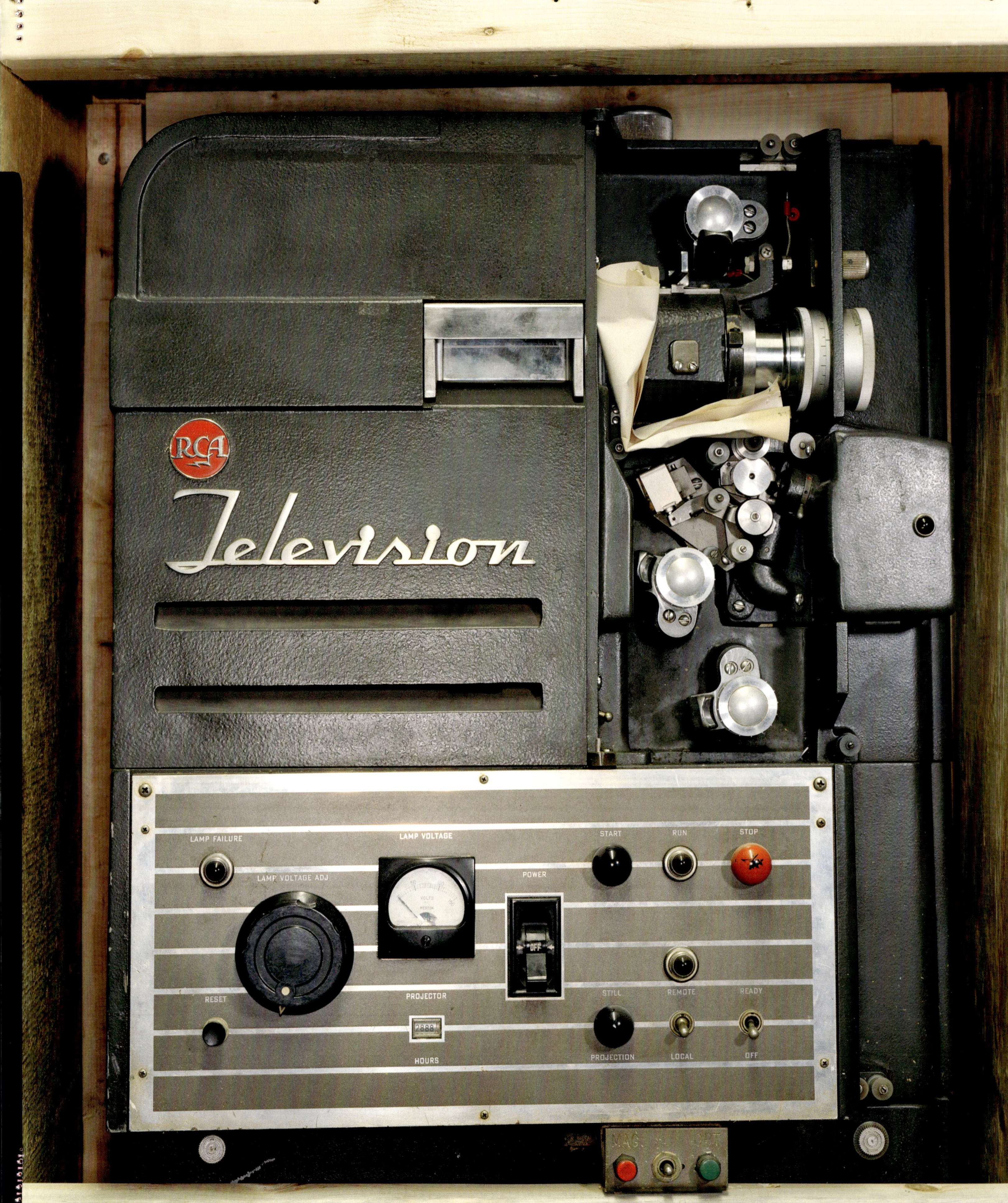
RCA
Television
LAMP FAILURE
LAMP VOLTAGE
START
RUN
STOP
LAMP VOLTAGE ADJ
POWER
OFF
RESET
PROJECTOR
HOURS
STILL
REMOTE
READY
PROJECTION
LOCAL
OFF

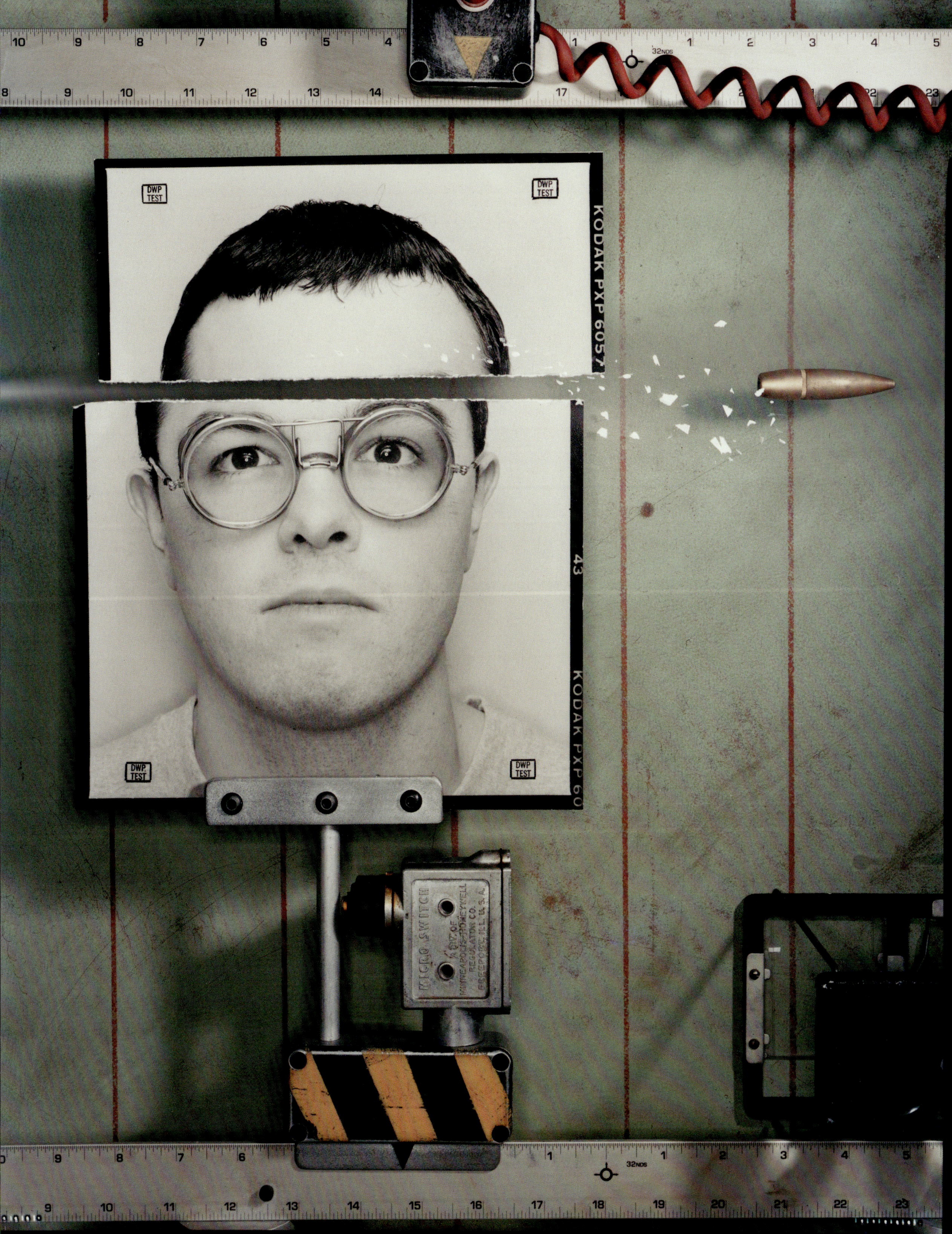

DWP TEST
DWP TEST
KODAK PXP 6057
43
KODAK PXP 60
DWP TEST
DWP TEST
MICRO SWITCH
A DIV. OF MINNEAPOLIS-HONEYWELL REGULATOR CO.
FREEPORT, ILL. U.S.A.

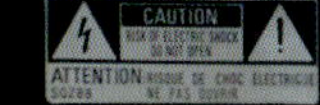

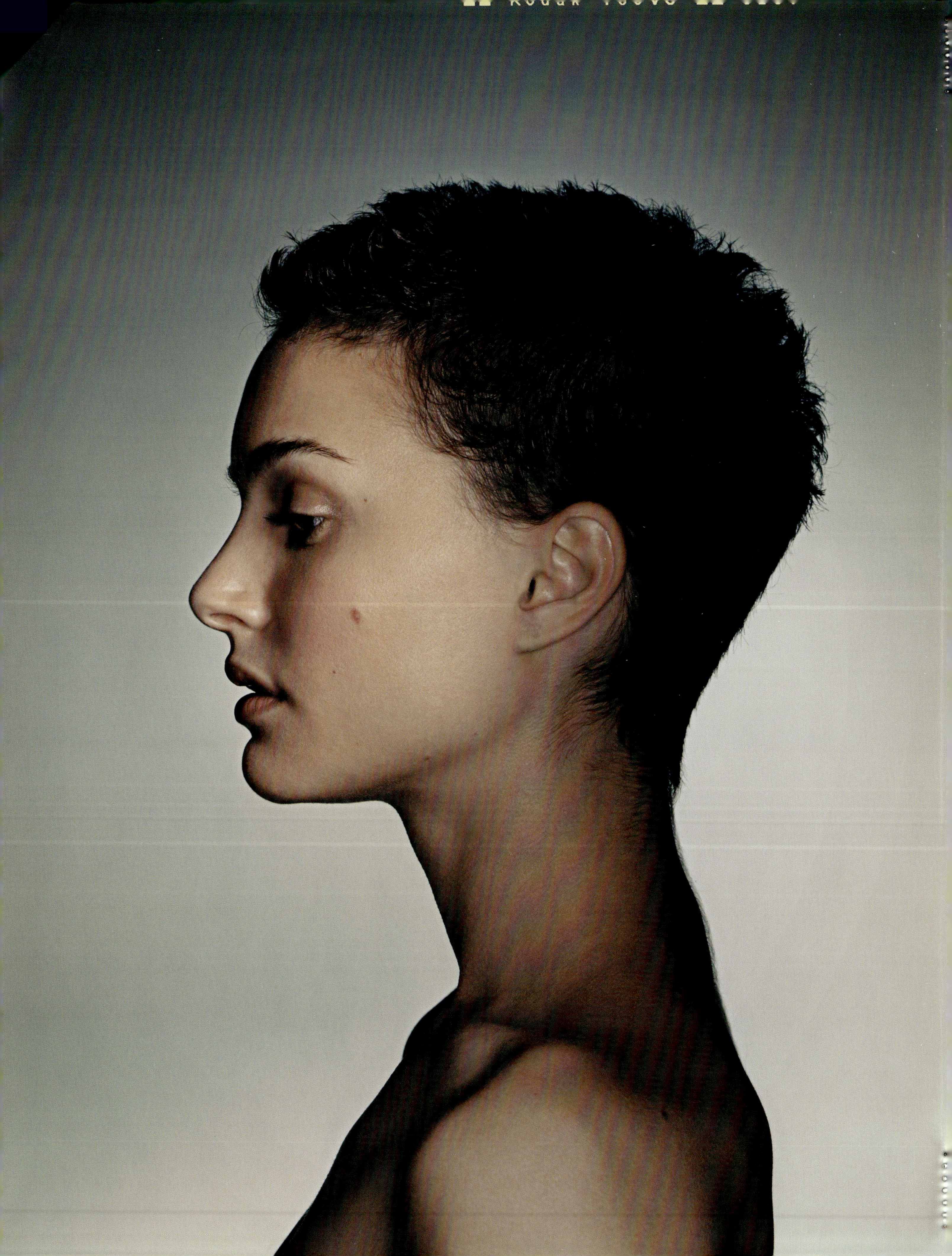

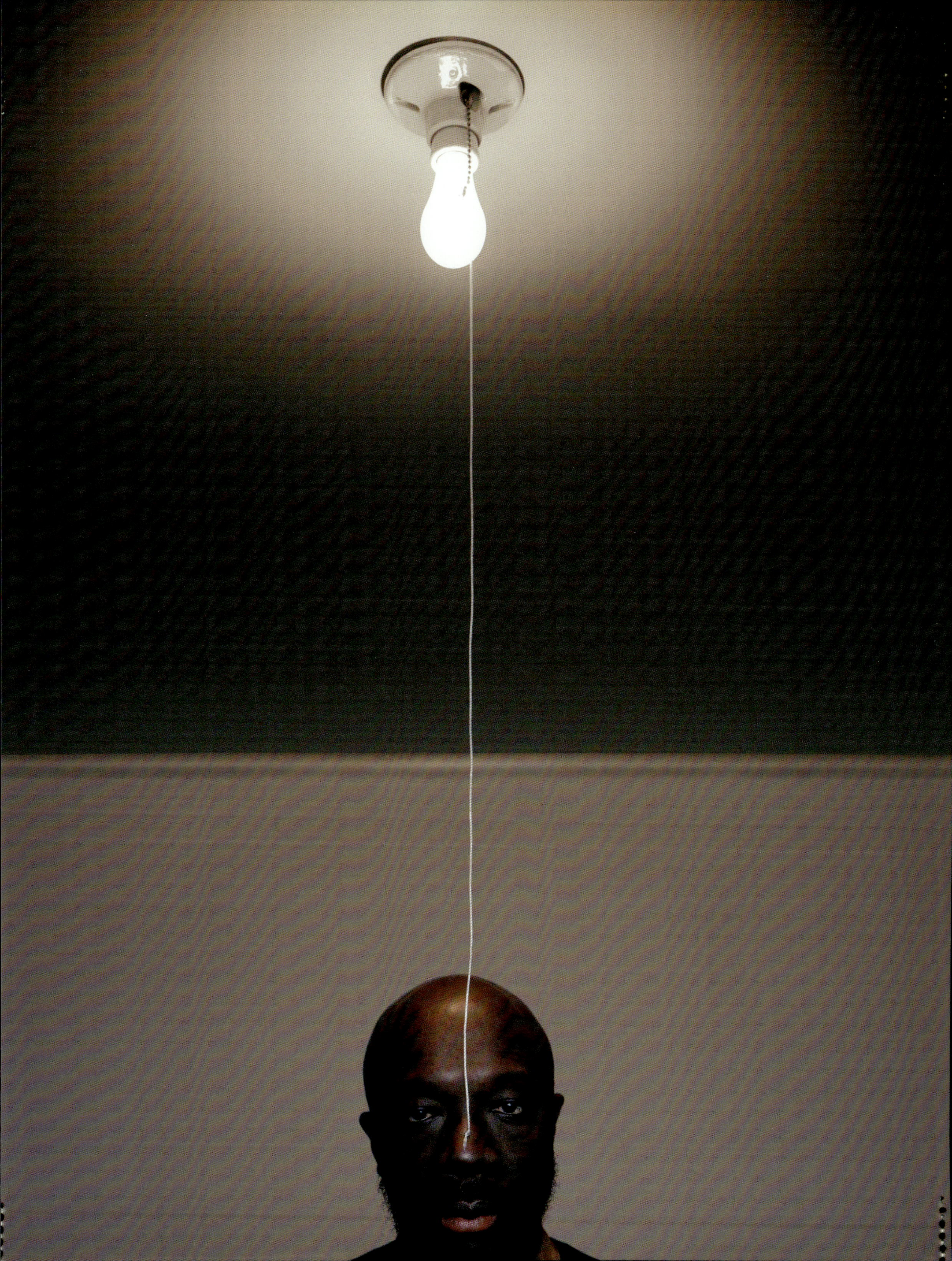

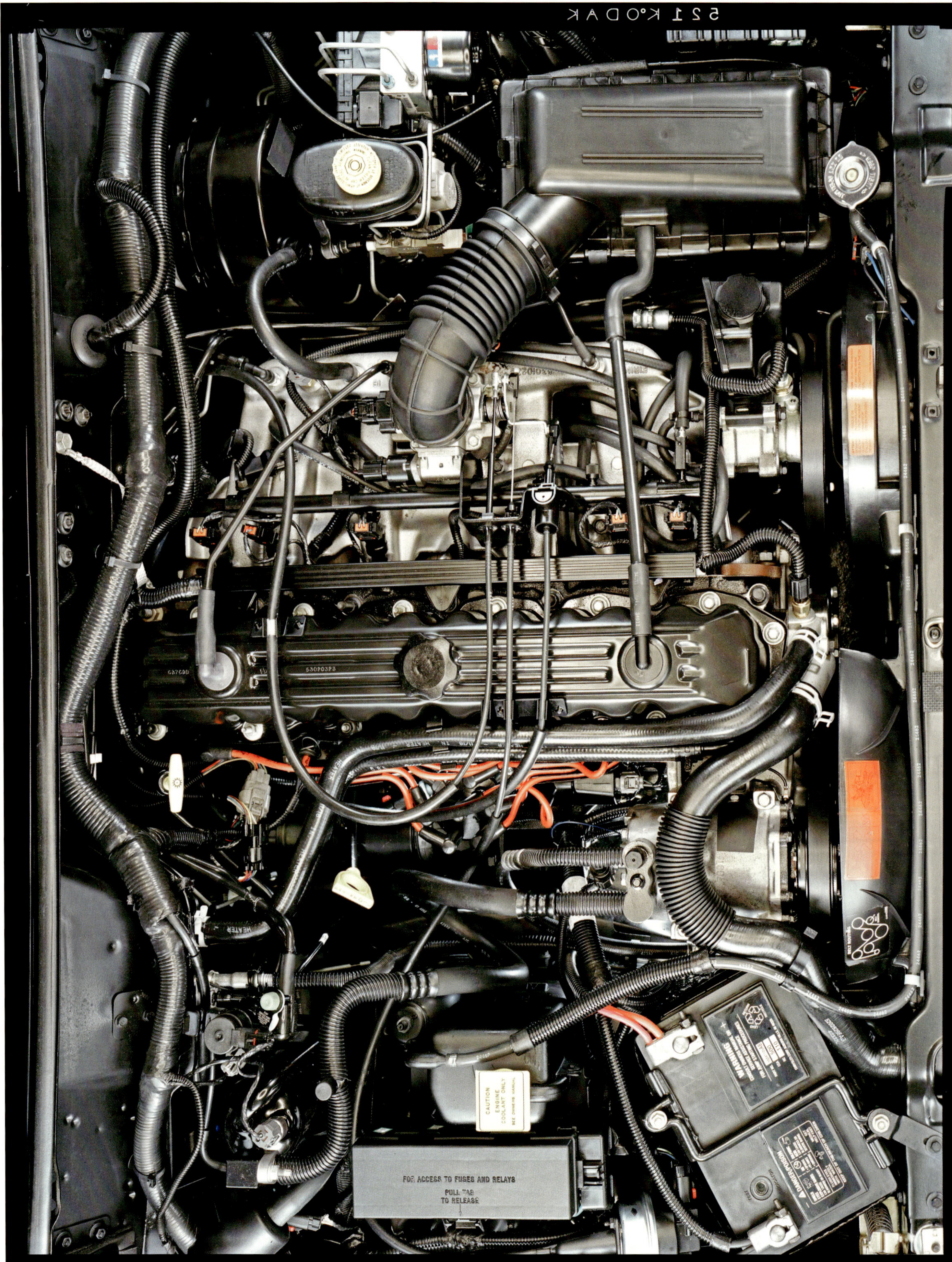
FOR ACCESS TO FUSES AND RELAYS
PULL TAB
TO RELEASE

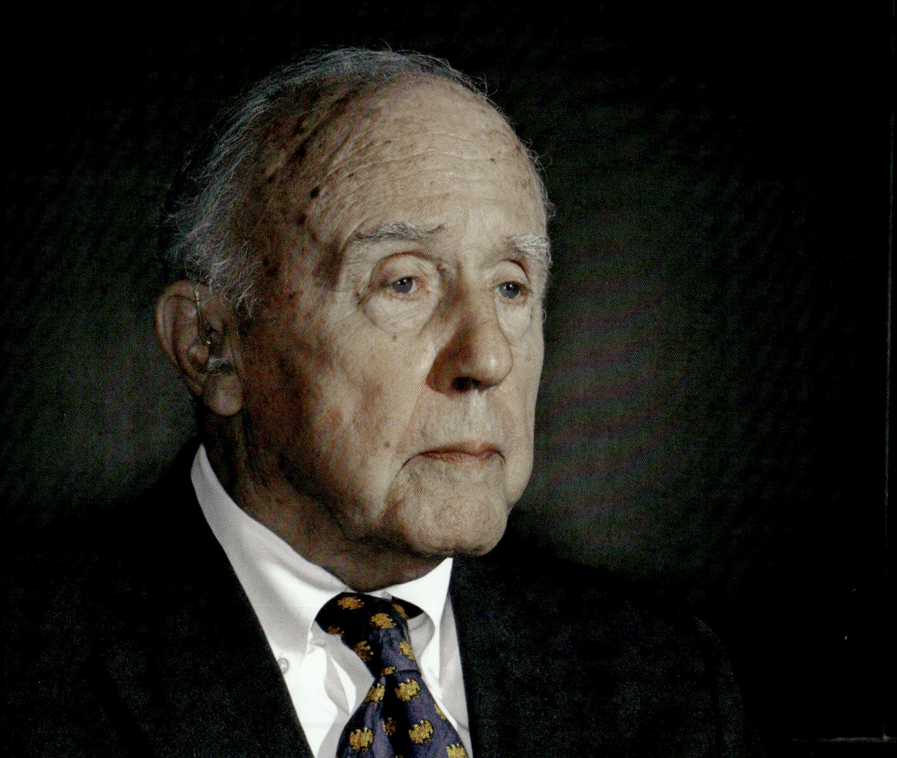
Kodak 160VC 3161

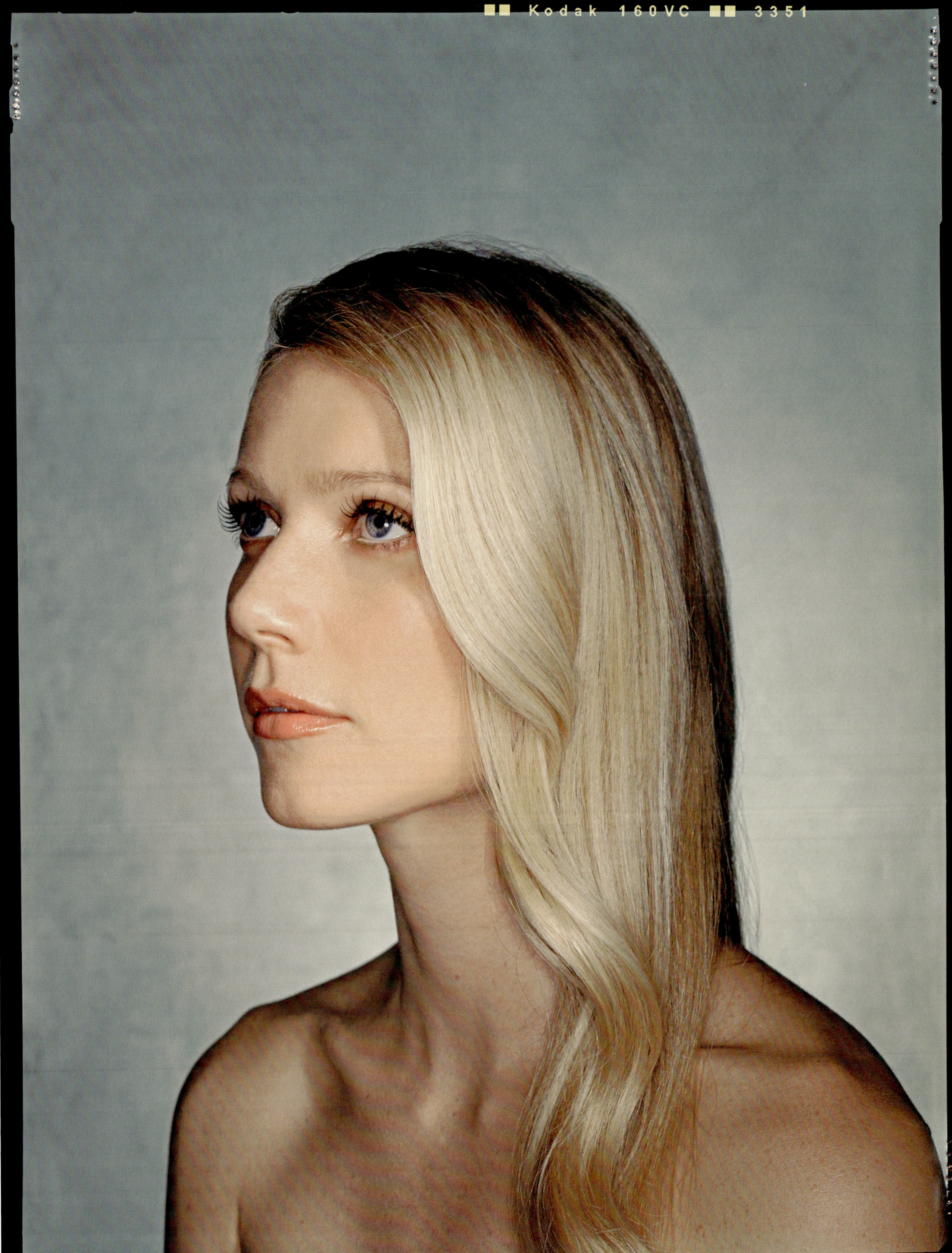
Kodak 160VC 3351

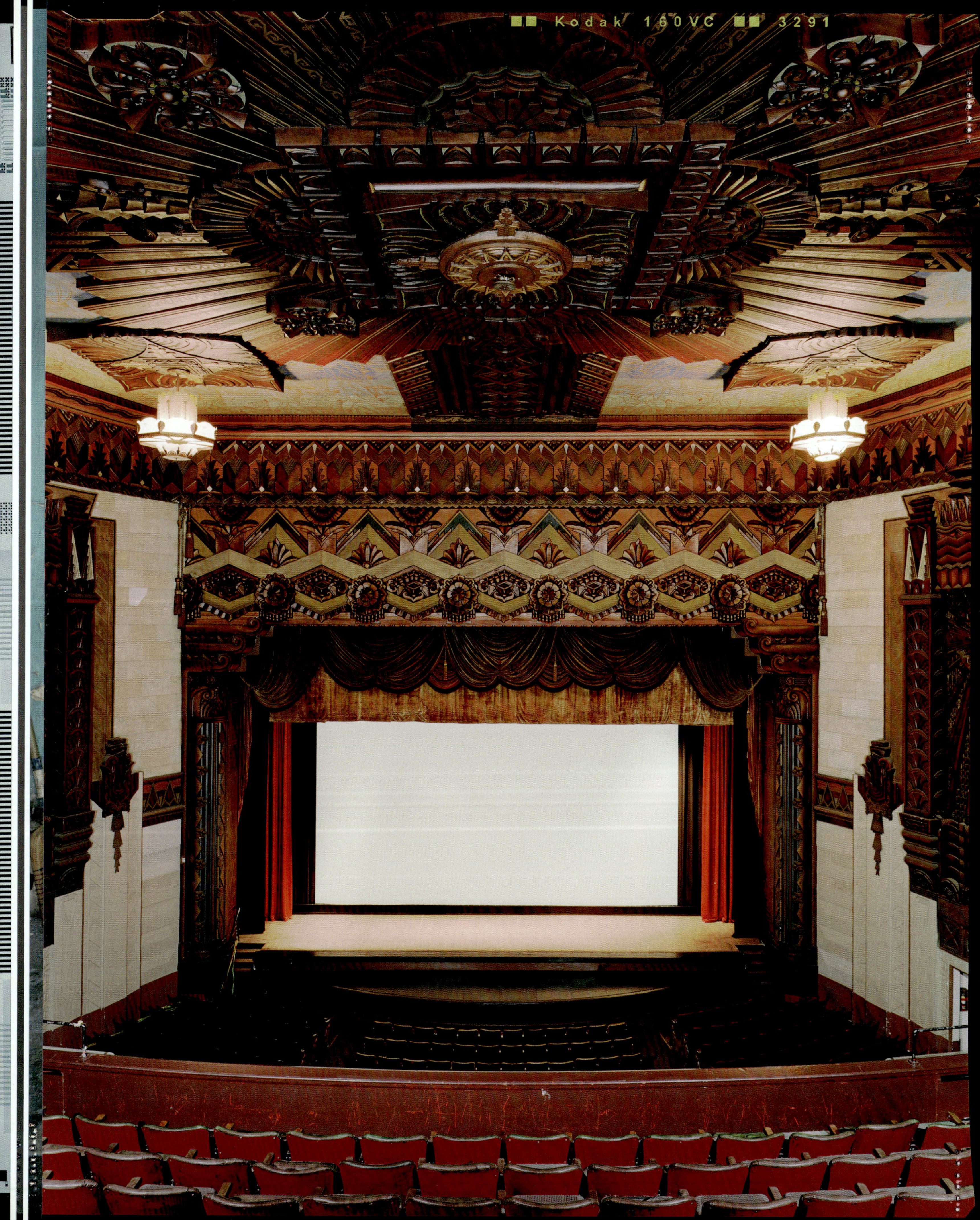
Kodak 160VC 3291

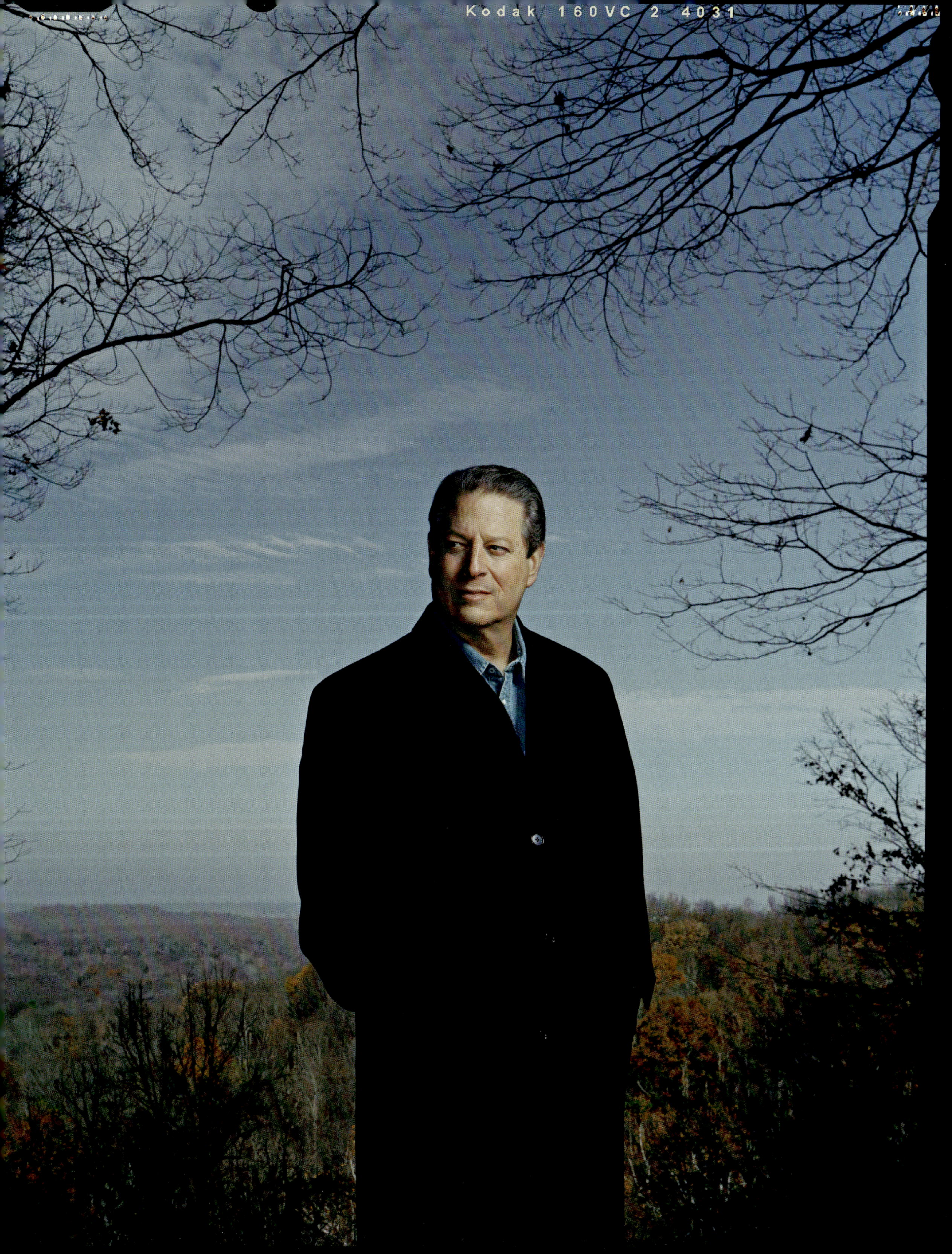
Kodak 160VC 2 4031

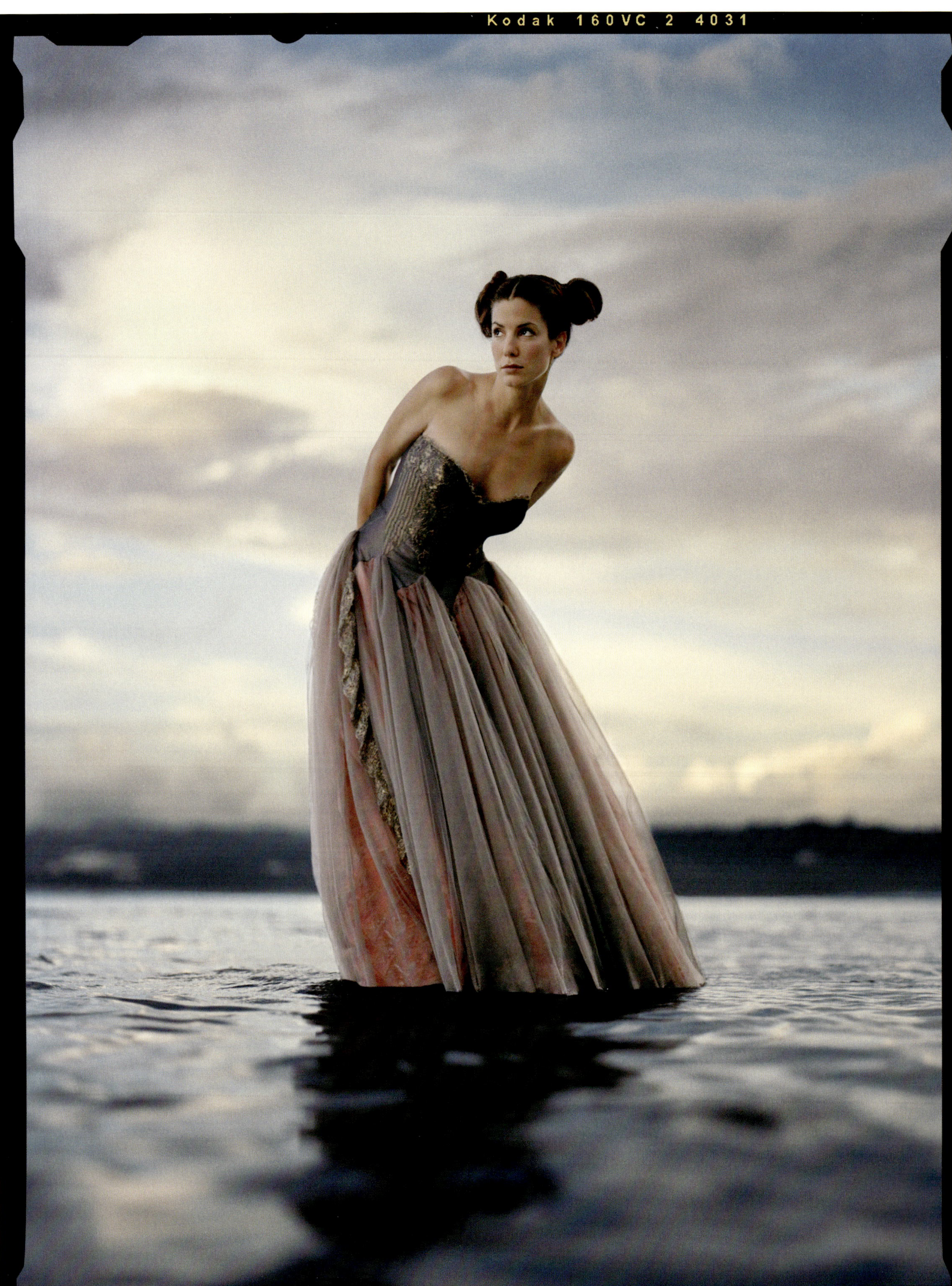
Kodak 160VC 2 4031

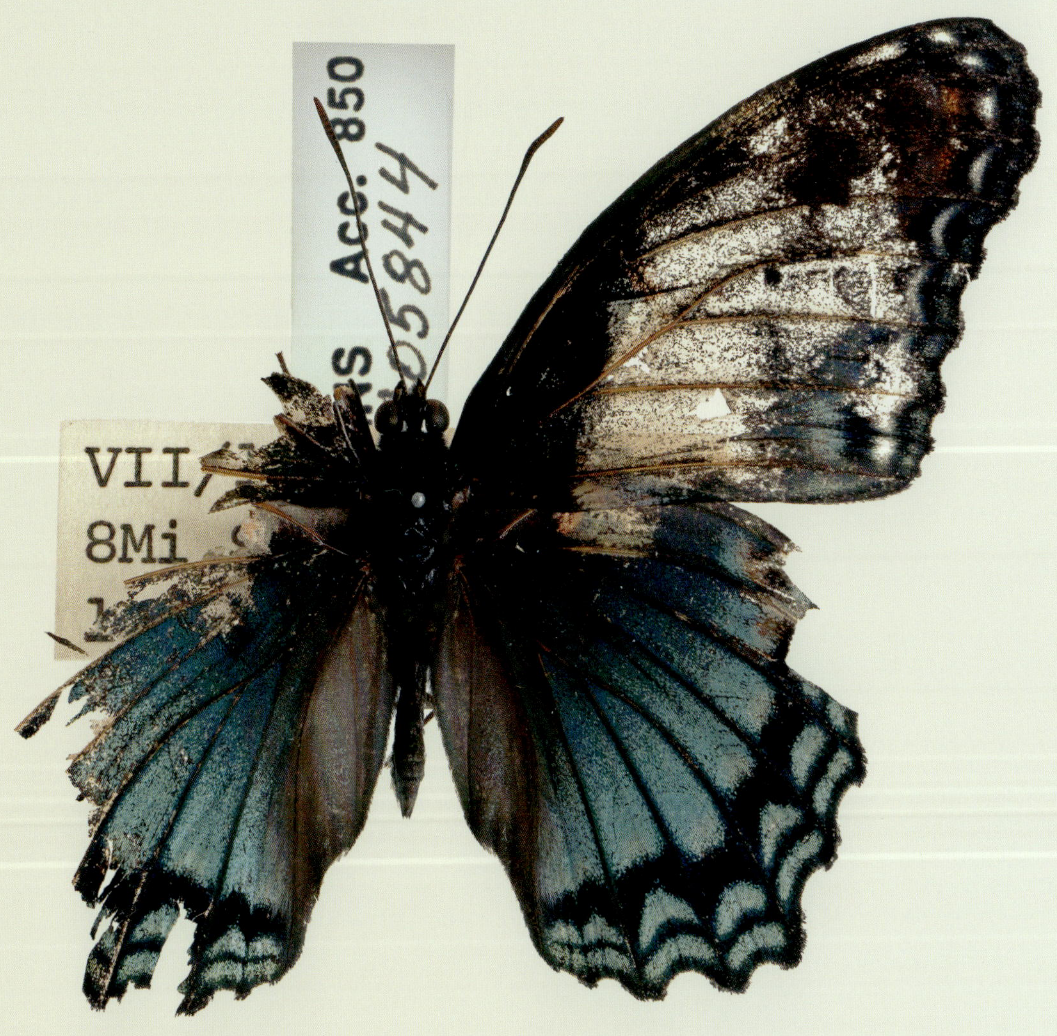
Kodak 160VC 3371
Acc. 850
05844
VII/
8Mi

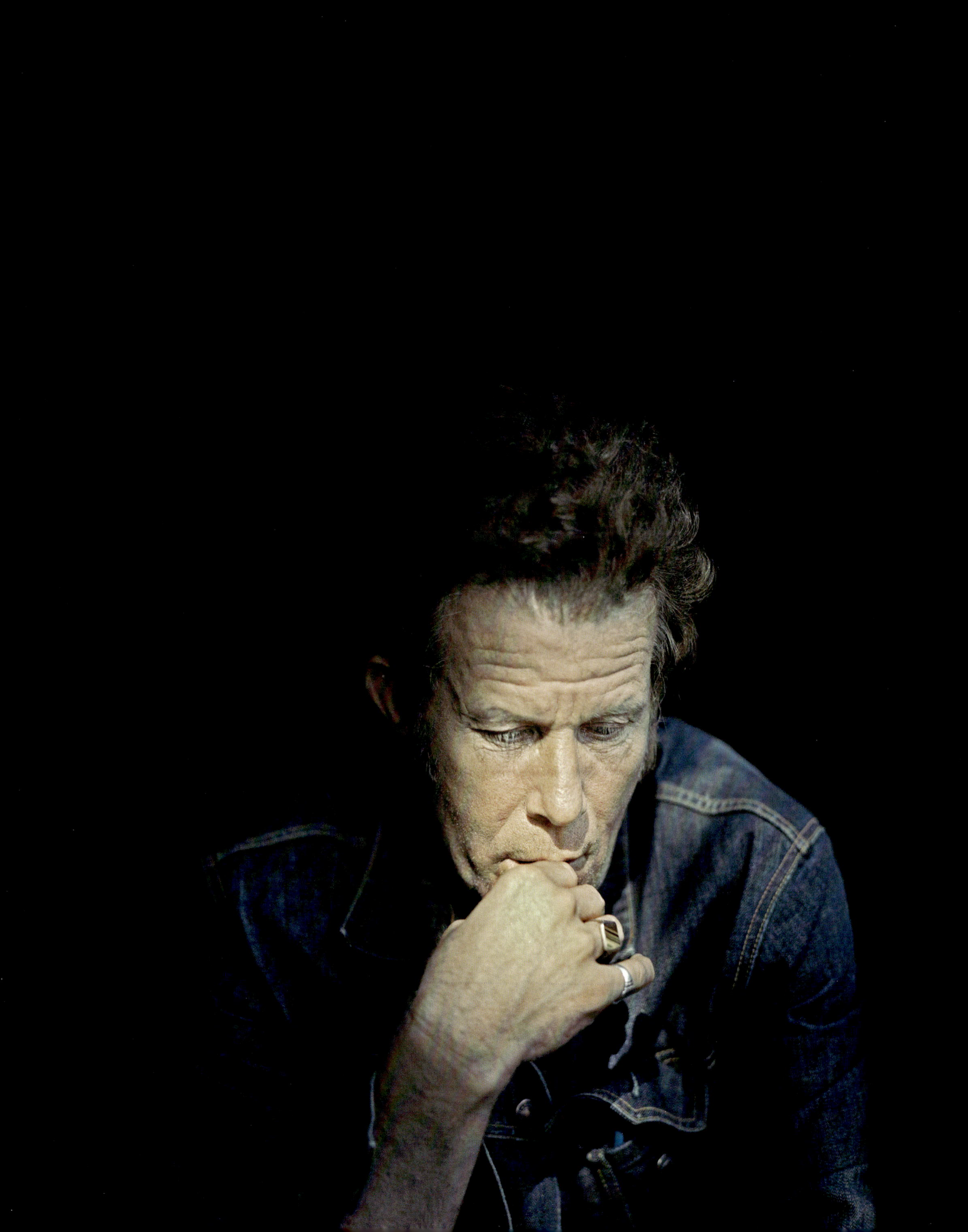

JETPACK
Constructed by Gary Tanhauser and Dan Winters, July 27, 2002
GQ

HELEN MIRREN
Los Angeles, January 11, 2007
New York Times Magazine

ROLLER GIRLS
Seattle, October 6, 2006
ESPN The Magazine

LEONARDO DICAPRIO
Los Angeles, November 2, 2002
New York Times Magazine

NEIL YOUNG
Waimea, Hawaii, July 17, 2000
New York Times Magazine

TAKASHI MURAKAMI'S *INOCHI*, UNDER CONSTRUCTION
Tokyo, March 3, 2005
New York Times Magazine

TAKASHI MURAKAMI
Tokyo, February 29, 2005
New York Times Magazine

CHINATSU BAN'S *VWX YELLOW ELEPHANT UNDERWEAR* UNDER CONSTRUCTION
Tokyo, March 2, 2005
New York Times Magazine

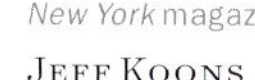

YOSHITOMO NARA
Tokyo, March 3, 2005
New York Times Magazine

WILLIAM CHRISTENBERRY
Washington, D.C., April 24, 2007
Stop Smiling

JOYCE CAROL OATES
Princeton, New Jersey, May 17, 2007
Entertainment Weekly

DEBBIE HARRY
New York, September 9, 2008
New York magazine

JEFF KOONS
New York, November 17, 2000
Ogilvy & Mather

AMBASSADOR HOTEL
Los Angeles, April 9, 1998
Los Angeles magazine

HEATH LEDGER
Hollywood, March 12, 2001
W

ANGELINA JOLIE
Hollywood, October 16, 1999
Entertainment Weekly

MAJOR GENERAL FRANCES C. WILSON, U.S. MARINE CORPS
Quantico, Virginia, January 28, 2003
New York Times Magazine

SERGEANT DONNA BRAVEBOY, DRILL INSTRUCTOR, U.S. MARINE CORPS
Paris Island, North Carolina, January 26, 2003
New York Times Magazine

U.S. ARMY MEDICAL TRAINING FACILITY
San Antonio, February 17, 2003
New York Times Magazine

PRIVATE HEIDI SHENK, U.S. ARMY
Fort Jackson, South Carolina, January 25, 2003
New York Times Magazine

THE PLATES

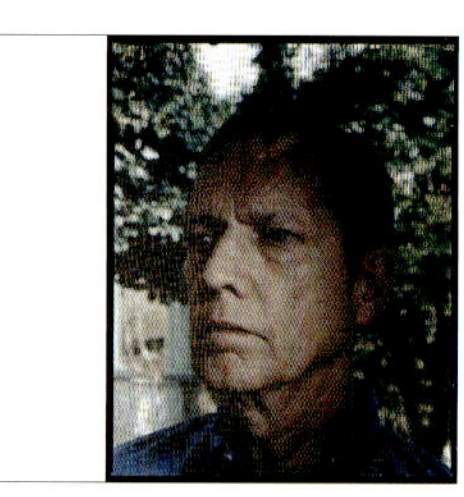

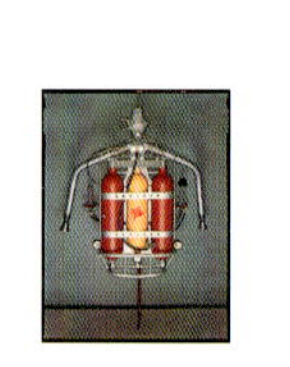

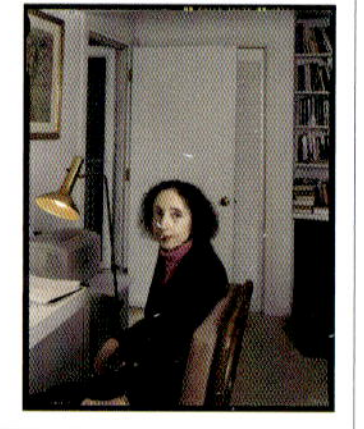

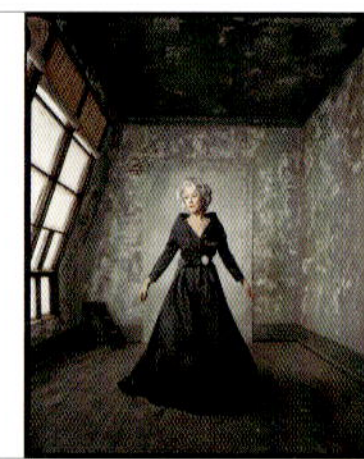

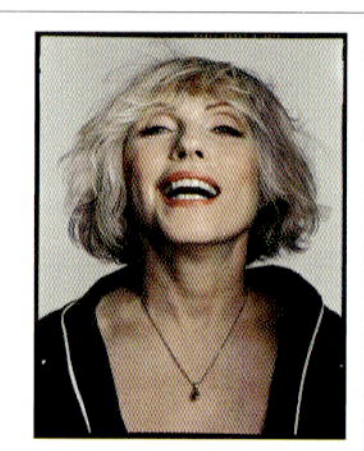

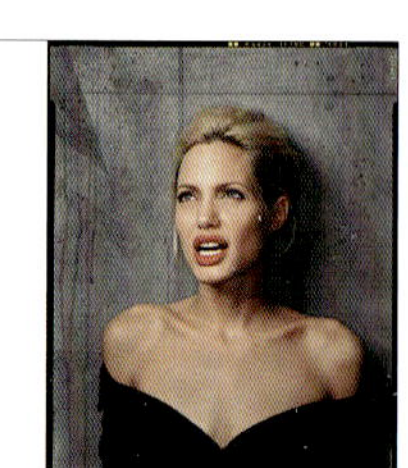

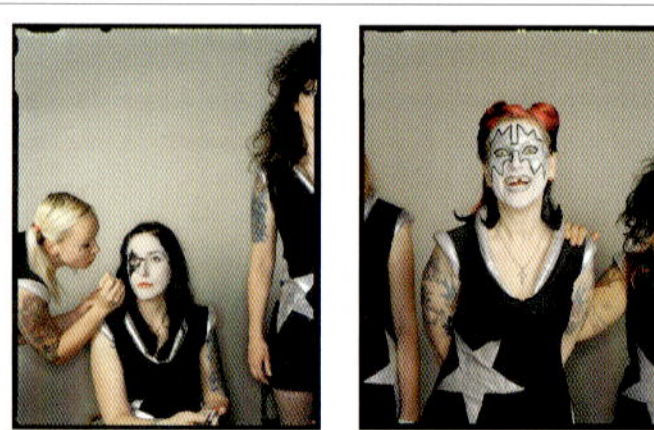

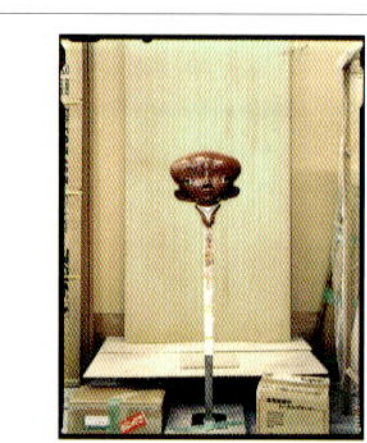

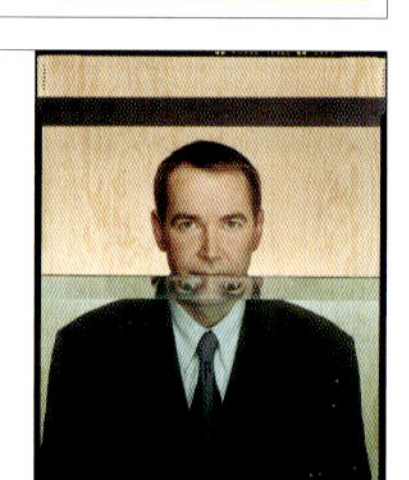

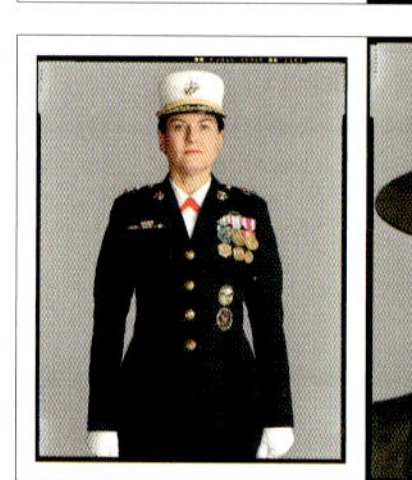

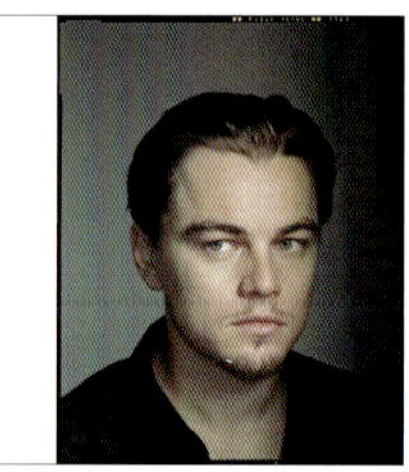

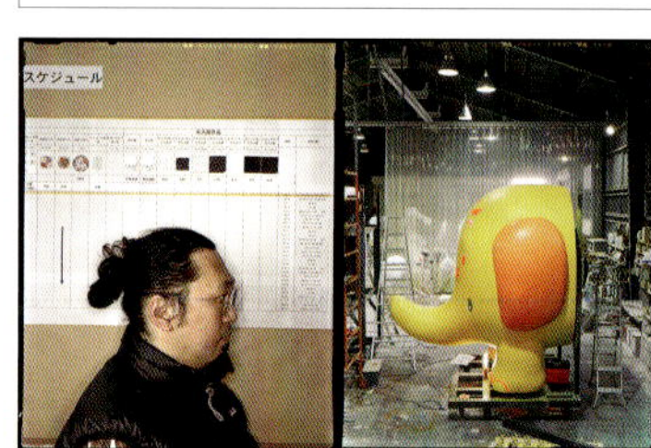

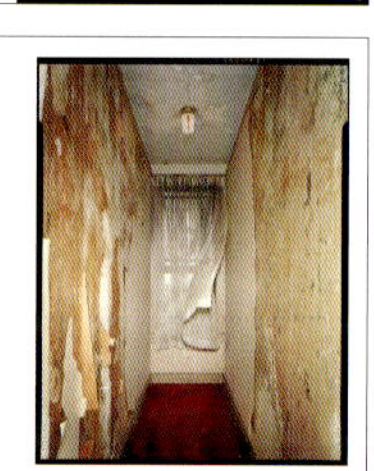

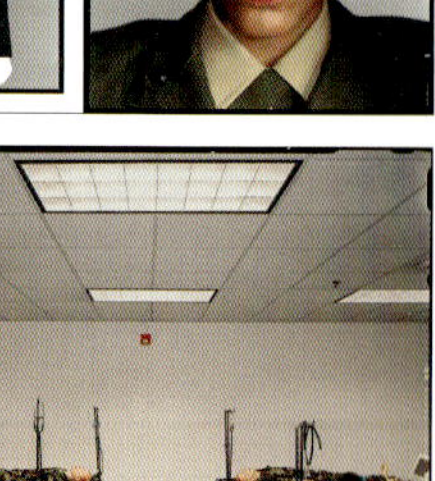

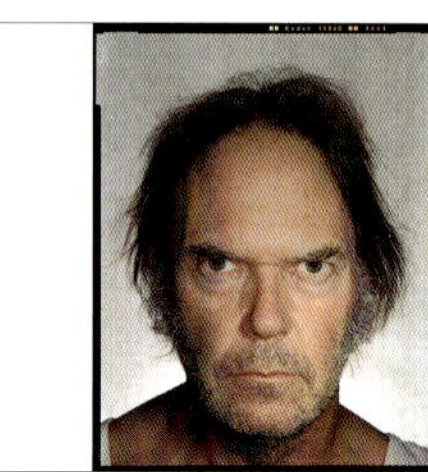

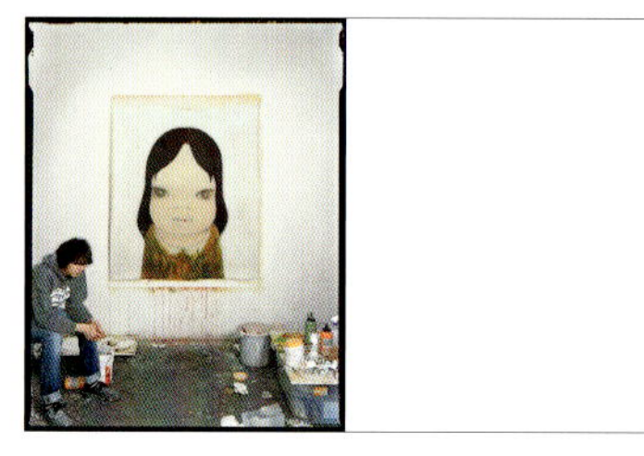

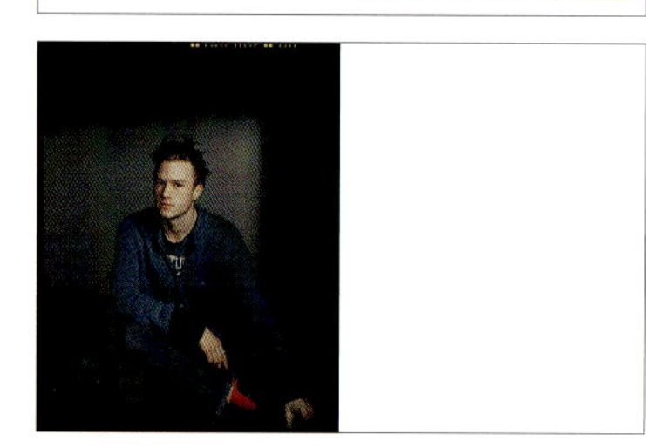

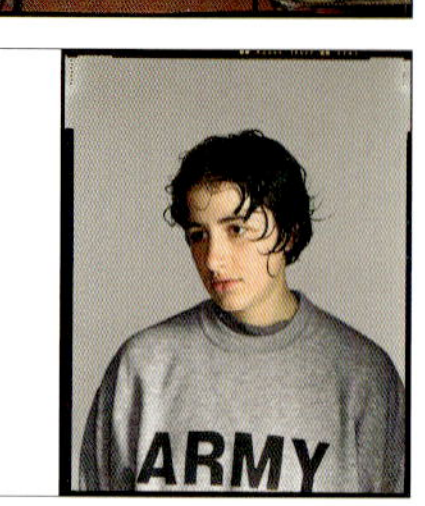

Kate Winslet
Los Angeles, November 10, 2004
V Life

His Holiness the Dalai Lama
Tucson, Arizona, February 23, 1993
New York Times Magazine

Barack Obama
San Antonio, Texas, March 5, 2008
Time

U2
Amsterdam Arena, the Netherlands, July 15, 2005
New York Times Magazine

Daniel Johnston
Waller, Texas, December 3, 2004
Texas Monthly

Fred Rogers
Pittsburgh, August 17, 1998
Esquire

Fred Rogers's sweater
Pittsburgh, August 17, 1998
Esquire

Talon of a Cooper's Hawk
El Segundo, California, January 10, 2008
Backpacker

Bald Eagle
El Segundo, California, January 11, 2008
Backpacker

Morrissey
Los Angeles, March 29, 2004
New York Times Magazine

Johnny Depp
New York, April 7, 1998
Rolling Stone

Laura Dern
Hollywood, July 21, 1999
Detour

Denzel Washington
Hollywood, October 7, 1992
New York Times Magazine

R.D. Horn and his son Bronc
along Route 66, outside Adrian, Texas, March 23, 2002
Texas Monthly

1949 Ford
along Route 66, Bushland, Texas, March 22, 2002

Plowed field
along Route 66 outside Conway, Texas, March 24, 2002
Texas Monthly

Candy rack
Adrian, Texas, "Midpoint USA," March 23, 2002
Texas Monthly

Sharla Lewis
Conway, Texas, March, 23, 2002
Texas Monthly

Lonnie Blankenship
outside of Glenrio, Texas, March 26, 2002
Texas Monthly

Willie Nelson
Bakersfield, California, January 24, 1998
Texas Monthly

Rick Rubin
Malibu, California, July 28, 2007
New York Times Magazine

Free climber Dean Potter
Yosemite Valley, California, September 10, 2007
ESPN The Magazine

Walt Disney Concert Hall
Los Angeles, June 28, 2003
Los Angeles magazine

Frank Gehry
Los Angeles, June 29, 2003
Los Angeles magazine

Walt Disney Concert Hall
Los Angeles, June 28, 2003
Los Angeles magazine

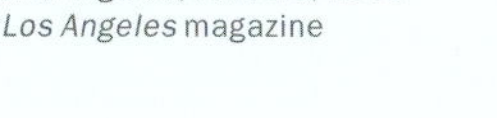
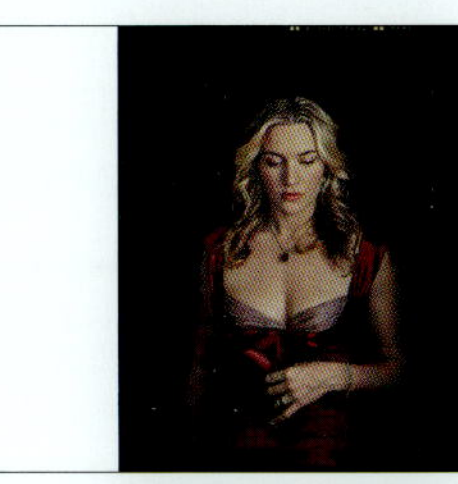
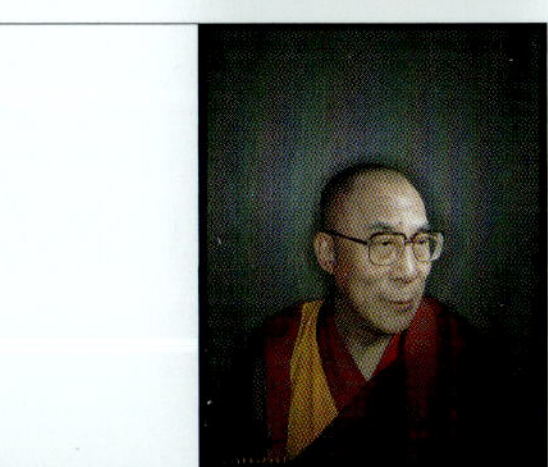
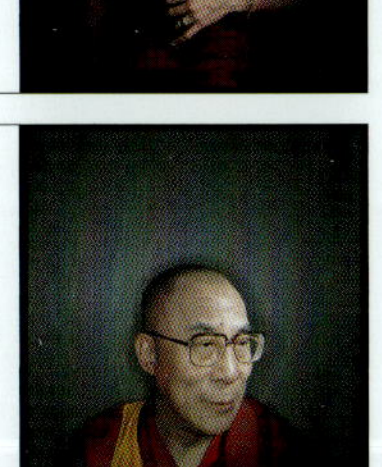
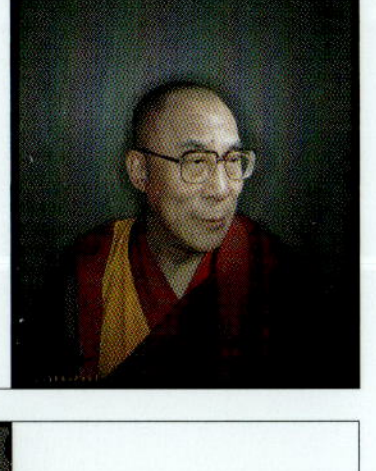
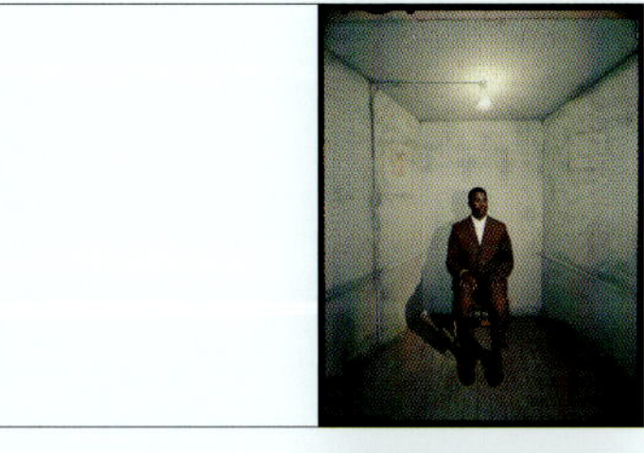
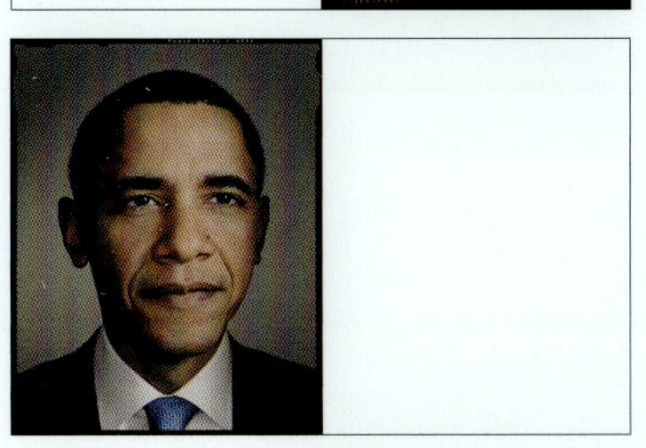
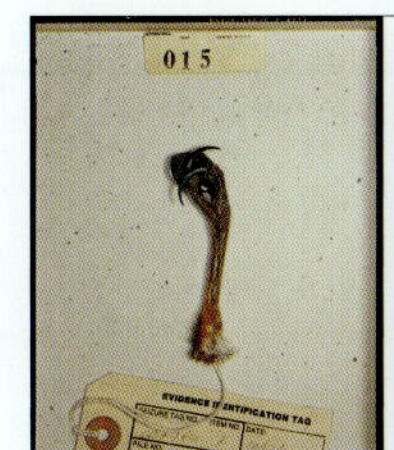
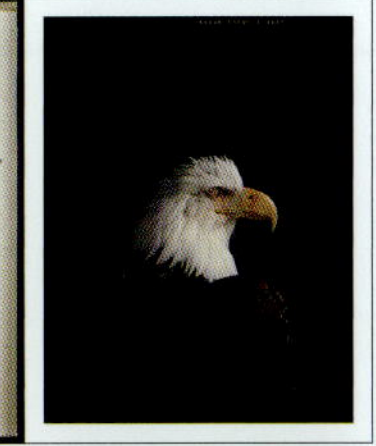
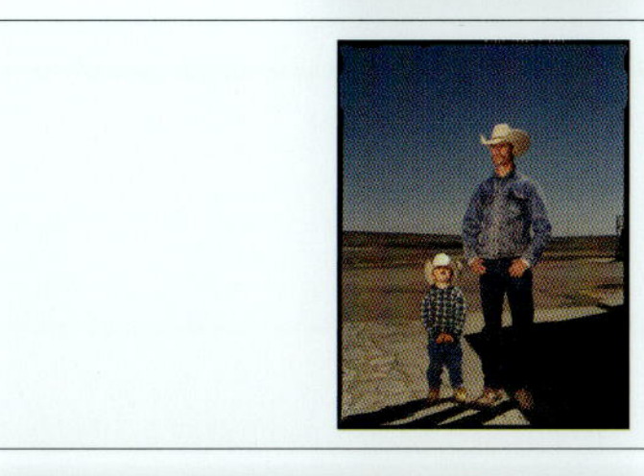
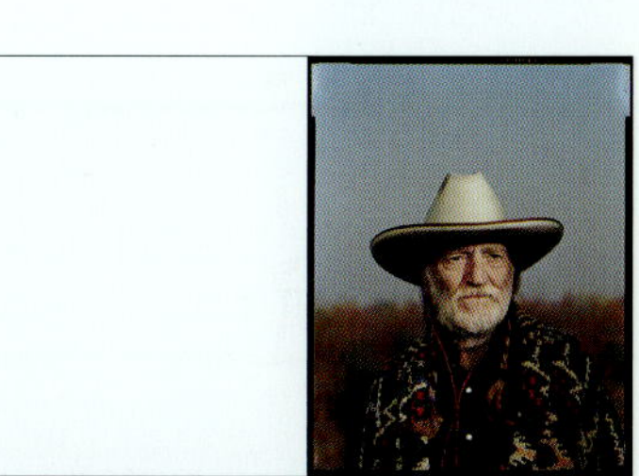
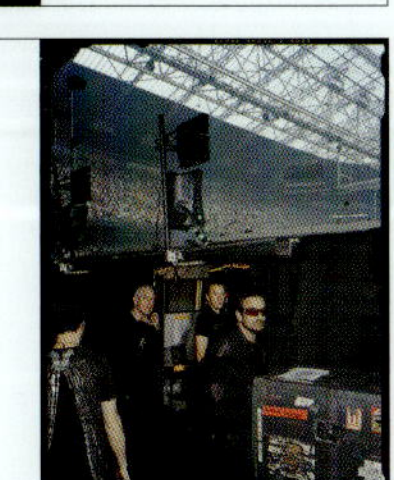
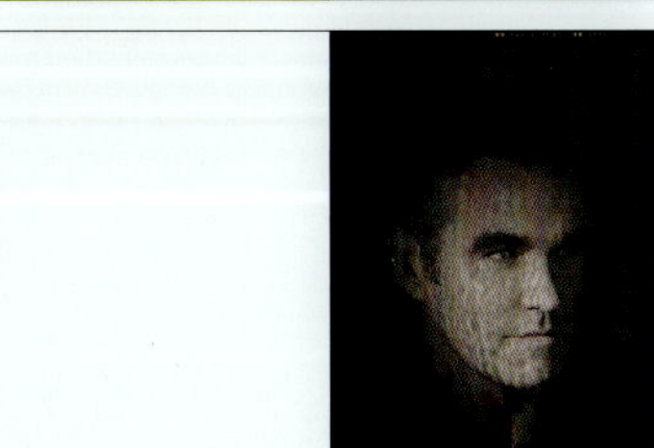
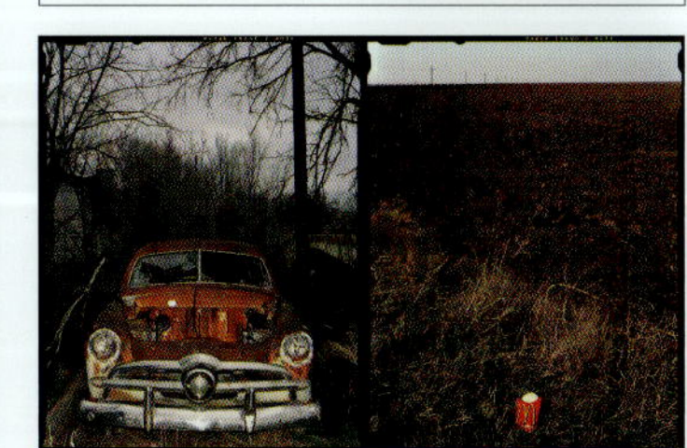
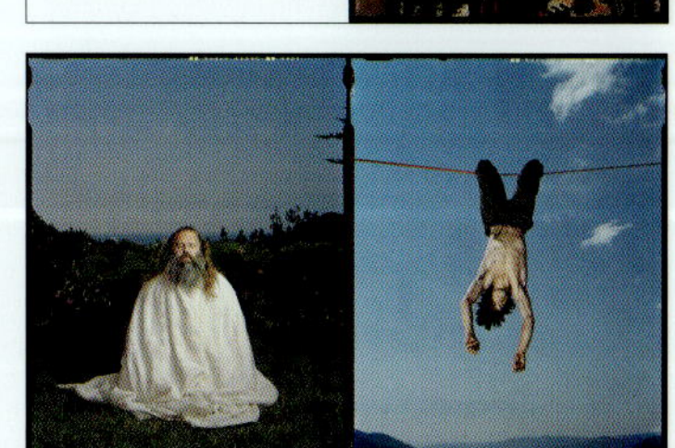
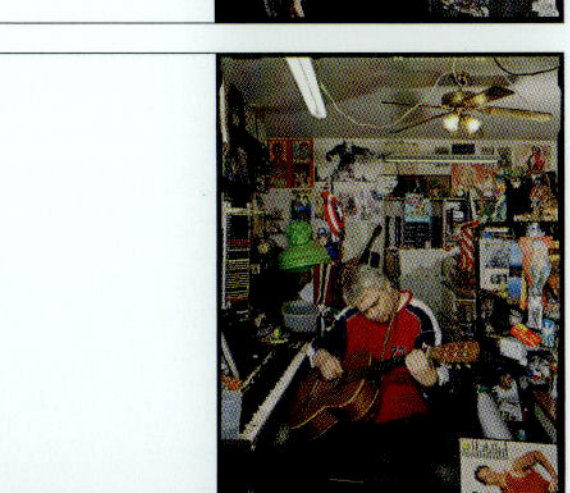
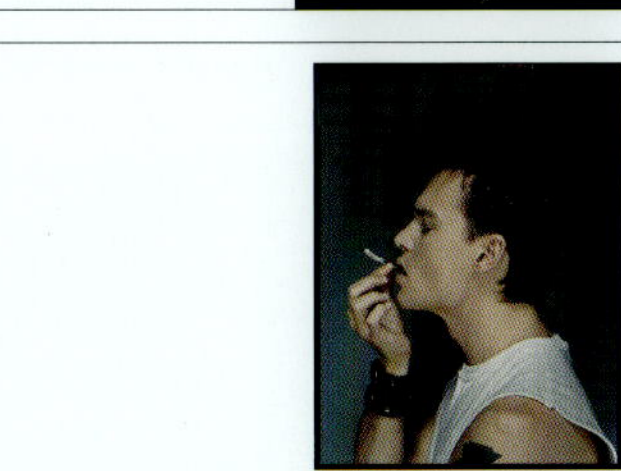
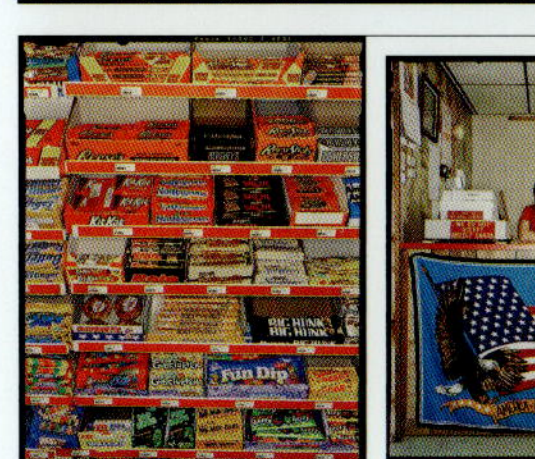
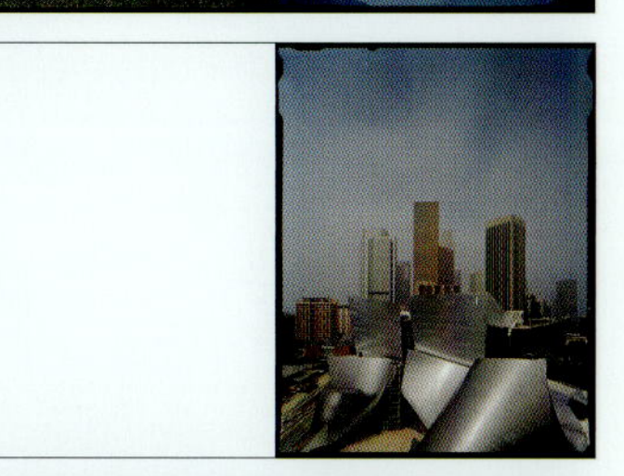
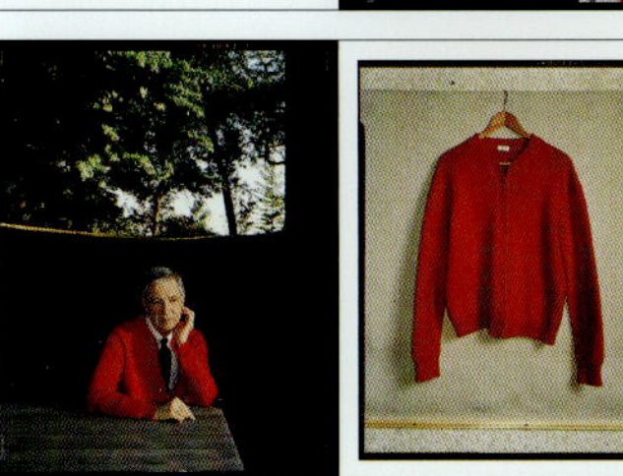
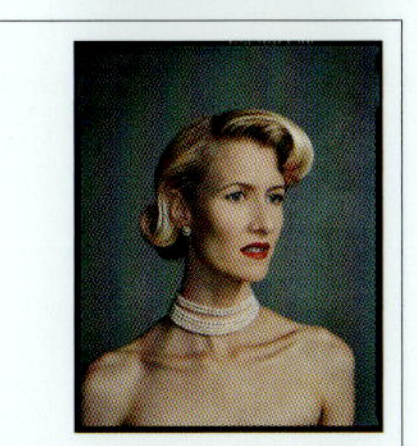
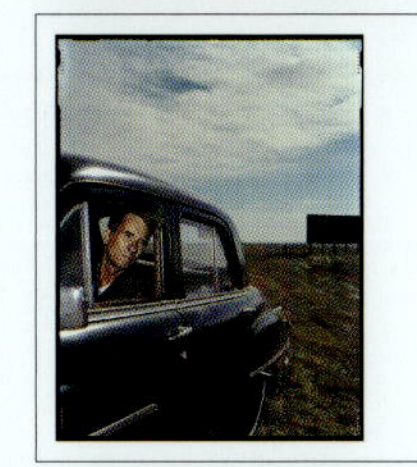
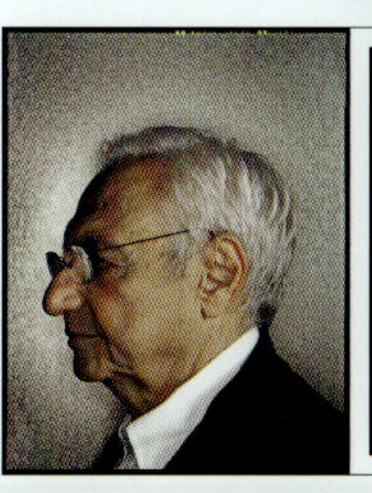
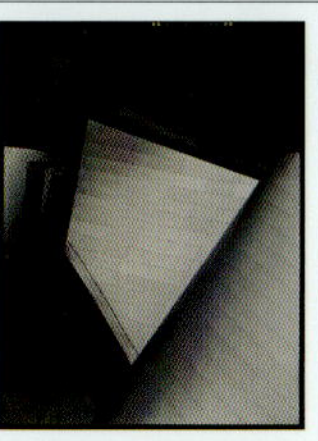

Djimon Hounsou
Los Angeles, October 24, 2005
Entertainment Weekly

Photo booth
constructed and photographed in
Austin, September, 2003
Entertainment Weekly

Window display
Leon Studio, Seguin, Texas, January 28, 1998
Texas Monthly

Darkroom sink
Leon Studio, Seguin, Texas, January 26, 1998
Texas Monthly

Enlarger
Leon Studio, Seguin, Texas, January 26, 1998
Texas Monthly

Leon Kubala
Seguin, Texas, January 29, 1998
Texas Monthly

Hand of Kong
Stop-motion animation puppet armature from
RKO's original 1933 production of *King Kong*
Collection of Bob Burns
Burbank, Califonia, October 25, 2007
Los Angeles magazine

Prop from *Rocketship X-M* (1950)
Collection of Bob Burns
Burbank, California, October 25, 2007
Los Angeles magazine

Prop from George Pal's 1951 film *When Worlds Collide*
Collection of Bob Burns
Burbank, California, October 25, 2007
Los Angeles magazine

Alien's head from *This Island Earth* (1955)
Collection of Bob Burns
Burbank, California, October 25, 2007
Los Angeles magazine

Tim Burton
Culver City, California, October 20, 2003
New York Times Magazine

Shuttle launch
Kennedy Space Center, Cocoa Beach, Florida,
October 27, 1998
Esquire

Wayne Newton
Las Vegas, August 17, 2003
Entertainment Weekly

Arnold Schwarzenegger
Los Angeles, April 21, 2003
V Life

Acid peel
Palm Springs, California, July 28, 2000
Esquire

Toupee
Hollywood, August 2, 2000
Esquire

Gorilla
Bronx Zoo, New York, June 31, 2001
Audubon Magazine

The Hymenoptera box of the late George Merriken, rancher, citrus grower, and amateur entomologist
Fillmore, California, July 22, 2000

Projector
San Francisco, June 22, 2001
Arena

Seth MacFarlane
Hollywood, January 22, 1999
Details

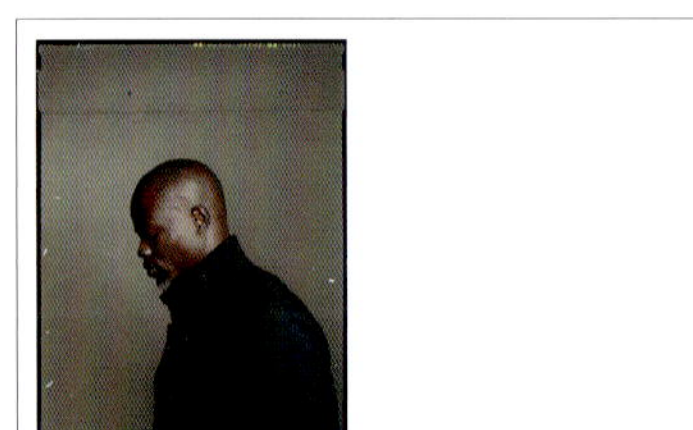

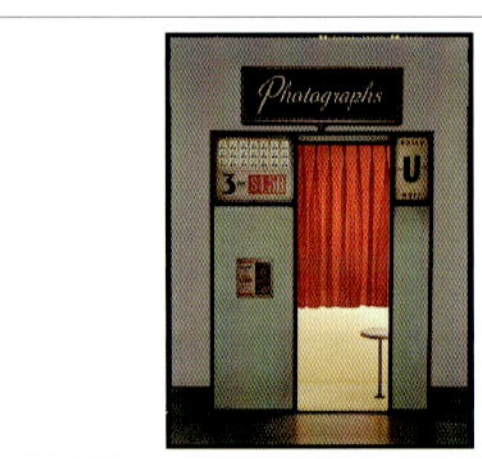

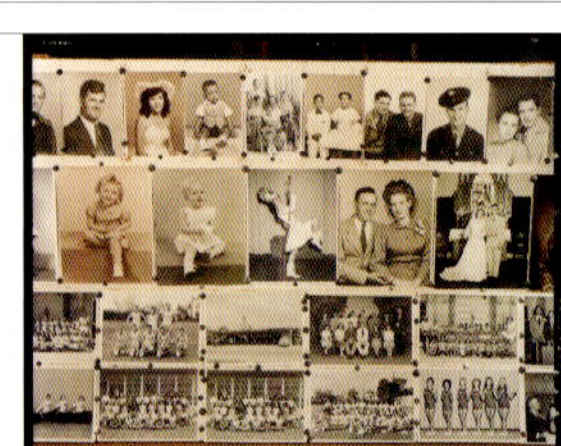

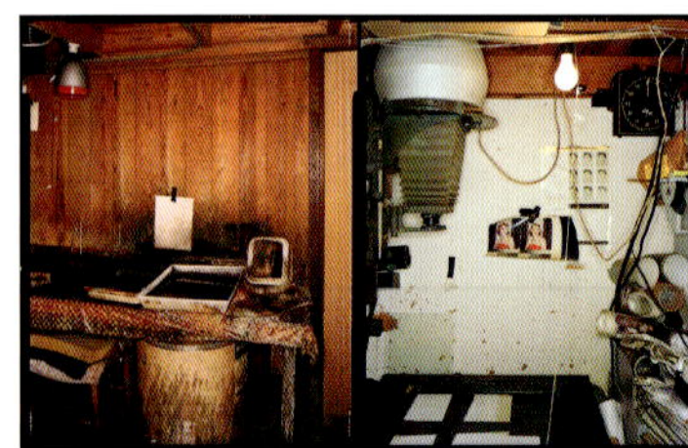

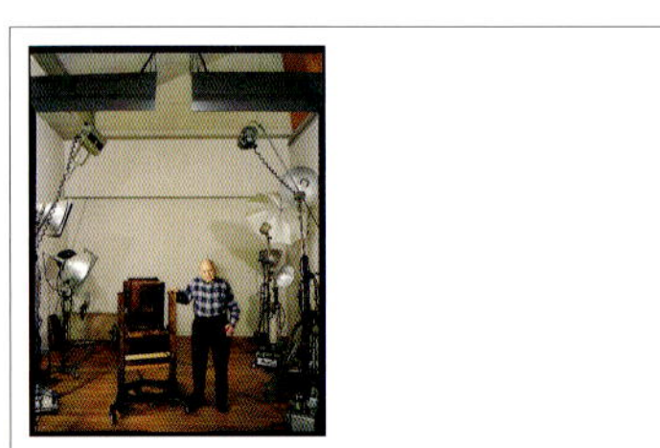

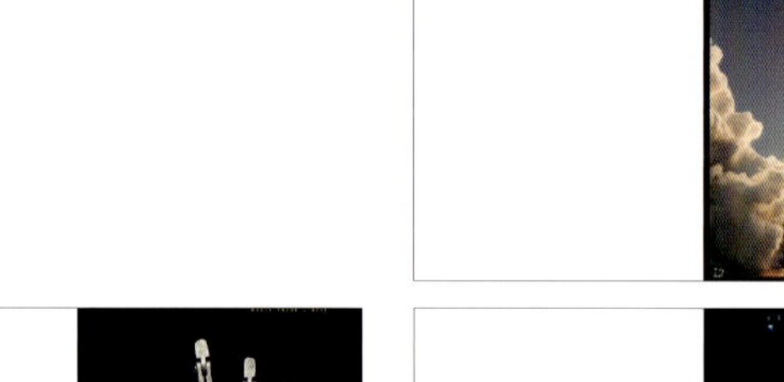

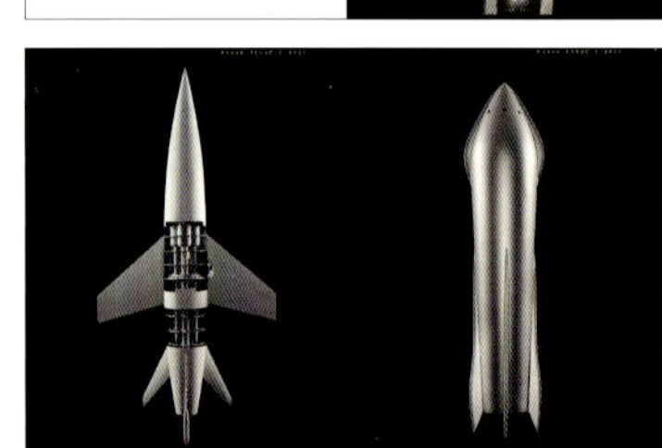

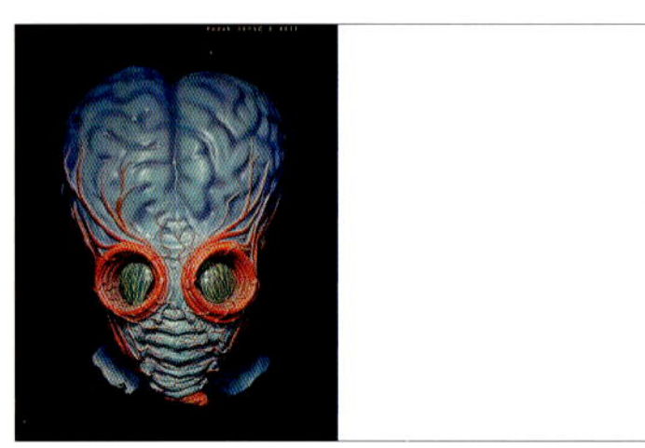

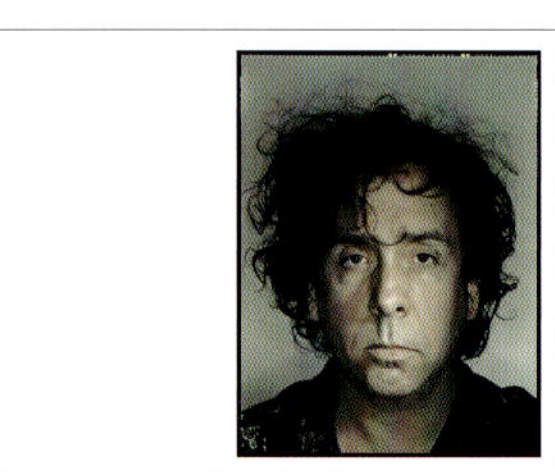

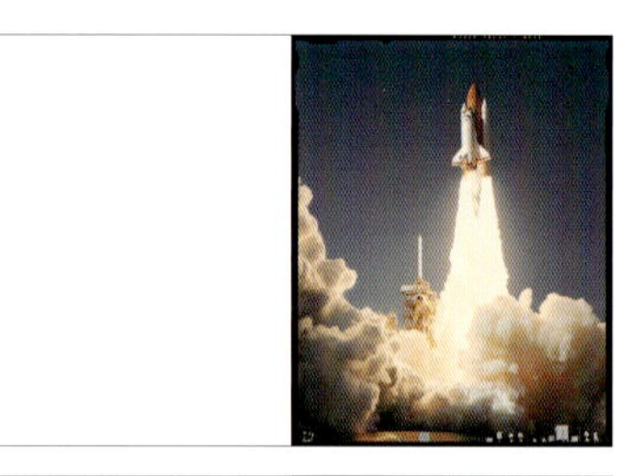

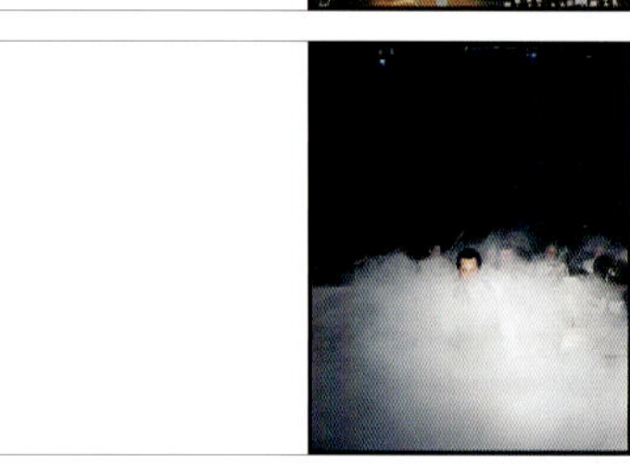

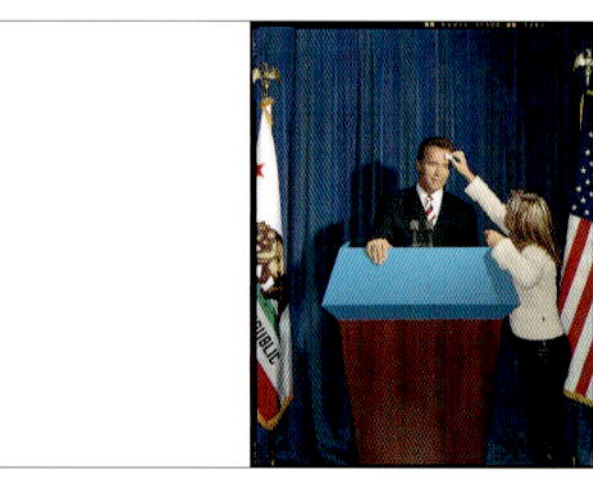

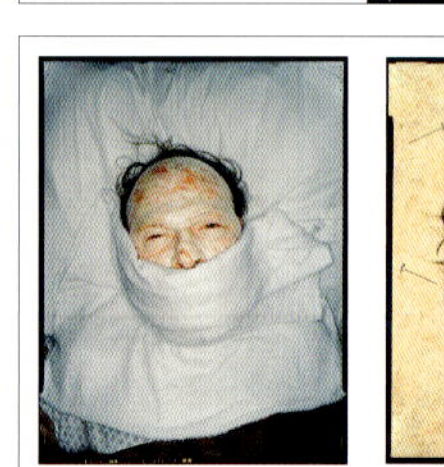

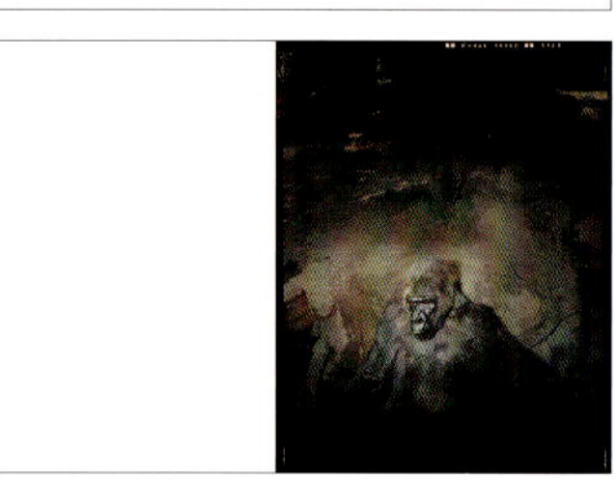

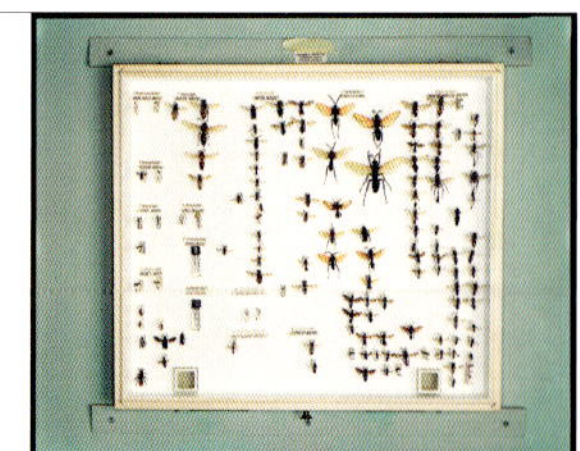

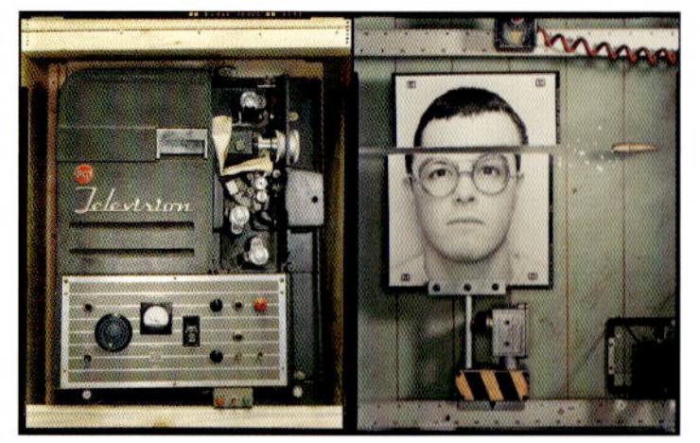

Beck
Los Angeles, January 20, 1997
New York Times Magazine

Vera Farmiga
New York, July 14, 2006
New York Times Magazine

Natalie Portman
New York, August 9, 2005
New York magazine

Isaac Hayes
Los Angeles, March 2, 1995
Interview

Engine
Los Angeles, October 2, 1997
Weiden+Kennedy

John Wheeler
Theoretical physicist and colleague
of Albert Einstein
Princeton, New Jersey, March 19, 2002
Discover

Gwyneth Paltrow
Santa Monica, California, August 23, 2006
New York magazine

Warner Grand Movie Palace
San Pedro, California, April 29, 2004
Los Angeles magazine

Alejandro González Iñárritu
Mexico City, February 20, 2001
New York Times Magazine

Tom Hanks
Los Angeles, September 23, 1999
Entertainment Weekly

Jay Z
New York, October 10, 2003
Vibe

Nicole Kidman
Los Angeles, December 7, 2004
V Life

Shunpei Yamazaki
The world's most prolific inventor.
Tokyo, July 17, 2007
Portfolio

Circuit on glass
Shumpei Yamazaki's laboratory,
Tokyo, July 17, 2007
Portfolio

The Asbury Hotel
Los Angeles, December 9, 1997
Esquire

Al Gore
Nashville, December 6, 2007
Time

Sandra Bullock
Vanua Levu, Fiji, December 27, 1998
Movieline

Broken butterfly
Houston, March 21, 2006
Texas Monthly

Tom Waits
Santa Rosa, California, March 2, 2002
Stern

Self Portrait after Walker Evans
2004

Movie theater
Midland, Texas, March 25, 1995
Texas Monthly

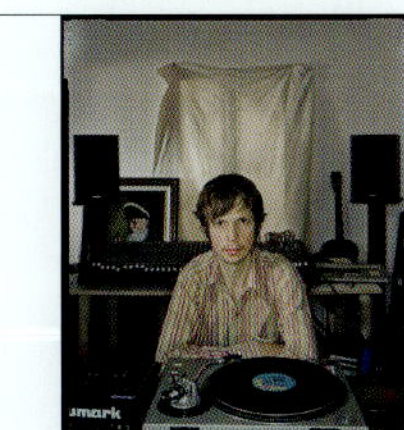
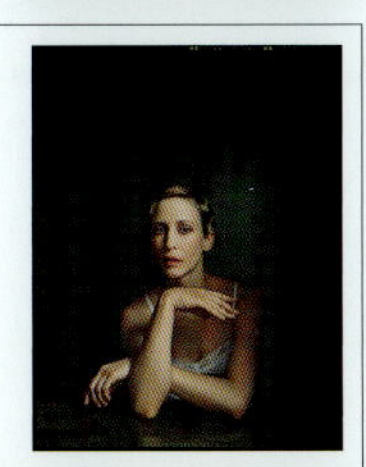
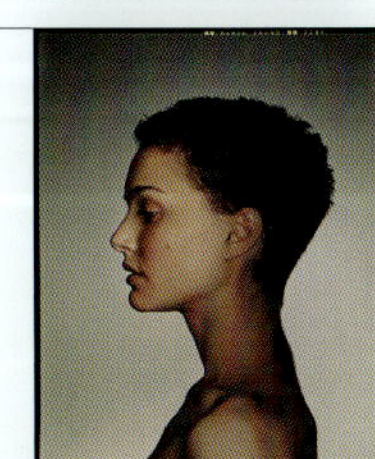

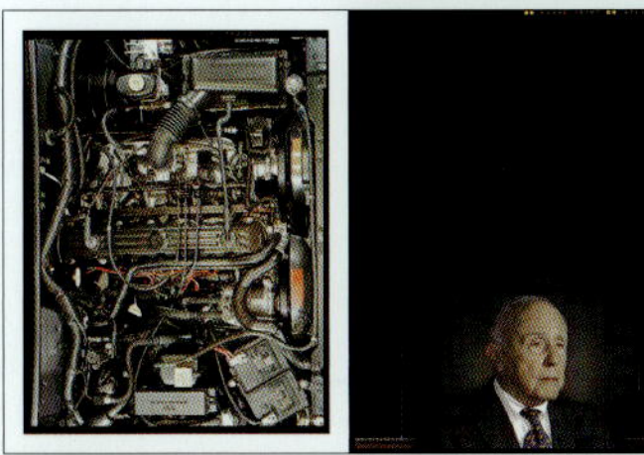
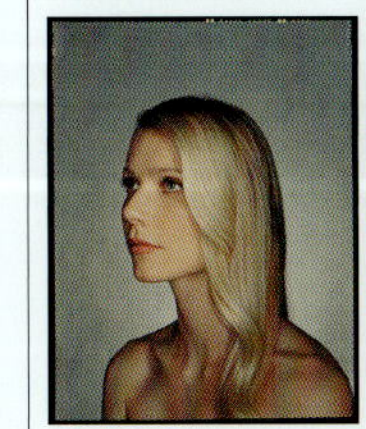
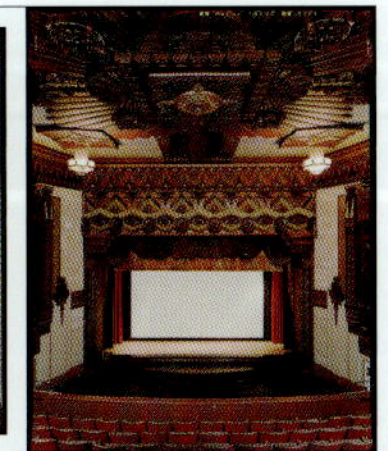
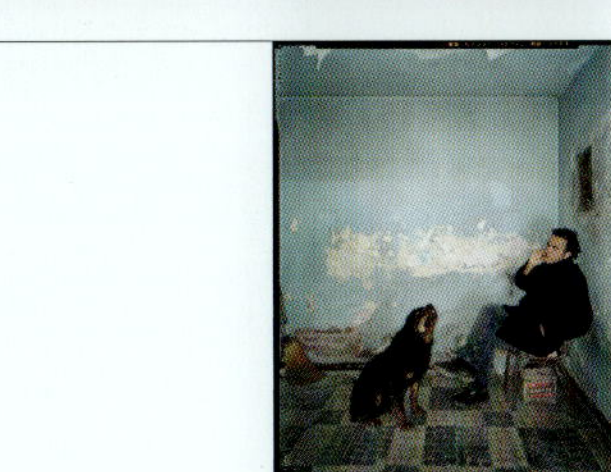
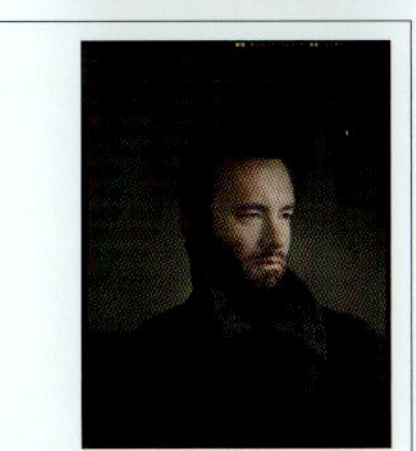
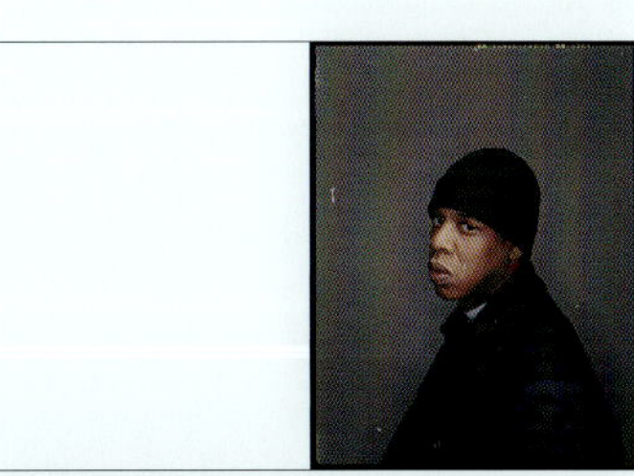
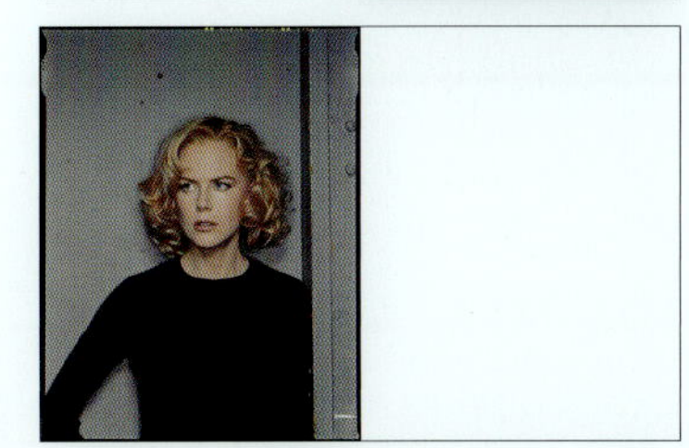
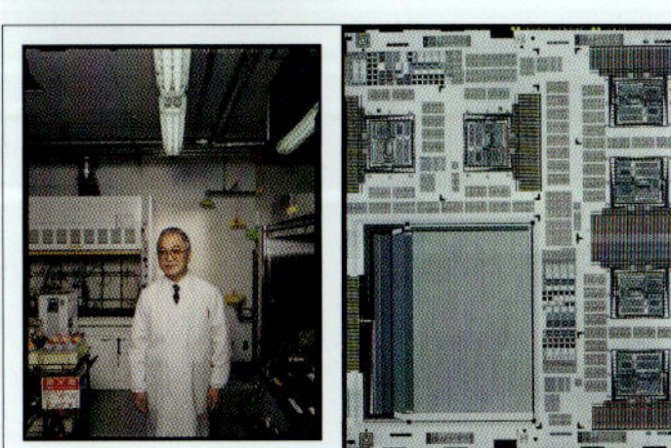
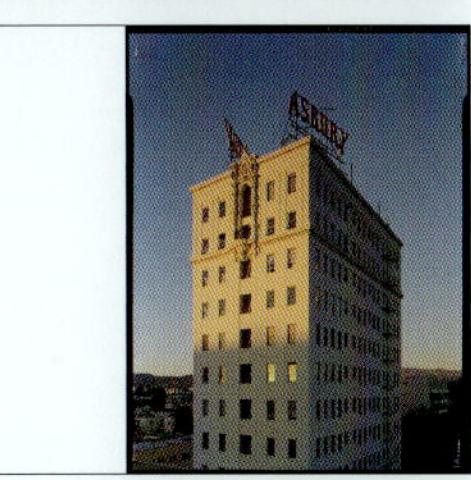
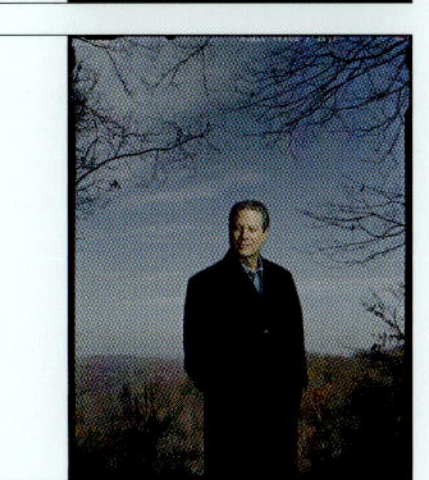
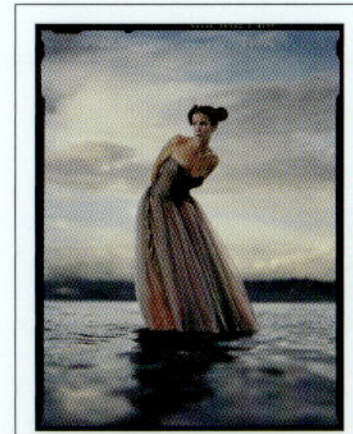
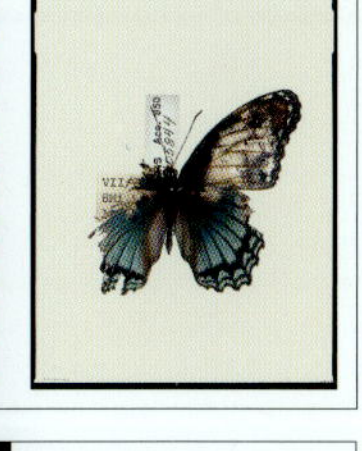
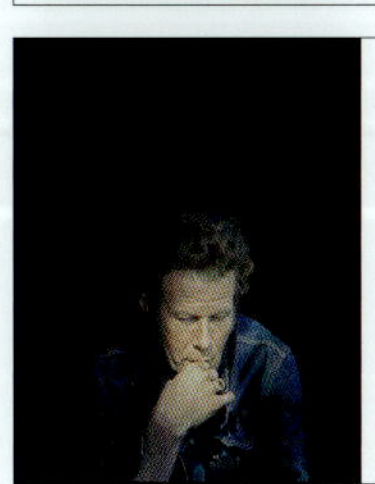
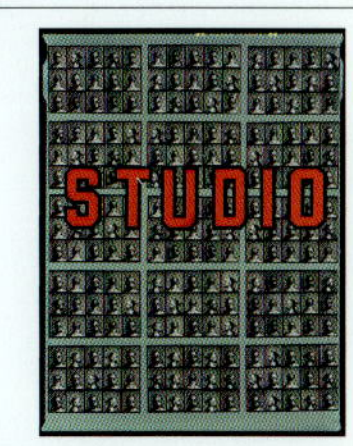

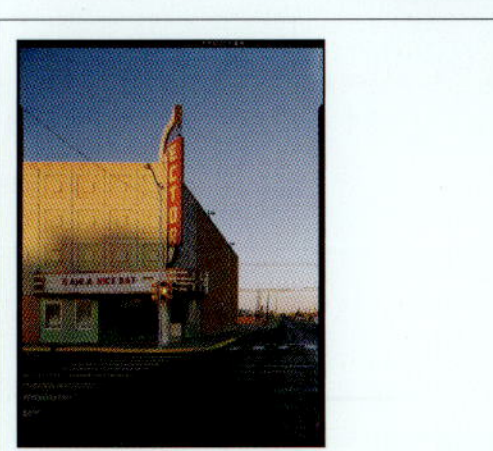

Biography

Selected Client List
ABC
Atlantic Records
Audubon Magazine
BLT
Columbia TriStar
Details
Detour
Discover
Disney
DreamWorks
Elektra
Entertainment Weekly
Epitaph
ESPN. The Magazine
Esquire
Fast Company
Fortune
Interscope Records
Life
Los Angeles magazine
MCA Records
National Geographic
Newsweek
New York magazine
New York Times Magazine
New Yorker
O. The Oprah Magazine
Outside
Paramount
Condé Nast Portfolio
RCA Records
Rolling Stone
Scientific American
Sony Music
Texas Monthly
Time
Universal Records
Vibe
Vogue
W
Warner Bros.
The Washington Post
Women's Health
Wired
20th Century Fox

1962 Born, Ventura County, California

1971 First exposed to photography and the darkroom process while in the 4H-Club under the tutelage of Clarence Dalrymple, a former Vietnam War combat photographer.

1972 Begins making 8mm films and studying entomology.

1973 Starts a small apiary and begins raising honeybees

1976 Studies internal combustion engines: also begins raising and selling livestock.

1977 Studies motion picture special effects, and begins experimenting with miniature effects and in-camera composite photography.

1978 Begins a three-year project studying the protective response of the Eleodes beetle (*Eleodes acuticada*) and places first in county, regional, and state science fair. Continues constructing and photographing miniatures, both with still and motion cameras, and continues experimentation in mechanical, miniature, and explosive special effects.

1979 Still a high school senior, begins working full-time in the motion picture special effects industry, focusing mainly on miniature construction and design.

1980 Graduates high school and continues working in the motion picture effects field.

1981 Attends classes at Moorpark College in Ventura County. Begins serious photographic studies under John Gray, who introduces him to the work of Atget, Bresson, Arbus, Eggleston, Callahan, Evans, Strand, Stieglitz, Penn, Avedon, Gene Smith, Bruce Davidson, and many other influential masters of the medium.

1982 Decides to make photography his life's work. Begins intensive study of photo chemistry and darkroom technique as well as large- and medium-format photography. Begins collecting early photographic negatives, initially focusing on large-format glass negatives. Works during the day as a carpenter.

1984 Earns associate arts degree from Moorpark College. Receives the Jim Sebeck Memorial Scholarship for Photographic Studies.

1985 Begins working as a photo laboratory technician at the *Thousand Oaks News Chronicle* in Ventura County. Applies to documentary studies program at Ludwig Maxmillian University in Munich. Moves to Germany and attends classes at LMU, focusing mainly on narrative photojournalism.

1986 Returns to Southern California and obtains a staff position at the *Thousand Oaks News Chronicle* as a general assignment photographer.

1987 Attends Eddie Adams Workshop in Upstate New York, where he meets with professional photographers, including Gregory Heisler, who encourages him to move to New York. In New York, he takes a full-time position as first assistant to editorial and advertising photographer Chris Callis. Studies the laws of light and their role in the medium.

1989 Receives first magazine assignment from Jeff Christiansen of *Metropolis* magazine. Sets up a studio in Greenwich Village. Starts working regularly with Tibor Kalman of *Interview*. Begins working regularly with magazines such as *Rolling Stone*, *Esquire*, *GQ*, *Vanity Fair*, the *Washington Post Magazine*, and others.

1991 Moves from New York to Los Angeles. Sets up a studio in Hollywood. Marries Kathryn Fouts, who becomes his partner and manages all of his business affairs.

1993 Son Dylan is born.

2000 Maintains home in Los Angeles, but moves to Austin. Sets up studio in Driftwood, Texas (pop. 27) in an historic building that has served the community as a general store, gas station, and post office since 1903.

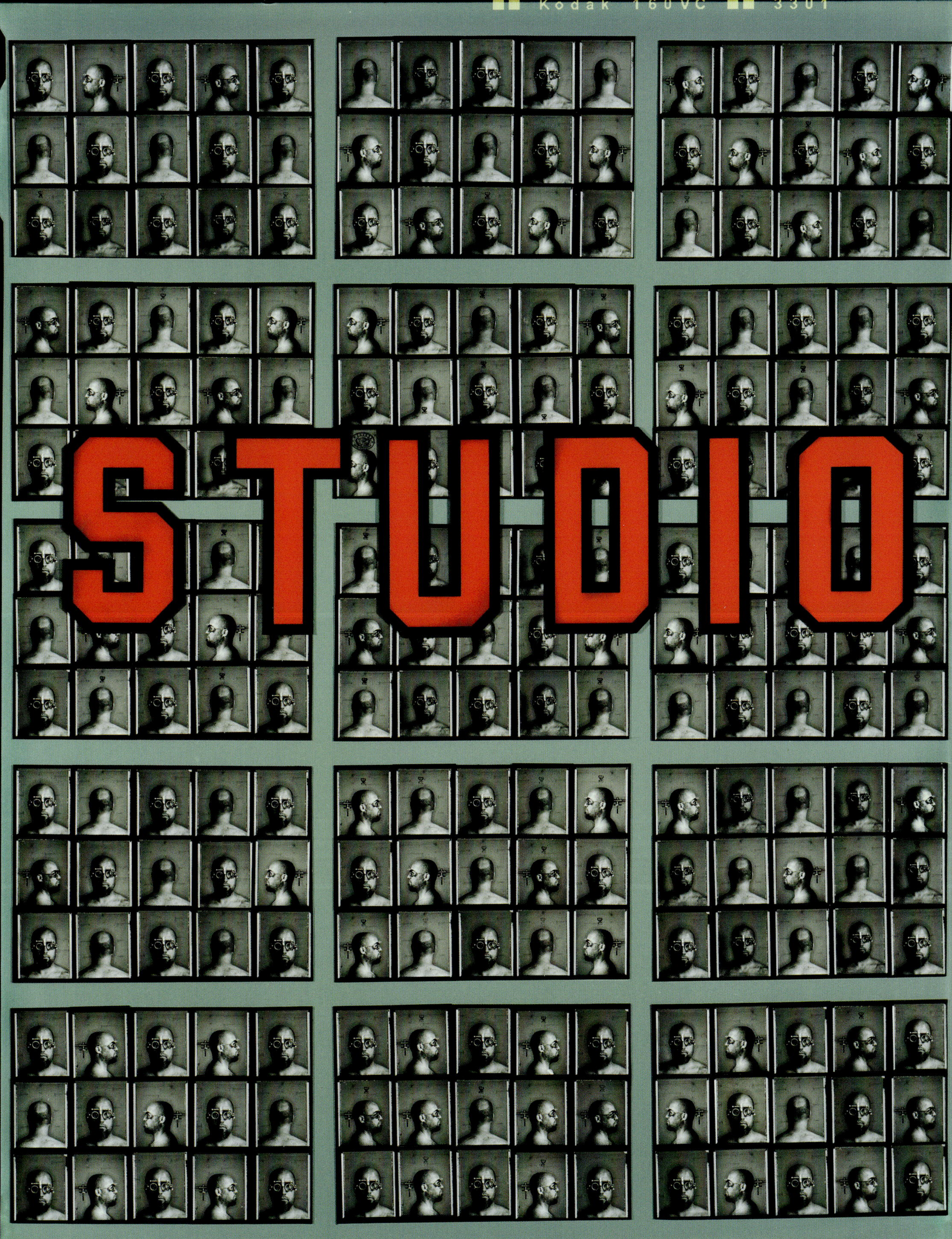
Kodak 160VC 3301
STUDIO

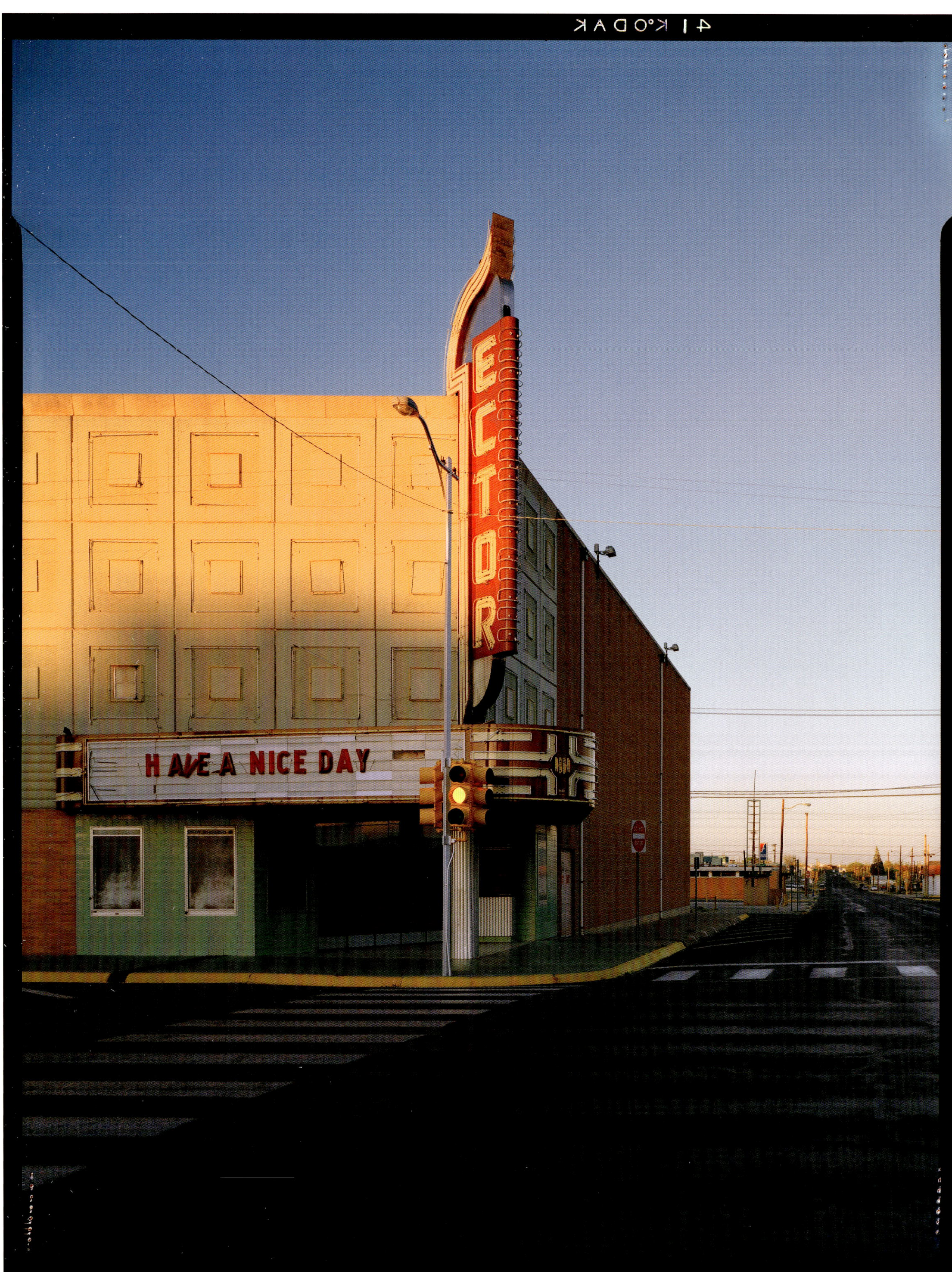
ECTOR
HAVE A NICE DAY

My deepest gratitude and sincere thanks to my family: Larry, Nancy, Paty, Matt, and Mike Winters for your constant love and support over the years. Thank you to my beautiful wife Kathryn and son Dylan, both of whom I love with all my heart. Thank you Dave Yeager. You are the calm in the storm. Thank you for your kindness and devotion. Thank you to my mentor John Gray for showing me beauty in two dimensions. Thank you Harry Callahan for showing me my path. Thank you Gary Tanhauser, my brother from another mother, who is one of the most talented people that I know. Thank you Joe Luper. Thank you Scott Harrison. Thank you Greg Heisler for urging me to jump off the cliff. Thank you Chris Callis for catching me on my way down. Thank you Kevin Amer, a truly wonderful photographer, for the hundreds of hours we spent talking about photography and roaming the streets of New York together making photographs. Thank you John Wells. Thank you Jeff Christiansen for giving me my first assignment. Thank you Tibor Kalman for throwing me to the wolves, knowing that I would come back alive. Thank you Matt Mahurin for inspiration beyond measure. Thank you Geraldine Hessler. Thank you Fred Woodward for teaching a magazine page how to sing. Thank you Laurie Kratochvil. Thank you Jody Peckman. Thank you Nancy Iacoi. Thank you Carl Lehman Haupt for the beautiful concerto in my apartment. Thank you Elisabeth Biondi. Thank you DJ Stout for starting my love affair with Texas. Thank you Allison Morley. Thank you Karen Frank, your voice on the phone always makes me smile. Thank you, Robert Priest for giving me my first raise. Thank you George Pitts. Thank you David Armario. Thank you Welch Golightly for sharing your vast knowledge and your great company. Thank you Tom Gugler. Your pictures live with me and make my life better. Thank you Rita Rago. Thank you George Good. Thank you Mary Klimek. Thank you Leslie Poling. Thank you Gillian Whitlock. Thank you Glenn Chivens for all of the time and insight that you have given to me. Thank you Greg Pond for a great collaboration at *Details*. Thank you Bob Newman. Thank you Michael Kochman. Thank you Gary Koepke. Thank you Greg Carter. Thank you Tom Junod. Thank you Mike Sager. Thank you Denise Sfraga. Thank you Freyda Tavin for being a true original. Thank you Sarah Rosen. Thank you Chris, Ed, and Leena for the worlds that we have made together. Thank you Dan George. Thank you Karen McHugh for always taking such good care of me. Thank you Patti Wilson. Thank you Gerald Lewis. Thank you Peter Wood. Thank you Michelle Romero. Thank you Nelson Anderson. Thank you Leslie Meyer. Thank you John Fulbrook. Thank you Greg Carter. Thank you Phillip Nardulli. Thank you Taylor Jones. Thank you Lisa Berman. Thank you David Granger. Thank you Mike Norseng. Thank you Maisie Todd for solving problems with me month after month. It was fun while it lasted. Thank you Simon Barnett. Thank you Sean Carnegie. Thank you Travis Smith. Thank you Marcel Saba, Leslie and everyone at the Saba Gallery. Thank you Marc English for the intense light you shine on the universe. Thank you Kim Hubbard. Thank you Rob Haggart. Thank you Hannah McCaughey. Thank you Dean Abatemarco. Thank you Ken DeLago. Thank you Scott Thode. Thank you Kathleen Clark for being one of the best there is. Thank you Larry Fink. Thank you William Eggleston. Thank you Bill Christenberry. Thank you Robert Adams for your words and images. Thank you Joe Kimberling. Thank you Adam Moss for your strong and unwavering voice. Thank you Chris Dixon. Thank you Leslie Baldwin. Thank you Evan Smith at *Texas Monthly* for always making me feel special. Thank you Laura Dern. Thank you Leo DiCaprio. Thank you Fred Rogers for making my time in Pittsburgh the most enjoyable four days of my career. Thank you Angelina Jolie for all that you gave me to work with. Thank you Nicole Kidman for our wonderful conversation about Irving Penn and Stanley Kubrick. Thank you Diana Edkins for bringing me together with Aperture, and for all of your support over the years. Thank you Jan Kessner. Thank you T.J. Tucker for your kindness and gentle manner. Your commitment to your craft inspires me. Thank you David Fahey. Thank you Lesley Martin at Aperture for your guidance. Thank you Joanna Lehan for the commitment that you have made to this project, and the insight you have shared in the making of this book. Thank you Kevin Huvane, my most loyal patron. Thank you to my doppelganger, James Hughes. Thank you to Tracy Boychuk. Thank you to my friend Platon for your vision and your kindness. I am extremely grateful to Jody Quon for years of collaboration and support. A very special thanks to Kira Pollack, Joanna Milter, Arem Duplessis, Janet Froelich, Clinton Cargill, Gerry Marzorati, and my family at the *New York Times Magazine*. Thank you to my dear friends Brett Kilroe and Loren Finkelstein, it feels safe when the three of us are together. Thank you to Jeff Wilson for your devotion and friendship. It has been a great gift to watch you grow as a photographer. Thank you Cassandra and Manon for sharing Jeff with me. Thank you Bear Guerra for the many hours in the shop. Your photographs make the world a better place. Abrazos. Thank you to Pat and Courtenay for making my family a part of your family. Thank you to Jesse and Sandy B for all of the kindness that you have shown to me and my family over the years. You are both profound artists and I live in gratitude for our friendship. Thank you to Lynn Hirschberg for allowing your talent and kind words to live in this book. To my close friend Scott Dadich, I am grateful for your incredible contribution to this project and for all of the collaboration and exploration that we have had over the years. Finally, I am deeply indebted to my dear friend Kathy Ryan for providing me with a home at the *Times* and for helping me to grow up as a photographer. *Thank You.*

Front cover
Laura Dern, Hollywood,
July 1999, *Detour*

Back cover
Photo Booth, constructed and
photographed in Austin, September 2003,
Entertainment Weekly

Frontispiece
Jet pack constructed by Gary Tanhauser
and Dan Winters, Austin, July 2002, *GQ*

Endpapers
Pattern by Marian Bantjes

SCOTT DADICH
Designer

JOANNA LEHAN
Editor

MATTHEW PIMM
Production

The staff for this book at
Aperture Foundation includes:

JUAN GARCÍA DE OTEYZA
Executive Director

MICHAEL CULOSO
Director of Finance and Administration

LESLEY A. MARTIN
Publisher, Books

SUSAN CICCOTTI
Senior Text Editor

NIMA ETEMADI
Editorial Assistant

ANDREA SMITH
Director of Communications

KRISTIAN OROZCO
Director of Sales and Foreign Rights

DIANA EDKINS
Director of Exhibitions and
Limited-Edition Photographs

INGER-LISE MCMILLAN
Staff Designer

ALEX FREEDMAN, MATT MINOR,
BEN REICHENBACH
Work Scholars

First Edition
Printed in Singapore
1 0 9 8 7 6 5 4 3 2 1

Library of Congress Control Number:
2008939808
ISBN 978-1-59711-092-1

Aperture Foundation books are
available in North America through:
D.A.P./Distributed Art Publishers
155 Sixth Avenue, 2nd Floor
New York, N.Y. 10013
Phone: (212) 627-1999
Fax: (212) 627-9484

Aperture Foundation books are
distributed outside North America by:
Thames & Hudson
181A High Holborn
London WC1V 7QX
United Kingdom
Phone: + 44 20 7845 5000
Fax: + 44 20 7845 5055
Email: sales@thameshudson.co.uk

aperturefoundation

547 West 27th Street
New York, N.Y. 10001
www.aperture.org
The purpose of Aperture Foundation, a non-profit organization, is to advance photography in all its forms and to foster the exchange of ideas among audiences worldwide.

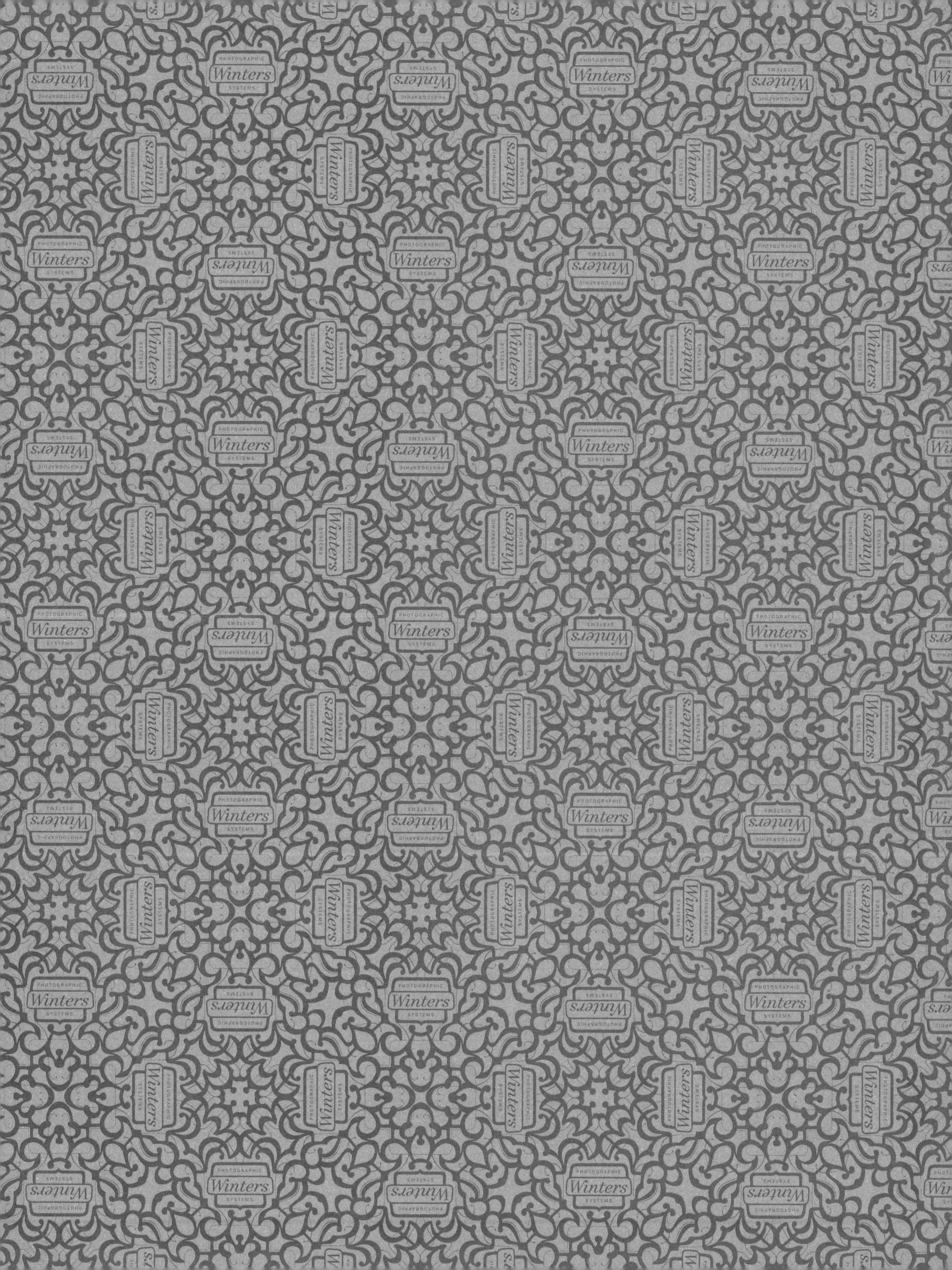
PHOTOGRAPHIC
Winters
SYSTEMS

PHOTOGRAPHIC
Winters
SYSTEMS